SALADIN AND THE FALL OF JERUSALEM

Saladin and the Fall of Jerusalem

GEOFFREY REGAN

CROOM HELM
London • New York • Sydney

© 1987 Geoffrey Regan
Croom Helm, Provident House,
Burrell Row, Beckenham, Kent BR3 1AT

Croom Helm Australia, 44–50 Waterloo Road,
North Ryde, 2113, New South Wales

Published in the USA by
Croom Helm
in association with Methuen, Inc.
29 West 35th Street,
New York, NY 10001

British Library Cataloguing in Publication Data
Regan, Geoffrey
  Saladin and the fall of Jerusalem.
  1. Saladin, *Sultan of Egypt and Syria*
  2. Egypt – Kings and rulers –
  Biography   3. Syria – Kings and rulers
  – Biography
  I. Title
  956'.01'0924   DS38.4.S2
  ISBN 0–7099–4208–7

Library of Congress Cataloging-in-Publication Data
Regan, Geoffrey.
  Saladin and the fall of Jerusalem.

  Bibliography: p.
  Includes index.
  1. Jerusalem — History — Latin Kingdom, 1099–1244.
2. Saladin, Sultan of Egypt and Syria, 1137–1193.
3. Islamic Empire — History — 750–1258. 4. Egypt — Kings
and rulers — Biography. I. Title.
D184.8.R44 1987   956.94'403   87-24562
ISBN 0-7099-4208-7

Typeset by Photoprint, Torquay, Devon
Printed and bound in Great Britain by Mackays of Chatham Ltd, Kent

Contents

For Andrew and Victoria

1

Introduction

Eight hundred years ago, on the rocky slopes of the Horns of Hattin in Galilee, the army of the crusader kingdom of Jerusalem was wiped out by the Saracens of Salah al-Din Yusuf ibn Ayyub, better known to Western historians as Saladin. Not only was the battle of Hattin decisive in the entire crusading period but it was also one of the most decisive battles of the Middle Ages. It put an end to a period of medieval colonisation that had seen the establishment of a viable Christian civilisation in the Near East, combining features of oriental and occidental culture. Although the Third Crusade (which followed the loss of Jerusalem in 1187) succeeded in regaining some parts of the land that the Christians had lost, it was only a temporary reprieve and Outremer never again flourished as it had during the twelfth century. In place of the Palestinian Christians came newcomers from the West whose contempt for what they saw as eastern effeminacy contrasted sharply with the attitudes of those whom they were replacing. At Hattin not only the army of the kingdom was lost but much of its identity as well. Jacques de Vitry, a rabid crusader during the Albigensian Crusade and later patriarch of Jerusalem, was particularly scornful of the eastern Franks whom he came to know well, comparing them unfavourably with their forefathers from the West, who had won the kingdom from the Muslims.

It was an evil and perverse generation, wicked and degenerate sons, corrupt men who proceeded from the aforesaid pilgrims, religious men, acceptable to God and full of grace, even as lees from wine, dregs from olives, tares from wheat, and rust from silver; they succeeded to their fathers' property but not to their good morals; they squandered the

1

worldly wealth which their fathers had won by the shedding of their own blood, fighting manfully against the infidels for the honour of God. Their children, who are called *pullani*, were brought up in luxury, soft and effeminate, more used to baths than battles, addicted to unclean and riotous living, clad like women in soft robes, and ornamented even as the polished corners of the Temple; how slow and slothful, how timid and cowardly they proved themselves against the enemies of Christ is doubted by no one who knows how greatly they are despised by the Saracens. . . . They make treaties with the Saracens, and are glad to be at peace with Christ's enemies.[1]

Contrary to the impression given by de Vitry and the historians who have accepted his views, the lands of Outremer were not peopled or governed by a degenerate race. Indeed much of the discord within the kingdom resulted from the influx of Western crusaders, whose attitudes had changed little since the time of Godfrey of Bouillon and the First Crusade, and who refused to come to terms with their new environment. To them the Muslims were merely infidels, to be converted or slain. Their aim was to win the wealth of the East and to gain fiefs denied them in the West, where land was scarce and knights plentiful. Prominent among these were men like Reynald of Châtillon, Gerard of Ridefort and the Lusignan brothers, Amalric and Guy. In contrast, the native barons (who represented the ancient families of the kingdom) no longer saw Outremer as a frontier outpost of Christianity. They had adapted to their environment and had adopted customs, laws and institutions which reflected a mingling of East and West. As Raymond of Tripoli's ancestors had helped to establish the kingdom so he, as their descendant, was committed to preserving what they had won, even if this meant compromising with the enemies of his religion. This was not treachery but rather common sense. To men like Reynald of Sidon, Baldwin of Ramla and Balian of Ibelin, Outremer was their home and they had no other. They knew little about France, or the West in general, except what they learned from the fierce knights who visited Jerusalem so regularly, often seeking to expiate their sins with Muslim blood. As early as 1127, Fulcher of Chartres conveyed the feelings of native Jerusalemites.

We who had been Occidentals have become Orientals; the

man who had been a Roman or a Frank has here become a
Galilean or a Palestinian; and the man who used to live in
Reims or Chartres now finds himself a citizen of Tyre or
Acre. We have already forgotten the places where we were
born; already many of us know them not or at any rate no
longer hear them spoken of. Some among us already possess
in this country houses and servants which belong to them as
of hereditary right. Another has married a wife who is not
his compatriot — a Syrian or an Armenian woman perhaps,
or even a Saracen who has received the grace of baptism
. . . . Why should anyone return to the West who has found
an Orient like this?[2]

Military necessity meant that the crusader kingdom needed
continual reinforcement from the West, and yet the newcomers
brought with them attitudes which were certain to conflict with
those of the native barons. As Usamah ibn Munqidh wrote,
'Everyone who is a fresh emigrant from the Frankish lands is
ruder in character than those who have been acclimatized and
have held long association with the Muslims.'[3]

The Christian states of Outremer had benefited from the lack
of unity in the Muslim world after the First Crusade, particularly
the decline of the Selchuk sultanate and the enfeeblement of the
Fatimid dynasty in Egypt. Although the Atabegs Zangi and Nur
al-Din had proved notable opponents of the Franks, neither had
been able to threaten the actual existence of the Christian lands.
Consequently, the Syrian and Palestinian Franks had flourished,
learning much from the Muslims and adopting Eastern customs
that were well suited to their new environment. For long periods
they were able to live in peace and friendship with their Muslim
neighbours, often learning Arabic and absorbing the Islamic
knowledge of medicine. Where fighting occurred it was not
necessarily religion that was the main issue; land, cattle and
crops were often the cause of frontier fighting and it was possible
for Christian and Muslim to side with one another against their
co-religionists if the situation demanded it. Far from resembling
the fierce, brutal soldiers who had followed Godfrey of Bouillon to
Jerusalem in 1099, the inhabitants of the kingdom in 1187 had
moved far towards an understanding with the Muslims, which
had given them a breadth of view and a tolerance not found in
Europe at this time. Although at an early stage, they were in the
process of becoming a distinct people. As Fulcher of Chartres so

admirably expressed it, 'Those who were strangers are now natives, and he who was a sojourner now has become a resident'. The tragedy of the battle of Hattin was that this conciliatory, evolutionary process was doomed: though defeats had been suffered before, no other defeat had been so complete. Stripped of available manpower, which could not be restored locally, the kingdom again became a battleground between the brutal crusaders of the West and Saladin's Muslim zealots.

It was not until the emergence of a single leader to unify the disunited forces of Islam that the existence of the Christian lands of Outremer was threatened. That man was Saladin; he achieved his aim not only through his ruthless use of force (as had been typical of conquerors down the ages) but by a rare combination of personal factors which baffled and disturbed lesser men. They could only attribute to him the motives they themselves possessed. His personal courage and resolution were undoubted. He had shown on many battlefields that death held few fears for him and that defeat was no more than an experience to be studied and learned from. However, such warlike virtues would not have been enough in themselves. Saladin was also a very honest man who inspired respect from those who had little reason to love him. His generosity became proverbial in an age when the personal pursuit of power and wealth were the accustomed aims of successful men. His unselfishness and humility disarmed those critics who accused him of simply playing politics and attempting to establish an Ayyubid dynasty in Egypt and Syria. Although much of his life was occupied by wars against his fellow Muslims, Saladin never lost sight of the overriding aim of his life: to liberate the coastal lands from Christian rule and to retake Jerusalem. However, his intellectual nature could find no ultimate satisfaction in a task achieved but not done well. To win Jerusalem was not a task in itself so much as a means to a greater end. Saladin hoped that by unifying Islam in the *jihād* ('holy war') he would be able to persuade Muslims to sink their petty, local differences and restore the political fabric of a single united empire under the Abbasid caliph.[4] Gradually his Zangid opponents began to recognise that in Saladin they were dealing with someone whose moral qualities could not be belittled. He was a man of integrity, whose oath was his bond; the hold that he exerted on men's hearts as well as their minds enabled him to succeed; and it was from his manipulation of the Muslim concept of *jihād* that Saladin was able to find the strength both to conquer the crusader lands and then resist the tremendous challenge posed by the Third Crusade.

The Arabic word *jihād* means 'striving' and originated in the very earliest days of Islam, at a time when Mohammed's followers were trying to establish their power over the people of Mecca.[5] It was then that the religious element of fighting for the faith became linked with the traditional Arab activity of *razzia*. As the need for more specialised military personnel increased it became necessary to make military service a religious as well as a civic duty for all Muslims. By the eleventh century, the religious nature of the Islamic states was reflected in the duty of the head or caliph to maintain religion, protect Islamic territories and to defend the frontiers from the assaults of non-Muslim invaders. Additionally, the head of state had a duty to fight against those who, having been invited to adopt Islam, had refused. In such a case *jihād* would be waged until the enemy had been converted or had accepted the status of a protected minority under Muslim rule.[6] In reality, the political or military power of the caliph had declined to such an extent, both in Cairo and Baghdad, that they had to leave the prosecution of *jihād* in the hands of such warlords as Nur al-Din and Saladin, who fought as Commanders of the Faithful. Nevertheless, though it was obvious that many Muslim leaders paid lip-service only to such ideas as *jihād*, they found it difficult to resist the moral pressures which a man like Saladin was able to bring to bear on them. Once he had made *jihād* his clearly avowed intention it became obvious to his opponents that unless they could impugn his integrity they were bound to be seen to be resisting the Commander of the Faithful, self-appointed though he might be. Thus, by functioning within a firm moral framework and by using *jihād* as a banner for his movement, Saladin was able to unite the separate and hostile Muslim states in a single purpose: the recapture of Jerusalem and the destruction of the Christian lands of Outremer. The present work traces the story of Saladin's pursuit of that aim.

Following his victory at Hattin, Saladin conquered almost the whole of the crusader kingdom of Jerusalem; only Tyre and a few scattered castles resisted him. The capture of Jerusalem, held for only 88 years by Christians, signalled that the victory of Islam over Christianity in the Holy War was complete. Apart from a brief period in the thirteenth century when Jerusalem was sold to the German emperor, Frederick II of Hohenstaufen, the holy city was to remain in Muslim hands until 1917, when General

Allenby captured it from the Turks.

The story of the fall of the kingdom of Jerusalem is an epic in many ways, containing characters who, though they may seem larger than life, were typical of their age. On the Christian side it is also a tragic story of intrigue and political jealousy. As if to symbolise the 'cancer' within the kingdom, young King Baldwin IV (1174–85) fought not only traitors at home and Muslims abroad, but the dreadful disfiguring disease of leprosy. Heroically ignoring the decay of his own body, he led his armies in person until he was no longer able to stand or ride and had to be carried in a litter. The blindness to which he eventually succumbed spared him the sight both of his own and his kingdom's physical disintegration.

2

Jerusalem the Golden

Friday, 15 July 1099

At noon, the hour Christians traditionally associate with the crucifixion of Jesus Christ, the (movable) siege tower of Godfrey of Bouillon was in position at the eastern end of the northern walls of Jerusalem. At this point, east of Herod's Gate, the walls were some 50 feet high and the tower overlooked them by some seven to ten feet. In the upper section of the tower were Duke Godfrey himself, his brother Eustace of Boulogne and a company of knights; while in the middle section were Ludolph and Engelbert of Tournai. Amidst the noise of war — the crashing of great boulders on the timber of the tower, the crackling sounds of burning thatch, the curious whirring and hissing noises as the pots of 'Greek fire' flew through the air like shooting stars, emitting fiery tails — the grim crusaders had little time for reflection. As they crouched low to the floor the siege tower was moved to within a few feet of the walls of Jerusalem. The goal of their journey and all their suffering was now just feet away; and yet these last few steps would be the hardest of any they had taken since they left France two years before.

Crouching, and occasionally crossing themselves or wiping the sweat from their eyes in the burning heat, the Frankish knights could sometimes make out the faces of the Muslims on the walls, faces contorted by fear and hatred, just as theirs must have seemed to their enemies. They were hardened soldiers, bred to their trade, veterans of a dozen such sieges and many battles in the field and yet this was different. They had fought for their faith at Dorylaeum and Antioch but it had not been like this. The Muslims who manned these walls seemed in their eyes less than human, mere servants of Antichrist who were fighting now to prevent true believers from inheriting the city of God. Here, in

7

Jerusalem, there was to be salvation for all, forgiveness for sins, cures for physical and mental ills, and in the Church of the Holy Sepulchre a tangible link with their Saviour Jesus Christ. In the hearts of the crusaders there was a hatred more bitter than any they had known before.

The Muslim warriors on the walls — professional soldiers of the Fatimid caliph — knew none of this. They were fighting to defend their city from these Frankish barbarians. It is doubtful if they gave much thought to why the Christians had come and if they did it was simply to dismiss such reasons as the misguided superstitions of infidels. However, within the city, among the ordinary people, there was a thrill of fear, for news of the prodigious strength and size of these Frankish invaders had already reached them from cities that, like Antioch, had succumbed. Once their walls were breached they could expect little mercy from the followers of the Christian God.

The Muslim defenders made a final effort to halt the inexorable progress of Godfrey's tower. Ropes were thrown over the wooden leviathan and efforts made to topple the whole structure, while rocks and pots of naphtha crashed onto its walls of hide. But the crusaders managed to keep the tower intact by scything through the ropes which threatened it, and by using vinegar to extinguish the flames of a combustible log swung out against the tower by the defenders. In the smoke and confusion opposite them the Franks began to detect a slackening resistance. At once, Ludolph and Engelbert pushed out tree trunks from the middle section of the tower to the top of the walls and clambered onto the battlements, soon followed by Duke Godfrey and his knights. With a shout of triumph from the waiting troops below, a dozen ladders were placed against the walls and selected soldiers now scaled them to join the Lorrainers on the battlements. It was hand-to-hand fighting now in which there was little skill. Men wrestled with each other, sometimes toppling together from the battlements, sometimes gouging at each other's eyes or tearing at throats. The press was too close for sword strokes and handles were used like hammers. But the longer Duke Godfrey and his men held the wall, the longer it gave the Lorrainers and Normans to use their ladders, while across the perilous bridge of logs first tens, and then hundreds, of warriors flooded onto the walls. Soon, by sheer weight of numbers, the Muslims were pressed back and then turned to flee. At last Godfrey of Bouillon raised his banner above the walls as a signal that the city had been entered.

While Godfrey and his troops secured the northern walls and fought their way deep into the Jewish quarter of the city, Robert of Normandy and Tancred headed for the Temple Mount. Here the Muslim defenders held out for a few hours in the al-Aqsa Mosque. Although Tancred had promised them their lives and left his banner with them as token, the Christian soldiers forced aside his guards and massacred everyone so that 'they were wading in blood up to the ankles'. The soldiers were inspired by such a fanatical hatred of both Muslims and Jews that as soon as the individual Christian leaders lost control of them in the narrow streets of the city a dreadful massacre developed which ranks with the most notorious in history and forever coloured relations between Christianity and Islam. It is easy to stand in judgement on the simple soldiers who followed the cross to the Holy Land and fought their way through incredible hardship to the walls of the Holy City itself. Modern examples of genocide should warn us of the power of religion and ideology to indoctrinate whole peoples. The men who slaughtered the Muslim population of Jerusalem were inspired by apparently higher motives than their leaders. Where the dukes and barons looked for a chance to take prisoners and earn ransoms as was customary in European warfare, the common soldiers thought only that in this city their Saviour, Jesus Christ, had been crucified by the Jews and that its holy places had been desecrated by the Muslims. They had come not only to liberate Jerusalem but to cleanse it and this could only be achieved by a general slaughter.

Thus Jerusalem had taken on a more than an earthly significance. To the simple men of the eleventh century the very name conjured up visions of the heavenly city itself, with gates of pearl and precious stones, as they had heard described by their village priests in France. Jerusalem was the centre of the spiritual world just as medieval maps depicted it as the centre of the physical world. In here the people of the world, scattered for so long, met again in pilgrimage. It was the place to which the elect of God ascended, the resting place of the righteous, the city of paradise. To the uneducated minds of the landless poor (who had followed the knights in 1099) Jerusalem was the city of eternal bliss.

For the rest of the day and through the night the killing went on as the crusaders hunted down every living thing: man, woman, child, even animal. Much of the slaughter was carried out by the pilgrims who had accompanied the Crusade and now fell to their work with any weapon that came to hand: axes, clubs and even sharpened staves. Almost intoxicated by the killing, they hacked at everything in their path. By torchlight the Muslims of Jerusalem were hunted down, some dying by fire, some by the sword and others, abandoning hope, chose to leap to their deaths from the highest buildings. To the disgust of the knights, the Christian Tafurs — followers of the Norman knight known as 'King Tafur' — even slaughtered the beautiful Arab stallions which were kept in the city. It was as if they could not rest until everything that had profaned the holy places had been slain. These terrible fanatics, who fought naked with faith alone as their shield and ate the flesh of their victims, drove the Muslims before them in greater terror than even the armoured knights of Duke Godfrey or Raymond of St Gilles.[1] As they moved through the city it was as if the Angel of Death had passed by leaving nothing living. Even the pots and jars of oil or grain were smashed, and sacks of corn ripped open like the bellies of their human victims.

In the Muslim holy places of the al-Aqsa Mosque and the Dome of the Rock, the bodies lay so thickly that they formed a veritable mound of flesh. Moreover, the Christians had hacked their victims horribly, slashing open their stomachs in search of the gold coins that, it was rumoured, the Muslims had swallowed to avoid losing them to the invaders. The result was that the blood was literally ankle deep in some areas of the city, where drainage was impossible. For the Jews a different fate was reserved. They were herded together into their chief synagogue and burned alive in the great conflagration that followed the assault on that building. It was as blood-soaked butchers that the crusaders eventually went to the Church of the Holy Sepulchre to celebrate their victory and to thank God for his great goodness, while around them in the streets were the unburied corpses of the Muslim population of Jerusalem, the first martyrs in the *jihād* that was to rage for the next two centuries. William of Tyre records the impact on the crusaders themselves.

> It was impossible to look upon the vast numbers of slain without horror; everywhere lay fragments of human bodies, and the very ground was covered with the blood of the slain. It was not alone the spectacle of the headless bodies and mutilated limbs strewn in all directions that roused horror in all who looked upon them. Still more dreadful it was to gaze upon the victors themselves, dripping with blood from

head to foot, an ominous sight which brought terror to all who met them.[2]

And yet, as cultivated and civilised a churchman as William could justify the actions of the Christians as the just judgement of God, because these same Muslims had profaned his holy places with their rituals. The bloodshed and the slaughter, however shocking, expiated this sin. Although they would have found it difficult to express their views so clearly, this was how the ordinary soldiers had felt while they were killing. Had they not felt themselves to be tools of God, absolved of any responsibility for what they were doing, it is doubtful if, even in so pitiless an age, they could in common humanity have slaughtered so many women and children.

The shock waves caused by the fall of Jerusalem were felt throughout the Muslim world. Those few refugees who had escaped from the general massacre took the dismal news to the Abbasid caliph. In the great Mosque of Baghdad they described the sufferings of the Muslims in Jerusalem, the slaughter of the innocent and the desecration of the holy places. They reported that the Muslim holy men who lived in the city, the ascetic Sufis, had been killed along with everyone else. The Dome of the Rock had ben stripped of its silver candelabra and all of its treasures, while the al-Aqsa Mosque had been subjected to barbarous treatment. The poet Abu l-Muzaffar al-Abiwardi composed these lines which reflected the shame felt by most Muslims that their leaders had allowed the Holy City to fall to the Franks while offering such feeble resistance.

> Sons of Islam, behind you are battles in which heads rolled
> at your feet.
> Dare you slumber in the blessed shade of safety, where life
> is as soft as an orchard flower?
> How can the eye sleep beneath the lids at a time of disasters
> that would waken any sleeper?
> While your Syrian brothers can only sleep on the backs of
> their chargers, or in vultures' bellies!
> Must the foreigners feed on our ignominy, while you trail
> behind you the train of a pleasant life, like men whose
> world is at peace?[3]

Yet, though the Muslim world mourned the loss of Jerusalem, it was too divided to organise an effective response. Those of the Franks who had come to stay in Palestine were given time to consolidate and extend their territory, until it seemed that they no longer represented simply a temporary intrusion into the Muslim world but were a major factor which could no longer be ignored. Nor could they easily be removed.

Jerusalem had been conquered because of Islamic disunity; only a revival of its religious unity could inspire Muslims to retake it. To thoughtful Muslims it had been apparent that part of the Christian victory had been because the city meant so much more to them than it did to the Muslim defenders. No ordinary army could have sustained such pressures both from within and without as had the crusaders of 1099. There had to be a unifying force of such strength that it overrode every other consideration. The Frankish leadership had proved notably quarrelsome and greedy in the past, and yet for this one purpose they had subdued personal objectives in the interests of the general welfare. Never again would the Franks achieve such a pitch of enthusiasm and commitment. Nevertheless, Muslim complacency had allowed them to develop into formidable opponents and it was inconceivable that their grip on the coastal lands could be broken without total co-operation throughout the Islamic world.

Jerusalem's importance to Islam needed to be emphasised. During the early twelfth century Muslim divines, particularly those in Syria, began to make the recapture of Jerusalem the vital task facing Islam. As the focus of the Old Testament prophets, Jerusalem was already a city deeply respected by Muslims, to which Christ's death added significance: figures like Abraham, Moses and Jesus were all seen as forerunners of Islam. Moreover, Jerusalem was the second house of God after the Kaʿaba at Mecca, and the Prophet had named it as one of the three directions of prayer which a horseman should face before mounting. Any Muslim who passed through the Gate of Mercy in the Temple Precincts at Jerusalem was assured of paradise and some Islamic divines believed that Jerusalem would be the site of the Last Judgement (when the angel Israfil will blow the ram's horn, standing upon the Rock). However, most important of all was the fact that it was in Jerusalem that the Prophet had made his mysterious ascent into heaven. The first verse of Sura 17 of the Koran describes the Prophet's Night Journey. Tradition states that while sleeping near the Kaʿaba in Mecca, Mohammed was awoken by the Angel Gabriel who led him to the winged charger,

Buraq, which transported him in spirit to Jerusalem and there, from the Rock, he was borne into heaven. Muslim tradition also relates that the Holy Rock is located directly beneath Allah's throne and above a cave where all the souls of the dead congregate. As a place of such significance to Islam it was unthinkable that it should remain in the hands of the Christian infidels. In time it would serve to rally the disparate forces of the Muslim world when a leader arose worthy of the title Commander of the Faithful. But how long must Islam wait for such a leader? In the middle of the twelfth century the Islamic world continued to be deeply divided and the triumph of her faith seemed to be as far away as ever.

3
Saladin's Early Life: 1138–74

Saladin's historical reputation has been based to a large extent on his qualities as a general. He has often earned inclusion in books of great commanders, as if he contributed something special to the military art or was notably successful as a leader of armies. He is remembered for his great victory at Hattin, for his lightning conquest of the kingdom of Jerusalem and for his epic struggle against Richard I of England during the Third Crusade. The main problem which faces the historian is, therefore, to penetrate this military façade to see if there was anything in Saladin other than the 'hero of Islam . . . dynastically-minded politician [and] war-band leader' by which labels he is generally known.[1] Was he merely the most successful of a group of powerful Eastern conquerors, equipped with great armies? I am inclined to answer in the negative. It is hoped that the present work will show that though Saladin may have begun in this way (as an ambitious man, keen to expand his own power), he developed individual weapons of persuasion far more powerful than mere force. He learned to use his own distinctive moral qualities to win the loyalty and affection of more traditional princes and managed to inspire them with his own vision not only of a successful *jihād* to retake Jerusalem but a moral rebirth of a united Islam.

His early experiences under Nur al-Din deeply affected him. Although his master was motivated by a desire to fight a successful holy war against the Franks of the coastal lands, he was restricted in how far he could commit himself because of the failure of neighbouring Muslim princes to unite in a common cause. The break-up of the Selchuk sultanate at the end of the eleventh century had led to the fragmentation of the Near East. Petty local princes established themselves in the ruins of the once

14

great empire, constantly warring against each other in the pursuit of land. At this time of Muslim disunity the great threat from the West came in the form of the crusaders who proved far too strong for a sundered Islam. Both Nur al-Din and, later, Saladin realised that only a united Islam could provide the military resources necessary to defeat the crusaders. In the Muslim world at this time power rested on the capacity to raise and maintain professional armies of mamluke warriors, and princes kept a predatory eye on their neighbour's lands for any sign of weakness which might merit intervention. For land brought not only taxes but *iqtas* which could be used to win the loyalty of troops.

In this world Nur al-Din was respected for his high abilities, both as a leader of armies and as a diplomat. He may have been more honest and sincere than his neighbours but he was forced to participate in the same struggle for power if he wished to build an army strong enough to challenge the crusader states. Yet his vision was limited in a way that Saladin's was not. When the opportunity to interfere in Egyptian affairs presented itself, Nur al-Din could see no further than that Egypt would provide a recruiting ground for troops; his thoughts were concentrated on Syria alone and he expected Saladin, as his vassal, to use Egyptian resources to strengthen his power base at Damascus. It was only after his death in 1174 that Saladin was able to begin to formulate ideas which had lain dormant during the previous decade. As a Kurd in an empire dominated by Turks, who considered themselves superior in every way to other Muslims, he had learned to keep his own counsel. But Saladin was emerging as an individual thinker whose aims transcended the petty squabbles that divided Muslims. His ideals worried friends and enemies alike because they did not resemble those of the previous great empire-builders. It was in his command of moral power rather than in the use of force that Saladin dominated his age.

Yet there was little in his early years that suggested that he was destined for greatness. The historical evidence on his boyhood is limited. He was apparently born in 1138 in the city of Baalbek, son of a Kurdish adventurer by the name of Ayyub. His father, and his uncle Shirkuh, must have been very able men; they cut their way through traditional Turkish prejudice against their race and rose to high rank. Early stories speak of the two brothers originating from near Dvin in Armenia. Finding service with the Selchuk sultan, Ayyub became the castellan of Takrit, a town on the River Tigris between Mosul and Baghdad. However, neither brother seemed to be able to settle for long in any allegiance and it is soon recorded that Ayyub was helping the Atabeg Zangi to establish his independent power at Mosul in 1132. Six years later Ayyub was expelled from his position after his brother, Shirkuh, was accused of killing a man in a fight. The two brothers now entered the service of Zangi, with Ayyub commanding the garrison at Baalbek in Syria. Here it was that Saladin was born. At the age of eight he went with his father to live in Damascus where his father and uncle made considerable progress in the service of Zangi's son, Nur al-Din.

He was a serious boy who apparently loved reading. Like many others of his class he was educated in genealogies, biographies and the histories of the Arab peoples, and is reputed to have learned the *Hamasa* of Abu Tamman by heart.[2] This collection of poetry contained an ethical basis for life deriving from the tribal background of the Arab people, and did not necessarily conform with strict Islamic principles. Nevertheless, between such reading and his studies of the Koran, Saladin emerged as a deeply thoughtful young man, serious beyond his years. Although he undoubtedly added physical exercises to his spiritual ones, and is reported to have been a fine horseman and excellent polo player, it is primarily as a scholar that he was remembered. The effect of Nur al-Din's deeply held religious beliefs, combined with the teaching of the many pious men who surrounded him, convinced the young Saladin that the pursuit of the holy war was the prime duty of every Muslim. According to one chronicler he spoke of little else.

Saladin must occasionally have suffered as a result of his Kurdish background at the hands of the Turkish upper classes. Although his father and uncle had won great renown for their service to Zangi and Nur al-Din, and had done as much as possible to distance themselves from their relatively humble origins, they were never to succeed completely. In 1174 when Saladin travelled to Damascus to try to piece together the wreck of Nur al-Din's lands after his master's death he was sharply put in his place by the accusation that he was only a dog barking at his master. It was just this social divisiveness which helped to keep the Islamic world divided. In the sight of God all were supposed to be equal — Bedouin, Arab, Syrian, Turk and Kurd — yet in the sight of man it was never so.

Though prominent in the Syria of Nur al-Din, Ayyub and Shirkuh were not so powerful that they could guarantee Saladin a better future than as a military commander in the wars against the Franks of Antioch, Tripoli and Jerusalem; if the young man was to advance further it would have to be through his own ability. We have a description of Saladin in his early manhood, as being of medium height, slender, with a dark complexion, dark eyes and a black beard, trimmed short in the Kurdish manner. In 1152 he had entered the service of Nur al-Din and had been allocated a fief, succeeding his brother Turan-Shah (four years later) as deputy to Shirkuh, the military governor of Damascus. His good sense and general steadiness recommended him to Nur al-Din and soon he was living in Aleppo as one of the Atabeg's trusted advisers. However, it was events in Egypt that were to catapult Saladin to prominence and enable him to put into practice some of the ideas which he had culled from his extensive reading and from his close acquaintance with his master, Nur al-Din.

The death of King Baldwin III in 1162 brought to the throne of the kingdom of Jerusalem his 27-year-old brother, Amalric, an able man and an ambitious one. William of Tyre has left a description of the king as tall and handsome, with the same thick beard and high colouring of his brother Baldwin, though he carried rather too much weight. He was not as widely read as Baldwin had been and suffered a stammer which made him less at ease in company. As a result, he was never as popular as his brother had been and was less scrupulous in his sexual morals.[3] Moreover, Amalric was not content to follow the policies of his brother, which had aimed to consolidate the Christian lands and hold at bay the rising power of Nur al-Din. Instead, Amalric was inspired by the idea of expanding his lands to the south and of interfering in the troubled affairs of Fatimid Egypt. Egyptian wealth had long been legendary; the highly developed agriculture of the Nile Valley, combined with the fishery, textile, slave and ivory trades, made the kingdom seem a great temptation to the land-hungry crusaders.

Confident in the support of the Byzantine Emperor, Manuel Comnenus, Amalric planned nothing less than the conquest of Egypt. He was politician enough to realise the importance of keeping the Islamic world divided and this meant that Syria must at all costs be prevented from extending her influence into Egypt. For the next decade the focus of the religious struggle between Christianity and Islam shifted southwards from Syria to Egypt, and at its end one figure was to emerge from the confused situation supreme: Saladin.

Fatimid Egypt was an empire in decline. Although she had once been powerful enough to challenge the pre-eminence of the Abbasid Caliph of Baghdad, by the mid-twelfth century her power had dwindled. However, if the will-power of her rulers was no longer strong enough to threaten her neighbours, her riches were enough to attract predators from both Christian and Muslim lands. In 1160 the eleven-year-old al-Adid became caliph and he left the running of Egypt's affairs to his vizier, Talai ibn Ruzzik. When Talai died in 1163 there was a dispute between two of his emirs, Dirgam and Shawar, for the succession. This power struggle within Egypt now took on international significance when Shawar was driven out of Egypt and travelled to Damascus to approach Nur al-Din for his help. Meanwhile, Dirgam consolidated his power by killing anyone who might have challenged his position, which resulted in a general massacre of the senior officers of the Egyptian army.

While Dirgham was in the process of destroying Egypt's power to resist her neighbours, Amalric I was already planning an invasion of Egypt on the pretext that three years earlier his brother had been promised a yearly tribute of 160 000 dinars, which Dirgam now foolishly withheld. Although the crusader force was well-equipped and contained a substantial force of Hospitallers, under their master, Gilbert d'Assailly, it was forced to abandon its invasion after the brief siege of Pelusium, when the Nile dams were broken and the surrounding country flooded. Amalric returned to Jerusalem claiming a victory but with little evidence to support him.

Meanwhile in Damascus, Shawar was promising Nur al-Din a third of all Egyptian revenues in return for an army strong enough to overthrow his enemy. Saladin's uncle, Shirkuh, was not slow to see the opportunity that presented itself. With the threat of a Latin takeover ever present, Egyptians were likely to prefer a Muslim ruler to Amalric of Jerusalem. If Dirgam now proved he was incapable of maintaining Egypt's independence then the opportunity was there for Nur al-Din to expand his influence into Fatimid territory. The combination of Egyptian and Syrian power would give Nur al-Din an enormous advantage in the holy war. With Egyptian seapower he might even be able to sever contacts between the Frankish lands and Europe, making the fall of Jerusalem far more likely. Yet if Amalric were to gain Egyptian power the holy war might be lost. It was a dangerous moment for Islam.

Shirkuh was the moving spirit throughout the confused struggle for Egypt. He was an ambitious man and it would be quite inappropriate to submit his motives to the scrutiny which one can use in assessing his nephew. In April 1164 Shirkuh was given the command of an élite force of Syrian troops, which succeeded in bypassing crusader territory, arriving in Egypt and installing Shawar as vizier. Although one Arab chronicler, Ibn Shaddad, refers to the young Saladin accompanying his uncle's first expedition, we cannot be certain: corroborative evidence is scanty.[4] Certainly, at 26, Saladin would have been considered ready to hold a command under his uncle, but further than that the evidence does not take us. Having achieved what he set out to do, Shirkuh was in no hurry to return to Syria. Shawar now realised that he had overthrown one enemy only to find that he was confronting another, far more dangerous. As a result, he decided to attempt to 'play off' his enemies against each other. In order to rid Egypt of Shirkuh, Shawar turned to Amalric. The Franks needed no second invitation and promptly invaded Egypt in July. Shirkuh now found himself at a grave disadvantage. For three months his small force was besieged at Bilbais and eventually he was forced to accept Amalric's terms and leave Egypt, with 30 000 Egyptian dinars and a safe conduct. Amalric had heard grave news from the north and was eager to leave Egypt himself. In a disastrous battle fought near Artah on 10 August, the army of Antioch under Bohemond III, aided by Raymond of Tripoli, Hugh of Lusignan and an important Byzantine contingent under the renowned general Constantine Colman, had been badly defeated by Nur al-Din and the leaders taken prisoner. Only Muslim fear of the power of the Byzantine Emperor Manuel Comnenus prevented the fall of Antioch itself.[5] Amalric needed to move his forces northwards to the defence of the principality.

In spite of his difficulties, Shirkuh was not downcast and continued to believe that his future lay in Egypt and not Syria. He applied again to Nur al-Din for permission to lead another expedition against Shawar. He was also successful in persuading the Caliph of Baghdad to declare his campaign a *jihād* against the heretical Shiites of Egypt. In January 1167, with an army of 2000 élite warriors, Shirkuh again set out for Egypt, avoiding crusader territory and crossing the Sinai desert, where he was confronted by the combined forces of Shawar and Amalric. In fact, Amalric had assembled almost the entire army of the kingdom of Jerusalem, making Shirkuh's task an extremely difficult one. After a period of skirmishing along the banks of the Nile, the two armies met in battle near Ashmunein. Shirkuh's army was made up almost entirely of light cavalry — either Syrian lancers or Turkish horse archers. Against this the Fatimid infantry and the heavy cavalry of the Franks provided quite inappropriate opposition. The mobility of the Turks enabled Shirkuh to pull back his centre, where Saladin was entrusted with command, and then having drawn the Frankish knights into the trap he encircled them by calling in the flanks. Amalric himself was nearly captured and many knights were either killed or taken prisoner. Nevertheless, the Frankish-Egyptian army was by no means defeated and continued to outnumber Shirkuh's force in spite of its losses.

More confused fighting took place along the Nile when Shirkuh moved northwards, skirting Cairo and heading for Alexandria where he was welcomed by Egyptians friendly to his cause. As his enemies closed in on the city, Shirkuh decided to break out with the main part of his army and head for Upper Egypt, leaving Saladin in command of the defence of Alexandria. Saladin was faced with great difficulties. In the first place he had a very small Syrian garrison of less than 1000 men and did not know to what extent he could rely on the Alexandrians themselves to defend their city against Shawar and Amalric. Secondly, his communications with Shirkuh would be rendered impossible by the fact that his uncle's *razzia* tactics would be designed to make it difficult for anyone to locate him in Upper Egypt, whether friend or foe. While he was absent Saladin decided that he would have to rely on the support of the Alexandrians if he was to ask them to stand a siege; as the Frankish-Egyptian forces moved towards Alexandria they prepared siege weapons, including great towers. Meanwhile, Shawar offered the Alexandrians every kind of financial incentive to overthrow Saladin and open the gates to him, and it says much for Saladin's level-headedness that he was able to maintain effective resistance against a foe many times his strength. For three months he held the city unaided. However, when news of Nur al-Din's attacks on the northern borders of his kingdom reached Amalric, the Frankish leader was eager to come to terms with Shirkuh. He negotiated an agreement for the evacuation of Alexandria and then headed north to counter the threat from Syria. Again Shirkuh had failed to secure control of Egypt and it was obvious that without substantially greater military support he could hardly hope to overthrow the power of

Shawar, particularly when supplemented by Amalric's Franks. Only the diversionary raids by Nur al-Din on the Syrian front had saved him from complete defeat.

Meanwhile, Shawar's policy of playing Amalric off against Shirkuh had achieved as much as it could. Amalric was now planning to change the ground rules and take Egypt for himself. Assured of the support of the Byzantine emperor, Amalric felt confident in his strength. On 29 August 1167 he married Maria Comnena, daughter of the Byzantine Emperor Manuel, in Tyre cathedral. With the young queen's party travelled important diplomats from Constantinople whose task was to negotiate an alliance with Jerusalem. Diplomatically, however, Amalric was making a grave mistake. By bringing Byzantine power into the equation he was in danger of overturning completely the delicate balance of power in the area. Egypt now had no alternative but to seek help from Nur al-Din.

In October 1168 Amalric set out once again to invade Egypt, though it is significant that he did so this time without Templar support. It is likely that the Templars were jealous of the part the Hospitallers were playing in the expedition and were annoyed at the news that their rivals were to be rewarded with the city of Pelusium.[6] In addition, the Templars had long been involved in a profitable trade with Muslim Egypt and did not wish to see their investments endangered. On 3 November the town of Bilbais, under the command of Shawar's son Tayy, refused Amalric entrance and was promptly besieged. Tayy, a young firebrand, impudently demanded of Amalric, 'do you think Bilbais is a piece of cheese for the eating?' Undaunted, the Frankish king replied, 'Yes, it is cheese and Cairo is butter'. Bilbais was soon taken by assault and an appalling massacre followed which was to have serious consequences for Christian military success in Egypt. Many of Amalric's fiercest warriors were followers of the Count of Nevers, who had only recently arrived in the Holy Land from the West. His men were fanatical opponents of the Muslims and showed them no quarter in battle. When the Count died of fever in Palestine, before the expedition started, his followers lacked a commanding figure who might have halted their excesses. In addition, their ignorance of the East was revealed by the way in which they indiscriminately killed Muslims and Coptic Christians alike. Whereas the opponents of Shawar had originally been willing to welcome the Franks as deliverers from the corrupt rule of their vizier, they hastily changed their minds when they saw the barbarism of the Frankish soldiers. The massacres at Bilbais and later at Tanis, where the victims were almost entirely Coptic, united the country in a way neither Shawar nor Shirkuh could ever have hoped to achieve.

The crusaders next turned towards Cairo. In desperation Shawar opened negotiations with the Franks, hoping to win enough time for the troops of Nur al-Din to reach Egypt. As a demonstration of his fierce determination to resist the Franks he burned the town of Fustat to the ground and threatened to do the same with Cairo if the Christians advanced any further. However, Shawar's power was dwindling and it was only the intervention of the Caliph al-Adid which saved the country. Under the Caliph's order a letter was sent to Damascus offering Nur al-Din a third of all Egyptian land and generous fiefs for his generals if he would send help. This was an offer far too good for Nur al-Din to resist and this time when Shirkuh set out he was equipped with 8000 of Nur al-Din's best troops. It is reported that Saladin was not personally eager to return to Egypt and that he had only complied under pressure from Nur al-Din.

On hearing the news of Shirkuh's advance, Amalric attempted to cut off the Syrians before they reached Egypt but failed to make contact with them in the desert. Once he heard from his spies that Shirkuh had made contact with Shawar's forces he was left with no alternative but to fall back on Bilbais and then quit the country on 2 January 1169. It was a humiliating military failure for the Franks and yet its significance went much further than anyone could have imagined at the time. Amalric had played into the hands of Shirkuh and by providing an external threat he had delivered a willing Egypt into the hands of the Kurdish adventurer and his able nephew, Saladin. They were both determined that Shawar would have no further opportunity for treachery.

On 8 January 1169 Shirkuh entered Cairo with Saladin, and the two Kurds were welcomed by the caliph himself. It seems possible that Shirkuh would have been prepared to share the vizierate with Shawar but his nephew was adamant. As Saladin told him, 'while Shawar holds power, we have no authority'. Within ten days of Shirkuh's entry into Cairo, Vizier Shawar had been murdered apparently on Saladin's initiative, although the orders had finally come from the Caliph al-Adid.

Shirkuh now became vizier with Saladin as his right-hand man. With minimal violence the Syrian takeover of Egypt had been effected and the springboard from which the successful *jihād* would be planned had been established. When Nur al-Din heard the news of Shirkuh's success he ordered celebrations throughout his lands; and yet he was not entirely happy when his vassal, Shirkuh, took service as vizier under the Fatimid caliphate. He had hoped that his trusted servant would return to Syria where his services were essential in the struggle against the Franks. However, it was not for Nur al-Din to dictate the future of his Kurdish commander. Shirkuh died within three months of his triumphant conquest of Egypt, apparently after taking a hot bath following a heavy bout of eating. Ibn Shaddad has left a description of the grizzly old warrior which reveals him as short, fat, and partially sighted: hardly the usual description of the heroes of history. Yet he had been a great soldier, respected by all and loved by his men.[7] He had achieved great things in the name of Nur al-Din and yet, had he not died, it is almost certain that he would have proved as difficult a vassal as his nephew was to be. Shirkuh was not as deeply complex a personality as Saladin and felt there was no shame in pursuing his personal ambition and the interests of his family. He would have been delighted to have seen how successful a leader of men his nephew was to be, but it is doubtful if he would ever have understood Saladin's idealism and deep commitment to *jihād*.

Shirkuh's dual role as Syrian army commander in Egypt and Fatimid vizier posed problems in the selection of a successor. The Turkish and Kurdish emirs who had accompanied him to Egypt naturally wished to choose the man who was to replace him as their leader. Nevertheless, so strong was the Syrian hold on the country that it was inevitable that whoever succeeded to the command of Shirkuh's army would also fill his role as vizier. After the required period of mourning, discussions took place among the Syrian leaders and as many as four other candidates were suggested besides Saladin. Eventually, however, Saladin was selected as army commander and accepted by the Fatimid caliph as Shirkuh's natural successor. So, at the age of 31, Saladin was the new Vizier of Egypt. And yet it was an honour which he had never sought. He had been unwilling to accompany his uncle on his third expedition to Egypt after his experiences in Alexandria during his second. Truly greatness had been thrust upon him. Yet he was an obvious choice. The great trust that Nur al-Din placed in him was well known, nor was his ability doubted by anyone. However, his modesty must have made him baulk at the title conferred by the caliph: that of El-Malik al-Nasir ('the conquering prince').

Saladin's initial problem was the need to establish his position in Egypt: a country that was hostile to the Syrian influence which he represented. If he had acted as no more than a pawn of Nur al-Din it is possible that he would have succumbed to a national rising. However, he made it clear from the outset that Egypt mattered to him more than simply as an outpost of Syrian power and a source of manpower for the holy war. While this attitude was naturally difficult for his master to understand, it showed considerable maturity for a man of limited experience. Certainly Saladin was an exponent of the holy war against the Franks and hoped for nothing more than to recover Jerusalem. But the ease with which Amalric had been able to invade Egypt when he chose showed Saladin that without a consolidation of his power base his hold on his new territory might prove as short-lived and difficult as that of Shawar and Dirgam. It is far too easy to reach the conclusion that most of his contemporaries did: that Saladin was motivated at this stage by an intention to further the interests of his family and found an independent dynasty. Saladin believed that Egypt was the weakest point in the holy war against the Christians, open to attack from both the Franks of Jerusalem and the Byzantine Greeks. Moreover, it would not be possible to achieve Muslim unity, and thereby greater strength against the infidels, if the Fatimids inside Egypt remained as a source of discontent. With these two threats ever present, Saladin had enough problems maintaining his hold on Egypt without immediately being able to make Egypt's resources in money and soldiers available to Nur al-Din for an assault on Jerusalem. Later events show how wise was Saladin's caution. The kingdom of Jerusalem was not ripe to fall in 1170.

As servant of the Shiite Caliph of Cairo as well as of Nur al-Din, the sword of the Sunnite Caliph of Baghdad, Saladin was aware of the ambiguity of his position. For two years he made no attempt to act against the Fatimite caliph for he realised that to act quickly might arouse both religious and national feelings in the Egyptian population which could sweep him from power. Even though Nur al-Din had ordered him to impose orthodoxy on his people, Saladin refused to be forced into acting before he was ready. In addition, the Shiite caliph had shown every sign of supporting his regime, which might prove essential if a clash with Nur al-Din should occur. In the event, Saladin was saved from the need to act in this difficult situation because in September 1171 the caliph died. Saladin had ordered that the young caliph's last hours should not be disturbed by the news that Sunnite prayers were being spoken at that moment in the great mosque in Cairo by a visiting priest from Mosul. 'If he recovers he will learn soon enough,' said Saladin, 'If he is to die let him die in peace.'[8] Freed of any personal obligation to the caliph, Saladin was now able to order that henceforth prayers in Egyptian mosques should be in the name of the Caliph of Baghdad. It says much for the effectiveness of the control Saladin had established that the changeover was achieved with minimal disruption. The remaining princes and princesses of the Fatimid dynasty were then placed in isolation, so that they would never find the opportunity to have children of their own.

It was noted by Arab chroniclers that at the time of his elevation to the rank of vizier, Saladin gave up his youthful interests in earthly pleasures and 'assumed the dress of religion'. It is difficult to be certain how much this tells us of the character of Saladin for the description of his pursuit of 'wine-drinking and . . . frivolity' may well be a standard description of any young man elevated to a senior position.[9] Moreover, it does not lie well with descriptions we have of Saladin as a somewhat grave and bookish young man. Nevertheless, from this time onwards Saladin makes a point of informing the Caliph of Baghdad at every opportunity of his commitment to the true religion and the holy war, as if to combat any rumours that he had been sidetracked by the material pleasures of Egypt.

Nur al-Din had been far from pleased when he heard that Saladin had accepted the rank of vizier in succession to Shirkuh, and wrote several letters to him, which complaints the young man ignored. Nevertheless, in other respects the Atabeg loyally supported his vassal in the period of his greatest trials, from 1169–73, sending reinforcements to quell internal unrest and creating diversions on the Syrian frontier to relieve pressure on Egypt from Amalric and from the Byzantines. Even the despatch to Egypt of Saladin's father, Ayyub, was an act of good faith by Nur al-Din, who escorted the old man's caravan through the dangerous lands of Oultrejourdain. Then he turned back to besiege the great castle at Kerak, from which the crusaders frequently came out to attack passing Muslim caravans and pilgrims.

During the summer of 1169, Saladin faced his greatest

challenge when a joint Frankish-Byzantine attack on Egypt was planned. A great Byzantine fleet (commanded by Andronicus Contostephanus) set sail from Constantinople and made for Cyprus; a smaller flotilla headed for Acre carrying money subsidies for the Frankish troops. Unfortunately, Amalric was slow to assemble his forces and the Byzantines were forced to wait until he could summon them to join him at Tyre and Acre. The Byzantine fleet, on the assumption that the campaign was to be a short one, had been issued with only three months of food supplies and the delay at Cyprus meant that they were already running short of some essentials. It was not until the middle of October that Amalric was able to lead his army down the coast, having inexplicably refused Andronicus's offer to transport the entire force by sea. The Byzantine fleet of over 200 vessels was an impressive sight. Some boats were equipped as landing craft with doors in the bow which let down allowing horses to be landed directly onto the beach; others were great dromons, packed with the complex siege machinery which was a feature of medieval Byzantine armies.

Meanwhile, Saladin faced an internal threat to his power. Realising the danger of a renewed Frankish assault he decided to purge the palace of servants on whom he could not rely. The replacement of Egyptian officials by his Syrians aroused great resentment and the caliph incited the Nubian troops to rebel and attack Saladin's men. For a while Saladin's position was imperilled and when his brother, Fakhr al-Din, counter-attacked the negro troops he was driven off. Only the burning of the Nubians' barracks had the required effect on them — as they rushed back to try to rescue their wives and families. Showing complete ruthlessness Saladin ordered Fakhr al-Din to massacre them and, once the caliph had assured Saladin of his complete support, the revolt crumbled. Saladin had revealed that beneath the cultivated exterior there lurked a man of iron resolution, who was prepared to eliminate political opponents like Shawar, massacre those who rebelled against him along with their families, and follow his own path in spite of his oath of loyalty to his master. Saladin had come of age as a ruler and was ready now to face the threat from the Christians.

By the end of October the allies had crossed into Egyptian territory near Pelusium. Saladin marched out to meet them near Bilbais but the Byzantines had already ferried the Frankish troops across the eastern branches of the Nile. The target for both

Christian commanders was Damietta, a rich port on the Nile whose capture would open the way to a river-borne advance towards Cairo. However, relations between the Byzantines and the Franks had become soured as the journey went on, so that by the time Amalric arrived at Damietta his allies were already accusing him of bad faith, by deliberately wasting time so that the Byzantines were forced to bear the bulk of the fighting. Although Saladin had been fully informed of the impending attack by numerous refugees who headed in to Alexandria by sea, he did not know precisely where it would fall and thus Damietta was poorly garrisoned and would have fallen to a prompt assault. However, in the time he was allowed by the caution of his enemies Saladin was able to buy the service of a large number of mercenary troops and rush them into position. Meanwhile, Nur al-Din stood by his young vassal by sending reinforcements from Syria.

The usual squabbles between the Frankish knights and the Greeks were splitting the allied camp. The 'Palestinian Knights' were renowned for their arrogance and the contempt in which they held both enemies and allies alike. While Andronicus had favoured an immediate assault on Damietta using scaling ladders alone, Amalric (a veteran of pointless sieges) insisted that no action should be taken until an enormous siege-tower, reputed to be seven storeys high, was ready. He had clearly been overawed by the powerful city walls of Damietta. Meanwhile, to the horror of the Latin Christians, their Greek allies had bombarded a quarter of Damietta where there was a chapel dedicated to the Blessed Virgin Mary.

As the siege persisted the Byzantine forces ran short of supplies, which their Frankish allies refused to supplement. At the end of 50 days the siege had still not advanced very far and both sides were eager to come to terms. The early arrival of the winter rains turned the besiegers' camps into morasses and it was apparent to all that little was to be gained in pursuing the siege through the winter. Nevertheless, the Byzantines felt obliged to complain that they had been betrayed by the Franks who, they claimed, had decided to make peace just as the Greek forces were on the point of success. Whatever the truth, the expedition ended disastrously for the Byzantines when their fleet, returning home, was wrecked by storms with many ships lost. William of Tyre writes that for weeks to come the coast of Palestine was littered with corpses of Greek sailors. Amalric escaped more lightly, reaching Ascalon on 24 December, having lost little more than his pride.

Saladin was now the undisputed ruler of Egypt, yet he was unwilling to precipitate a break with his master in Damascus; Nur al-Din seemed equally unwilling to believe that his trusted officer could possibly mean to betray him. A less trusting man than Nur al-Din would sooner have recognised what was clear to advisers and officials in both Cairo and Damascus. Saladin believed himself to be independent of Syria in all but name, yet if he were to meet his master how then would he react? Was he so secure that he could afford to alienate Nur al-Din and bring down the wrath of Syria on him, to add to the danger of a renewed Christian attack? It would be easier simply to avoid contacting Nur al-Din as far as possible and so Saladin made every effort to avoid meeting his former master in case it would lead to conflict.

By December 1170 Saladin felt confident enough to strike out at the frontier regions of the crusader lands in order to relieve pressure on Egypt. Darum and Gaza were subjected to attacks and though Amalric advanced to their relief Saladin was able to break off and make good his escape into Egypt. He had at least shown the Franks that they could not rely any more on Egyptian passivity. More important, though, was Saladin's recapture of the seaport of Eilat on the Red Sea, thus reasserting Muslim domination of the Gulf of Aqaba. Amalric was gravely concerned by developments in the south. Now that an able ruler was in control of Egypt there was a growing possibility that he would face attacks from both the south and the east, where Nur al-Din was an ever-present threat. During 1171 Amalric visited Constantinople to meet the Byzantine Emperor Manuel Comnenus, where he was cordially entertained and promised further assistance.

The rift between Saladin and Nur al-Din was becoming ever more apparent. Saladin seemed to time his attacks on the Franks to coincide with his master's campaigns in the far north of Syria, to prevent any opportunity of the two men meeting. The reason for this was clear: Saladin knew that if he met his master he could be ordered to some new commission and forbidden to return to Egypt. He knew that his authority in Egypt came from the Caliph al-Adil and not from Nur al-Din. During October 1171 Saladin advanced into Oultrejourdain to besiege the castle of Shaubak. When he heard the news, Nur al-Din hastened to join his vassal only to find that Saladin had promptly broken off the siege, complaining of heavy casualties and the dangers of a conspiracy in Cairo. Nur al-Din was no fool and was grudgingly giving credence to the arguments of his advisers that Saladin should be deposed. Saladin had already considered this eventuality and had concluded that a declaration of revolt against Nur al-Din would be politically harmful and should be avoided until the very last moment.

For nearly two years Saladin had been in independent control of Egypt and Nur al-Din had done little to interfere. Nevertheless, he had invested money and men in the conquest of Egypt and he clearly thought Saladin remiss in not sending a regular payment to Damascus. It has been suggested that Nur al-Din had provided Shirkuh with at least 200 000 dinars. In return Saladin sent 'gifts' rather than regular income. It was as if he considered himself to be an independent ruler dealing with an equal. He is reported as having sent Nur al-Din jewels from the Fatimid royal treasure, as well as an ass of the finest breed and an elephant.[10] Quite what Nur al-Din thought of this whimsical gift is not recorded but he was generally dissatisfied and obviously expected something resembling more of an annual subsidy from Egypt. This Saladin was unwilling to do as it would have weakened his own capacity to raise troops, either to fight the Franks or to resist Nur al-Din should this be necessary.

The campaigning season of 1173 again brought the two rulers very close to an open rift. While Saladin besieged Kerak, Nur al-Din moved to his support from the north. When he was informed of the movement of the Syrian troops Saladin promptly broke off the siege on the grounds that his father Ayyub had been taken ill. This was far from a convincing pretext and, even though he was trying to avoid an open rift, it was obvious that Saladin was defying his master. Nur al-Din was determined, however, to discipline his disobedient vassal and withdrew to Damascus to prepare himself for war. In May 1174, summonses were sent from Damascus to Mosul, Diyar Bakr and al-Jazira calling troops to prepare for a major expedition, and the general opinion was that this would be against Egypt. What the effects of a war between Saladin and Nur al-Din would have been on the future of Muslim unity is difficult to estimate. Certainly only Amalric of Jerusalem would have stood to benefit. However, fate had decreed otherwise. Before he could put into operation any plans for matching his strength against Egypt Nur al-Din fell ill and died on 15 May 1174, of a quinsy. His greatness was to be eclipsed by Saladin and yet it should not go unnoticed that William of Tyre expressed the opinion of most Christians when he said Nur al-Din was, 'the greatest persecutor of the Christian name and faith, but a just ruler, astute and far-sighted and, according to the traditions of his race, a religious man'.[11]

4

Saladin in Syria: 1174–86

The death of Nur al-Din in 1174 marked a watershed not only in Saladin's personal life but in the history of the crusades. Though Saladin may have viewed the Atabeg as an obstacle to his ambitions, in other ways Nur al-Din had exercised a profound influence on the younger man's political education. From him Saladin had learned to ally the holy war or *jihād* with a policy of gradual growth; to use religious propaganda as a weapon every bit as potent as armed force; and to value men's loyalty and seek to win it rather than merely to pursue a course of personal aggrandisement. The death of Nur al-Din, following so closely on that of his father, Ayyub, brought Saladin a degree of political independence he had never known before. He need no longer feel indebted to Syria for men and money; Egypt was his base. Now he could look forward to incorporating Nur al-Din's lands in an Ayyubid state, committed to the holy war.

However, Saladin could not long afford the luxury of contemplation for events followed fast on the death of Nur al-Din. The chief officers of Nur al-Din's army promptly set about trying to win control of his eleven-year-old son, al-Malik as-Salih. Meanwhile, Nur al-Din's nephews, 'Imad al-Din Zangi in Sinjar and Saif al-Din Ghazi in Mosul cast predatory eyes on as-Salih in Syria. For a while Saladin could do no more than keep abreast of the situation, for a naval attack by the King of Sicily on Alexandria kept him fully occupied simply holding what he had won in Egypt. Moreover, he had acknowledged as-Salih as his suzerain, as a mark of respect to his father; it would have been unwise to have appeared to covet Syria so soon after Nur al-Din's death. However, if Saladin's political sensibilities prevented him acting hastily, there were others who did not suffer from such scrupulousness. Facing a crisis in Damascus the ruling emirs made a truce with the Franks of Jerusalem so that they could turn their attention to their own domestic problems, which were many. Saif al-Din Ghazi of Mosul invaded and annexed all of as-Salih's territories beyond the Euphrates, in al-Jazira; while in August 1174 the eunuch Gumushtekin gained control of as-Salih and set himself up at Aleppo by imprisoning Nur al-Din's officers. Certainly the unity of Islam was now severely damaged and only the death of Amalric I (from dysentery) prevented the Franks exploiting the situation to their own advantage. The break-up of the centralised military command that Nur al-Din had created was a great blow to Muslim hopes of success in the holy war. None of the Atabeg's family possessed the necessary qualities to succeed him. However, although Saladin had such qualities he could not hope to achieve success within the Zangid structure created by Nur al-Din and Ayyub. As an outsider and a Kurd he would inevitably face opposition from legitimists who already felt that he had committed treason against Nur al-Din by his actions in Egypt. To them he was truly the 'dog barking at his master'. He had been the creation of Nur al-Din who repaid his master by stealing his lands and property.

Saladin was in a difficult position: he had to decide whether to operate inside or outside the existing Zangid structure. As the *de facto* ruler of Egypt he clearly possessed greater resources and stronger armed forces than any of the Zangid rulers. Moreover, he recognised the strategic advantages (in terms of the holy war) of operating from Damascus rather than Egypt. Logic surely demanded that he should succeed Nur al-Din as the leader of the *jihād*, and absorb the Zangid empire into a greater Ayyubite empire. However, as the vassal of Nur al-Din and now of his son, as-Salih, he would find it difficult to justify intervening in Syria unless he was either invited to do so by those representing the young ruler or forced to do so by anarchy within the late Nur al-Din's lands. The alternative was for him to create a new political structure, built on moral foundations and committed to the holy war which he could persuade the Zangid princes to join either by peaceful means or by force. If he chose the latter he would be upheld both by his inner conviction that he was doing God's work and by the public recognition granted to him by the Caliph of Baghdad.

When Saladin set off from Egypt in October 1174, it was with the intention of not only restoring the unity of Nur al-Din's lands but of creating a state incorporating Egypt, Syria and Mesopotamia with the single purpose of pursuing the holy war against the Franks of Outremer. To his contemporaries, who had none of the advantages of later commentators, Saladin's action seemed quite understandable. To them he was merely a successful commander who intended to exploit the chaos following the death of Nur al-Din by gaining as much as he could for himself and his family. However, in this they were wrong. They were attributing to him motives that they shared and which, in their view, were universal imperatives. But with Saladin they were dealing with that unusual figure — the honest man — who did not need to strike postures or adopt causes for political effect, because his qualities were the sort that inspired respect. Saladin's unselfishness was revealed on numerous occasions, as was his humility, his generosity and his deep morality. It was difficult to snipe at a man like him because his every gesture bore the stamp of the charismatic leader. Yet, though he was not a great general, diplomat, or politician, he was a man moved by simple ideals, who refused to compromise them in pursuit of personal gain. In time even his enemies would be forced to accept this.

Saladin moved quickly, taking with him a force of just 700 chosen riders. He expected to receive reinforcements as he advanced into Syria and in this he was not disappointed, being joined on the way to Damascus by emirs, soldiers, Turks, Kurds and Bedouin. As he approached the city a part of the Damascene army drew up to bar his way but they were unprepared to fight and after asking quarter from Saladin they dispersed and he entered the city.

It might appear that Saladin had taken a great risk by advancing into the territory of the Zangids with so slight a force and by committing himself so far from home. Yet he was right in believing that money, liberally and astutely applied, could achieve more for him than armed force. It is said that he spent the wealth of Egypt on the conquest of Syria. Nevertheless, Saladin must have been confident in the support he was likely to have in the city for he was a cautious man who was unlikely to risk everything on the simple chance that Damascus would fall to him without a struggle. Indeed there was one awkward moment when the Emir Raihan occupied the citadel in Damascus with his troops and Saladin was forced to order his brother, Tughtekin, to surround it. However, by assuring Raihan that he had come simply to support the house of Nur al-Din Saladin was able to arrange terms of agreement with him. It was a bloodless occupation and when the people compared the way that Saladin treated them with the way they had suffered recently under the Zangids they were immediately won over. His occupation of Damascus on 28 October 1174 was not an act of conquest but a first step on the path to the holy war. He had taken the city the Arabs called the 'Bride of the Earth' and the 'Garden of the World'.

But if Damascus was the key to southern Syria and the war against the Franks it would need to be defended from its Muslim foes to the north. Saladin could not simply rest after taking Damascus without attempting to liberate as-Salih in Aleppo. He did not have to wait long before he heard from the rulers of that city. While still in Damascus he received an envoy from the Zangids who threatened him with the direst consequences if he tried to move against them. When Saladin insisted that he had merely come to Syria to uphold the rights of as-Salih he was told: 'you want the kingdom for yourself; go back where you came from'.[1] Clearly the rulers of Aleppo were determined to portray Saladin simply as an aggressor, motivated by greed and ambition.

Leaving Damascus under the authority of his brother, Tughtekin, Saladin marched northwards, skirting the Jebel esh Sharqi (Anti Lebanon) mountain range to the east and avoiding the hostile garrison in Baalbek. Speed was essential and he had neither time nor the equipment for protracted sieges. Reaching Homs on 8 December, his army now numbered more than 7000, and he was further strengthened by the arrival of Nur al-Din's army commander, Fakhr al-Din ibn al-Za'farani, who held the *iqta* of Homs. After a brief siege he was able to occupy the town of Homs, but the citadel held out resolutely against him and he was compelled to leave a force to mask it. After negotiations with the governor of Hama it was agreed that the town but not the citadel should be surrendered to Saladin. Arriving at Aleppo on 30 December 1174, Saladin called on Gumushtekin to surrender both the city and the boy as-Salih to him as his rightful guardian. However, Aleppo was protected by formidable fortifications and its citadel was one of the strongest in the world. Moreover, the Aleppans had no intention of surrendering. Whatever rights Saladin believed he possessed were disputed by the members of the house of Zangi. As-Salih appealed to the people to protect him and in return he restored privileges to the Muslim Shiites which his father had previously withdrawn.[2] Meanwhile, the vizier, the eunuch Gumushtekin, made a treaty with Raymond of Tripoli, regent of the kingdom of Jerusalem, for the Franks to threaten Homs and so draw off Saladin's pressure on Aleppo. Not content with this, the Aleppans also appealed to Rashid al-Din Sinan, the 'Old Man of the Mountains', to send an assassin to kill Saladin. While he was encamped outside Aleppo a group of some 13 of these *fidawis* approached his tent but were fortunately recognised by one of Saladin's emirs, Khumartekin, who sounded the alarm before being cut down. One assassin forced his way into Saladin's tent but was swiftly decapitated by another emir. Although the attempt failed, Saladin was certainly shaken.

The Frankish feint towards Homs caused Saladin to relax his grip on Aleppo on 26 January 1175. He thereupon spent a month besieging the formidable citadel at Homs, one so high that it was said to wear the clouds as a turban. Casualties were unfortunately heavy on both sides until, at last, his sappers undermined the walls and forced an entry into the citadel. Saladin now showed just how much he differed from the picture painted of him by Zangid propaganda. He was no cruel and ruthless tyrant, for the lives of all the defenders were spared. Saladin was more concerned to conquer men's hearts than their cities.

Meanwhile, Saif al-Din Ghazi, Atabeg of Mosul, had sent his younger brother, 'Izz al-Din Mas'ud, with an army to the relief of Aleppo. But the Zangids were failing to present a united front against Saladin, for Imad al-Din, Zangi of Sinjar, had refused to come to the assistance of Saif al-Din, whereupon the strength of Mosul was split, with half going to the aid of Aleppo and the rest remaining with Saif al-Din to help him in his attacks on Sinjar. Nevertheless, Saladin did not underestimate the threat posed by the union of Aleppo and Mosul. In his negotiations with them he appeared as conciliatory as possible, offering to return into Aleppan control the fortresses of Homs, Hama and Baalbek (which he had recently taken) in return for Aleppan help in the holy war against the Franks. The Zangid emissaries took this as a sign of weakness and broke off the negotiations, hoping to overwhelm Saladin's small army. However, Saladin had been playing for time until his Egyptian reinforcements reached him. There was now no alternative but a bloody solution to be sought on the battlefield. On 13 April 1175 the armies came together at the Horns of Hama, a combined force of some 20 000 men, mostly horsemen. Saladin took up his position in the centre of his battle line and, after a preliminary skirmish, his cavalry routed their opponents who fled from the field in disarray, abandoning their camp, baggage and infantry to his mercy. There was no substitute for experience and Saladin's battle-hardened veterans were far too accomplished for the Zangid troops; his commanders outmanoeuvred the confused 'Izz al-Din Mas'ud, who showed courage but no military acumen. At one stage Saladin was forced to remark that 'Izz al-Din had placed himself in an impossibly dangerous position and was either the bravest man present or a complete fool.[3] Saladin had nothing to gain by pursuing his enemy and adding to the bitterness of their defeat by multiplying their casualties. He wanted no legacy of blood, and he knew that he would soon need these same men that he had defeated to make up his armies for the holy war against the Franks.

Saladin returned in triumph to Aleppo in April 1175. The Aleppan emirs broke off their alliance with the Franks and Gumushtekin now had no alternative but to accept Saladin's terms. Aleppo was to remain in the hands of as-Salih and his name was to be retained on the coinage throughout Saladin's lands, but Saladin was to hold his conquests in northern Syria and Aleppan troops were to combine with him in campaigns against the Franks. He was, however, far from content with the mere fact of conquest. He felt the need to have the sanction of law and holy writ. Yet in reply to his urgent letters demanding to be acknowledged as the leader of Islam in the holy war and rightful ruler of Nur al-Din's lands in the name of as-Salih, the Abbasid Caliph of Baghdad was unwilling to take sides against the Zangids. Soon after his return from Aleppo the caliph's envoys brought Saladin formal confirmation of his investiture with the combined governments of Egypt, Yemen and the parts of Syria he already held. However, the caliph made it clear that he must maintain friendly relations with as-Salih and by no means covet Aleppo or its possessions. He was reminded of his duty to the holy war and the fact that his Egyptian lands were as likely battlefields as those of Syria.

The real danger posed by Saladin was more clearly understood by the Franks than it was by his fellow Muslims. Where the latter saw him simply as a more than averagely successful warlord, the Franks saw that he had a wisdom and an incorruptibility which singled him out from other Muslim leaders. He spoke of holy war with a conviction which boded ill for the kingdom of Jerusalem. His Christian enemies feared and respected him, and were willing to support his opponents within the Muslim world. On the other hand, the jealousy of Saladin's Muslim rivals prevented them from seeing his true worth. Saif al-Din Ghazi of Mosul, for example, was outraged when he heard that the caliph had confirmed Saladin's rule in Syria. After all, Saladin was merely one of Nur al-Din's protégés. How could he dare to rise above the house of Zangi, to whom he owed everything? Saladin was a Kurd, hated and despised by the Turks, who took their supremacy in government for granted; he was the son and nephew of adventurers, who had wanted to establish their own family in the highest positions in the land; he seemed to be willing to challenge the Zangid dynasty and replace it with that of Ayyub, his father. Again his opponents misunderstood his motives, seeing in his actions simply the dynastic drives so prevalent in Muslim society in the years after the collapse of the Selchuk polity. Where Saladin wished to give power to those on whom he could rely, namely his kinsfolk, his enemies saw only a tyrannical nepotist. It is doubtful whether even Saladin's own family understood his true intentions.

In the spring of 1176 the struggle against Aleppo and Mosul was renewed. Saif al-Din Ghazi crossed the Euphrates with the army of Mosul and reached an agreement with Gumushtekin and as-Salih outside Aleppo. Saladin was in Damascus during this and was not slow to take up the challenge, advancing north with a force of 6000 men. At Tall as-Sultan, he broke the Zangid army and in al-Fadil's poetic phrase 'The trees of Saladin's spears bear fruit, while those of the enemy cast no shadow'.[4] In his encounters with Zangid troops Saladin never lost sight of the fact that he was fighting fellow Muslims. Necessary as the bloodshed was in welding together a unified state, he realised that every drop spilled made that unity more difficult. His co-religionists would never forgive him if he took more lives than was necessary and so he reined back his troops from pursuing the shattered Zangids. Instead he released the captives, recruiting many for his own service, and returned to Saif al-Din Ghazi the cages of doves, nightingales and parrots that had been found in his camp, suggesting that he confine himself to such amusements in the future as he was clearly unsuited to military adventures.[5] Saladin had been shocked by the decadence of the Mosuli camp, which he likened to a tavern, filled with wines, guitars, lutes, bands, singers and dancing girls. As Oliver Cromwell might have done in a later age Saladin displayed such worldly vanities to his troops and sternly warned them against ever succumbing to their like.

Saladin now returned to besiege Aleppo but his efforts were aimed at achieving a diplomatic rather than a military solution to the campaign. In fact, he withdrew after a while and attacked instead the strong fortress of A'zaz. It was here that he suffered a second attack from the 'Assassins'. Again he was only saved by the courage and quick action of his companions and the fact that he wore a mail head-dress under his fez. One Assassin managed to stab him in the head with a knife; failing here, he stabbed at Saladin's neck. Although all four Assassins were killed, one of Saladin's emirs died and he himself returned to his tent with his cuirass pierced through and blood streaming from his face. His whole camp was in turmoil. Saladin's nerve was tried far more than it had ever been in battle. For a while he seemed almost paranoid, suspecting every stranger of harbouring a knife and strewing chalk and cinders around his tent to detect secret footsteps. He was later driven to mount an attack on the Assassin stronghold in central Syria and began a siege of the fortress of Masyaf, high up on a cliff. One night Saladin claimed that he awoke from sleep only to see a dark figure slipping out of his tent. Looking round he noticed a tray of hot scones of the kind made famous by the Assassins and on them lay a paper bearing the following verses:

By the Majesty of the Kingdom! What you possess will
    escape you, in spite of all, but victory remains to us:
We acquaint you that *we hold you*, and that we reserve you
    till your reckoning be paid.[6]

He hastily raised the siege and from that time he never again threatened the Assassins, nor was he a target for their knives.

Meanwhile, after a siege of nearly six weeks A'zaz fell and Saladin was able to return to Aleppo where he renewed the agreement made the year before. A general peace followed between Damascus (in which Saladin's brother Turan-Shah had been installed), the cities of Mosul, Aleppo and the Artukid princes of Hisn Kaifa and Mardin. This allowed Saladin to return to Damascus where he married the widow of Nur al-Din, Ismat al-Din Khatunthus, further enhancing his claims to be the legitimate successor to the late Atabeg.

The truce with the Franks had allowed hostilities to be resumed 'if any king or great noble arrived' and 'the armistice should be renewed on his withdrawal'. In 1177 Philip, Count of

Flanders arrived in Palestine and the Franks had great hopes that he would use his considerable force to help them in a combined attack with the Byzantine navy on Egypt. In fact, Philip of Flanders was by no means an easy man to deal with. He appeared vacillating to the frustrated native barons of Jerusalem but clearly had designs that he did not reveal to them. Eventually, he allowed himself to be persuaded by the Christian rulers of Tripoli and Antioch to use his troops in a northern campaign to attack Hama and Harim. This presented Saladin with an opportunity to attack southern Palestine, particularly Ascalon and Gaza, while the bulk of the Christian army was occupied elsewhere. Unfortunately for Saladin, his Egyptian troops were over-confident and undisciplined. Consequently, Baldwin IV's surprise attack on them at Montgisard on 25 November inflicted on Saladin the most serious defeat of his career. Nevertheless, he was not slow to learn from his mistakes and his defeat did nothing to reduce his commitment to *jihād*. He also realized that the Franks presented a greater obstacle than he had originally supposed and now knew that only with the combined armies of Syria, Mesopotamia and Egypt could he hope to succeed against them. The withdrawal of the Count of Flanders meant that the truce with the Franks was automatically restored. However, it was not long before Baldwin IV, in August 1178, broke it again by attacking Hama. In situations like this Saladin showed the severity of his nature. With oath- or truce-breakers he showed no mercy and he had the Frankish prisoners who were captured at Hama executed by Muslim men of piety. It was to be a feature of his rule that, though this habit of using non-combatants to kill prisoners as an amusing spectacle was not of his invention, he permitted it to continue for oath-breakers.

In October 1178, Baldwin IV (with Templar support) began the construction of the strong fortress of Bait al-Ahzan, which controlled the crossing at Jisr Banat Ya'qub of one of the main routes to Damascus. The area it overlooked was known as the 'granary' of Damascus and contained rice and cotton fields as well as groves of lemon trees. The plain had previously been peacefully shared by Christian and Muslim and the actual border was marked by a single oak tree. Here flocks grazed side by side. The building of a fortress there was a definite act of provocation and Saladin could not let it go unchallenged. Firstly, he offered the Frankish king 60 000, then 100 000, dinars to stop work on it but when this was declined he determined to destroy the fortress.[7] It was situated a day's march from Damascus and if fortified it would have seriously threatened the peace of the Muslim frontier. In June 1179 Saladin heard from his spies that the Franks were planning a raid; therefore he ordered Farrukh-Shah, with his garrison of less than 1000 men at Damascus, not to engage the Franks but to retire before them, lighting beacons to warn of their advance, whereupon Saladin would march out with his full force. The Franks, eager to capture the unprotected herds on the pastures of the Golan Heights made a night advance which took Farrukh-Shah by surprise and involved him in fighting before he could retire as arranged. The Franks were overconfident and Baldwin led his men rashly against the Muslim vanguard, not realising the size of the force hidden on the rocky slopes. Farrukh-Shah's Mamelukes inflicted very heavy casualties on the Franks and drove them off the field in disarray. While covering the retreat, the old constable Humphrey of Toron was killed covering the young king with his body and being riddled with arrows. His loss was mourned by all alike: one Arab historian wrote that 'No words can describe Hunfary; his name was a proverb for bravery and skill in war. He was indeed a plague let loose by God for the chastening of the Muslims'.[8] Saladin, advancing rapidly to close the trap, was astonished to receive the news (by carrier pigeon) that the Franks had already been routed.

The Franks were stung by their defeat and Baldwin swiftly took the field again with a strong force. Moving north from Tiberias, he tracked west through the hills, past Safad and Tibnin and finally to a point overlooking the wide plain of Marj 'Uyun. His circuitous route had taken Saladin by surprise and the Franks were able to gaze down on the Muslim campfires. However, Baldwin now proceeded to waste his opportunity. Farrukh-Shah was sent out on a raid but Baldwin failed to trap either this force or attack Saladin's camp, while it was depleted. Eventually news reached Saladin from nomadic herdsmen that a substantial Frankish army was in the vicinity. Saladin acted with commendable speed, getting his troops into battle formation and sending his baggage to Banias for safety. Farrukh-Shah, meanwhile, had been trapped on the Christian side of the River Litani, and was trying to fight his way back to join Saladin. His baggage had been seized and plundered by Frankish infantry and this had resulted in the splitting of the Christian army. Baldwin and Raymond of Tripoli, who were commanding the Frankish troops, now found that they had badly misjudged the Saracen strength. As Farrukh-Shah's men forced their way across the Litani from the west they were joined by Saladin's troops advancing from the south-east. The Franks were ensnared in a trap of their own making. Many of the Christian knights were trapped on a hillside and forced to surrender. The great knight Baldwin of Ramla was captured single-handed by the Kurdish chieftain, Jamal al-Din Khushtarin. A total of 270 knights were taken prisoner, including the Master of the Templars, Odo of Saint-Amand: 'a haughty, arrogant man, with the breath of fury in his nostrils, who feared not God nor respected men'.[9] In some ways Odo had been the cause of the disaster through his rashness, but when Saladin offered to ransom him he replied, 'A Templar can give for his ransom nought but his belt and dagger'. Saladin kept him imprisoned until he died. His special hatred was reserved for the Templars and Hospitallers, whom he regarded as fanatical opponents of Islam and whom he generally killed when he took them prisoner.

Saladin now closed in on the fortress at Jisr Banat Ya'qub, which was built on a sizeable mound, about 875 yards in circumference, overlooking the River Jordan. Instead of bringing up his siege equipment he decided to try a swift assault and succeeded in capturing the settlement around the citadel and forcing the Frankish defenders inside the castle. So fierce was the Muslim assault that the Franks built fires behind their gate in case they were broken down by an immediate assault. Saladin ordered his sappers to begin undermining the castle walls, and after several days part of the stonework collapsed. Again the defenders lit a fire behind this breach in order to keep the attackers at bay, but the wind blew the flames back on them until the whole fortress seemed to be ablaze. The defenders now realised that the relief force that they had expected was not going to arrive in time and that they had no option but to surrender. Of the original garrison of 1500 more than 700 were taken prisoner and Saladin ordered the execution of those Muslims found within who had either adopted Christianity or had sold their services to the infidels. He also reflected the contemporary Muslim hatred of crossbowmen (whose efficiency against his lightly armoured warriors was fearful) by ordering these troops also to be put to the sword. Saladin personally supervised the destruction of this fortress and would not leave the scene until every stone had been removed. He later wrote to the caliph that he had pulled out the foundation stone with his own hands. The castle well, one of phenomenal depth, was then used to inter the bodies of the castle garrison, and finally filled up with earth and lime. Nevertheless, even in death the Frankish warriors inflicted a final blow on Saladin's army. The hot weather accelerated the decomposition of the bodies and produced an outbreak of disease which inflicted greater losses on the Muslims than either the successful siege of Bait al-Ahzan or the battle of Marj 'Uyun. Ten of Saladin's leading emirs died and his nephew, Taqi al-Din, barely recovered his health.[10]

For the operations of 1178–79, Saladin had been forced to rely on his Damascene and Egyptian troops, and the lack of support from the Zangid cities of Aleppo and Mosul showed him that he could not hope to overthrow the full strength of the Franks without their co-operation. There was no alternative but to continue his struggle to bring the military potential of Aleppo and Mosul under his control and if this meant delaying the *jihād* and even fighting fellow Muslims then so be it. He had clearly established his right as successor to Nur al-Din and this brought him support from people in Mosul and Aleppo who could not accept their own leaders' close relations with the Franks or their attempted use of assassination against Saladin. His close observance of legal rights and his obvious commitment to the *jihād* made him seem more worthy in their eyes. The complex campaigns that took up most of the years from 1179 until 1185 were designed to bring under Saladin's control the full potential of Muslim strength for the holy war to regain Jerusalem.

Saladin realised that his best hope of gaining control of Mosul would be by prising away the powerful vassals of the Mosul rulers, who supplied at least half of the city's military power. Prominent among these were the Artukid princes of Diyar-Bakr, particularly those of Hisn Kaifa and Mardin. When fate offered Saladin a chance to interfere between Nur al-Din, Prince of Hisn Kaifa, and the Selchukid Sultan Kilij Arslan II, he was not slow to accept. Nur al-Din, though a vassal of Mosul, appealed for help to Saladin, probably as a result of the general agreement of 1176. Secure in the knowledge that a truce had been arranged with the Franks, Saladin marched his forces to the borders of the Selchukid realm to threaten the Sultan Kilij Arslan and warn him to leave the affairs of Diyar-Bakr alone. The two sultans met on the River Sanja in June 1180 and there concluded an alliance. Saladin thereby removed another potential threat to his northern frontier as well as demonstrating his suzerainty over the princes of Diyar-Bakr.

On 29 June 1180 Saladin's implacable enemy, Saif al-Din Ghazi, died at Mosul, nominating his son Sanjar-Shah to succeed him. However, this wish was set aside by his brother 'Izz al-Din who seized power for himself. He sent envoys to Saladin asking him to accept the suzerainty of Mosul over the Mesopotamian cities that his brother had seized on the death of Nur al-Din in 1174. This was clearly provocative and Saladin refused absolutely to concede these cities which had been granted him by the diploma of the Caliph of Baghdad. Furiously Saladin informed the caliph that he needed these cities if he was to maintain pressure on the Franks. The caliph duly obliged by confirming the original grant. There could be no peace with Mosul while 'Izz al-Din refused to accept Saladin's pre-eminent position in Syria and Mesopotamia.

Matters were further complicated when as-Salih died in December 1181, at the age of 19. His death from colic was attributed by many to poison. Had the young man lived to rule in his own right, and father sons, then perhaps Saladin's route to supremacy in the lands of Nur al-Din would have been permanently blocked. As he lay dying as-Salih made his emirs swear fealty to his cousin, 'Izz al-Din of Mosul, the only remaining Zangid with the strength to hold off Saladin. For Saladin himself there could no forgiveness for the treachery he had shown to the dynasty which had raised him so far.

As it was, Saladin was again the beneficiary of a timely death. Yet it may not have seemed so fortunate to him at the time for he was in Egypt and too far from the centre of events to interfere. He sent urgent orders to his brother Farrukh-Shah at Damascus and his nephew Taqi al-Din at Hama to occupy quickly western Jazira and prevent the Mosulis from crossing the Euphrates. But for once fate was againt him. Farrukh-Shah had invaded the lands of Oultrejourdain to force Reynald of Châtillon, Lord of Kerak, to withdraw from his invasion of Arabia. Consequently he was unable to act in time to stop 'Izz al-Din entering Aleppo, pillaging its arsenal and treasury, and leaving his brother, 'Imad al-Din, there as governor. Saladin was impotently forced to resort to written complaints sent to the caliph's council at Baghdad, claiming that the Prince of Mosul had seized land not allocated to him and that his activities were weakening the *jihād*. He was now involved in a desperate propaganda battle with the

Zangids to win the support of the caliph. As he pointed out, while his troops under Farrukh-Shah were protecting the gateway to Medina and were defending the Prophet's tomb, the Mosulis were seizing land from their co-religionists and were allying with the Franks. Yet Saladin must have realised that his claims to Aleppo were based on nothing more solid than his view of himself as champion of Islam. He had never owned Aleppo and the fact that it was continuing in the hands of the Zangid family was

In May 1182, Saladin left Egypt with 5000 troops from his reformed Egyptian army and set out to march on Aleppo. This was to be the last time he saw Egypt and as he left Cairo an old Arab poet called out words of ill-omen to him:

> Enjoy the perfume of the ox-eyes of Nejd
> After tonight, there will be no more ox-eyes.[11]

It is doubtful if he was optimistic of taking the city, and he knew that resistance would be lengthy and determined. However, before he reached Aleppo he received a visit from the Zangid Governor of Harran, Muzaffar al-Din Keukburi, who advised him that instead of besieging Aleppo he should cross the Euphrates, where he was certain of a warm welcome. This was an attractive proposition. After all, if he besieged Aleppo the Mosulis would undoubtedly take the offensive against him, but if he crossed the Euphrates the Mosulis would be forced onto the defensive. Moreover, Saladin was confident because he already possessed the caliph's diploma for the trans-Euphratean territories and so he took up al-Din Keukburi's offer. 'Izz al-Din was furious and attempted to bring his army out to oppose Saladin but he was prevented by a mutiny among his own officers. Saladin now advanced on Mosul itself, hastily justifying his action to the caliph by accusing 'Izz al-Din of first bribing the Franks to attack him and, when this failed, of trying to persuade the Selchukid ruler of Persia to do so. There is little doubt that 'Izz al-Din was feverishly seeking allies and was not being very selective as to whom he chose. Eventually the caliph arranged a mediation between the two sides, hoping to persuade 'Izz al-Din to agree to support Saladin in any future holy war against the Franks.

'Izz al-Din's intentions during the negotiations were to retain his hold on Aleppo, but for Saladin a negotiated settlement posed certain problems. His supporters in the Jazira had risked much to

invite his protection and if they now saw him willing to negotiate
with Mosul their confidence in him would quickly have evapo-
rated. Saladin therefore broke off the negotiations and, helped by
Nur al-Din of Hisn Kaifa, besieged Sinjar, taking the city after 15
days when the garrison became careless. After seizing Dara,
Saladin went into winter quarters. 'Izz al-Din now called up all
his allies and Saladin retaliated by summoning Taqi al-Din to his
aid. On the arrival of Saladin's nephew the coalition formed by
'Izz al-Din promptly collapsed; in the words of one commenta-
tor, 'they advanced like men; like women they vanished'.

Thus encouraged, Saladin besieged the previously impregnable Mosuli fortress of Amid, defended by massive walls of black
basalt, iron gates and a moat provided by a loop of the River
Tigris. After a siege of three weeks Saladin's engineers made a
breach in the walls and the city was looted. It was a place of
immense value, possessing a library of 'a million volumes', which
greatly attracted al-Fadil, who removed selected volumes on the
backs of 70 camels.[12] What followed showed another side to
Saladin's character: to the amazement of his followers, he handed
over the city and all its vast treasure to Nur al-Din, his faithful
ally from Hisn Kaifa. Mosuli claims that he was inspired by
greed and personal ambition now seemed even further from the
truth.

Saladin's success in taking Amid had a major effect on his
opponents. The remaining Artukid princes — of Maiyafariqin
and Mardin — came over to his side and the outlying Aleppan
fortresses of Tall Khalid and Aintab fell to him without a
struggle. Saladin continued to send letter after letter to the caliph
insisting that the capture of Amid had owed much to the fact that
the population of that town had known that he held the caliph's
diploma. Mosul would fall to him likewise if only the caliph
would extend his diploma to include that city. While other
Muslim leaders spent their time in sports and idle luxury, Saladin
alone was the flag-bearer of Islam. Which of them, Saladin asked
the caliph, was the greater threat to the enemies of Islam, he
himself or the ruler of Mosul?[13]

All that remained of the campaign in northern Syria was to
close in on Aleppo itself. In May 1183 he camped before its walls
but it was with a heavy heart that he contemplated the bloody
struggle that might be needed before the city fell. Within the
walls were the *Nuriyah*, the old guard of Nur al-Din, whom he had
known well in his youth and who had fought so well for the *jihād*

in the past. He wanted these men with him not against him. His own army included many of the younger and more ardent soldiers of Islam, eager to fight any who stood in the way of *jihād*. In spite of Saladin's own feelings that bloodshed should be avoided if at all possible these hotheads rushed into the attack and in the savage fighting Saladin's own brother, Taj al-Muluk Buri, was killed. This loss affected Saladin greatly and in order to avoid unnecessary casualties he withdrew a short distance and erected a fortress within which he began to allocate Aleppan fiefs to his senior officers. Inside Aleppo 'Imad al-Din was unhappy at the turn of events. He knew he was unpopular with the Aleppans and had no wish to fight for a city that he did not care for; he simply wished to return to Sinjar, the city he loved. Secretly he approached Saladin about the possibility of an exchange and was well received. Saladin made it clear that he wanted only 'the stones of Aleppo' and was content to allow 'Imad-al-Din to remove the valuables and the stores from the citadel. On the basis of a promise that he would aid Saladin with his troops in the *jihād*, 'Imad al-Din was allowed to retire to Sinjar, amidst the hoots and derision of the Aleppans who likened him to an old washer-woman rather than a king, offering him a wash-tub rather than a crown.[14] On 11 June 1183 Saladin's great yellow banner was raised above the citadel of Aleppo and his followers took possession of the city to the enthusiastic cheers of the vast crowds. They seemed to recognise in him the qualities of the late Nur al-Din. Saladin's old comrades in arms, the *Nuriyah* troops, submitted to him with some alacrity and were welcomed with open arms. Thus only Harim remained in Zangid hands and when its commander tried to come to terms with Bohemond III of Antioch, his soldiers arrested him and surrendered the castle to Saladin's troops on 22 June.

Saladin had been away from Egypt for over a year and during that time matters had not been quiet on the border between the Franks and the Egyptians. Most notably, Reynald of Châtillon had launched his Red Sea campaign which had inflicted unprecedented shame on the Muslim world. Prompt action by Saladin's brother al-Adil had limited the damage caused by the Frankish fleet but the instigator of the raid, the Lord of Kerak himself, had escaped unscathed and retained his hold over the caravan routes between Cairo and Damascus, which ran through Oultrejourdain. Saladin was determined now to pursue the *jihād* against the Franks and his first object was to destroy the castle of

Kerak which had become a symbol alike of Frankish power and Muslim impotence. On two occasions, in November 1183 and August–September 1184, Saladin turned his full fury against Kerak; both times he failed. The second assault involved for the first time a combined army of Egyptians, Syrians and Mesopotamians, with Turkish cavalry, and was the strongest force he had yet raised. In spite of this, however, he had to accept that so long as the Franks operated on internal lines and refused to be drawn into precipitate action, it would be very difficult to defeat their field army if it was capably handled.

Meanwhile, 'Izz al-Din of Mosul had not remained inactive. He had received military assistance from the Selchukid rulers of Persia and Azerbaijan, and was proposing to attack the city of Irbil, whose governor called on Saladin for assistance. The time had come to settle finally matters with 'Izz al-Din and Saladin was fortunate that the severe drought which was affecting Palestine and Syria prompted Raymond of Tripoli, as regent of the kingdom of Jerusalem, to agree to a four-year truce. With his rear defended Saladin felt confident enough to march on Mosul in May 1185. The Selchukid Sultan Kilij Arslan, warned Saladin that if he attacked Mosul he would be opposed by a coalition of eastern princes; but in the event no one was willing to fight for the city. Saladin quickly encircled Mosul and began the siege which lasted (on and off) for seven months. 'Izz al-Din tried to soften Saladin's hard heart by sending him an embassy of the leading Zangid princesses but he refused to be moved. However, as winter drew on Saladin fell dangerously ill and in his weakened state he repented of his harsh dealing with the embassy. He therefore withdrew his troops from the city and despatched a mission to Mosul. 'Izz al-Din was by now as eager as his brother had been at Aleppo to achieve the best terms he could. He was able to obtain from Saladin the restoration of the small district of Baina-n-Nahrain, as well as recognition of his suzerainty over Mosul. In return he promised Saladin his full assistance in the *jihād* against the Franks of Palestine. Saladin had admitted, after the capture of Aleppo, that his great aim was not the possession of territory for its own sake but for the military forces it could provide. He had at last united Egypt with the lands of Nur al-Din and he was ready now to begin the *jihād* against the kingdom of Jerusalem. It had been a lengthy process but throughout Saladin had been sustained by an inner conviction that what he was doing was ordained by God.

5

The Kingdom of Jerusalem:
Dramatis personae

Reynald of Châtillon

The knights who followed Louis VII's crusade to the Holy Land in 1147 included many who had abandoned all pretence of being soldiers of Christ. Their motives were clearly acquisitive and they found in the Latin lands of Outremer opportunities denied them at home. Of those who chose to carve out for themselves a new life in the desert lands, none was to play a greater part in the future of the kingdom than Reynald of Châtillon, younger son of Geoffrey, Count of Gien, Lord of Châtillon-sur-Loing.

Reynald was not content with his lot as the younger son of a minor noble. Convinced that fortune had decreed that he should rule rather than serve, he decided to take his sword to where land and gold were available to a man strong enough to take and keep them. As a soldier of fortune he served under Baldwin III of Jerusalem and it was not long before his bravery had brought him to the attention of the young king. In 1151 he accompanied his lord to Antioch where his handsome appearance and restless spirit won him the affection of the recently widowed Princess Constance. Refusing the many distinguished husbands suggested to her by both the Byzantine Emperor Manuel Comnenus and King Baldwin, Constance set her heart on the young adventurer. It seems likely that they had become lovers before she asked permission of Baldwin to marry. Permission was granted and the marriage took place in the spring of 1153. From the beginning Reynald was unpopular with the nobles and people of Antioch, who viewed him as a low-born intruder. However, he had no intention of courting popularity.

Reynald was now thrust into the diplomatic affairs of kings and princes and found that in the relations between states his freebooting ways were wholly inappropriate. He was determined to be his own man and in his relations with the Byzantine emperor he showed an undisciplined nature which was to be a feature of his career in Outremer. In 1156 he allied with King Thoros of Armenia against Manuel and planned a piratical raid on the Byzantine island of Cyprus. Shortage of money prompted Reynald to take action against the aged Patriarch of Antioch, Aimery of Limoges. Aimery had spoken out against Constance's marriage and Reynald was determined to exact a cruel revenge. When Aimery refused to help finance his piratical foray, Reynald had the old man whipped, beaten about the head then smeared his wounds with honey, leaving him chained naked in the blazing heat for a day at the mercy of insects.[1] Reynald's brutality achieved the desired result and the patriarch gave him what he asked. When the news of the atrocity reached Jerusalem, King Baldwin immediately sent the Bishop of Acre to rescue the old man. Reynald, having achieved his aim, was content to let Aimery go.

Relations between the inhabitants of Cyprus and the Franks of Outremer had been generally good since the time of the First Crusade, when food supplies had been furnished by the islanders to help the crusaders. Since that time the island had prospered, secure in the protection of a Byzantine garrison and the knowledge that the Levantine coastline was in Christian hands. How great was the shock therefore when Reynald landed with his soldiers in the spring of 1156. The Byzantine troops led by the emperor's nephew, John Comnenus, and the general Michael Branas, were taken unawares and in spite of heroic resistance were overrun by Reynald's raiders. What followed shocked the whole of Christendom. Scarcely a building on the island remained unscathed, and churches and monasteries were particular targets for attack. Greek priests had their noses and ears cut off, apparently on Reynald's order, while nuns and young women were raped. Old people and young children were killed indiscriminately, and the fit and healthy were forced to ransom themselves. Reynald's soldiers showed a ferocity that 'the Huns or the Mongols might have envied'.[2] Throughout the island the crops were burned and herds seized, either to be carried off by boat or to be sold back to their owners. So much wealth was taken that eventually there was no money left to ransom the people and Reynald ordered that the island's governor, leading churchmen and citizens be taken to Antioch until more money was forthcoming. Rumours that a Byzantine fleet was approaching brought an end to the raid and Reynald ordered his troops to return to Antioch.

If Reynald believed he could escape the consequences of his actions he was mistaken. In 1158 Manuel Comnenus assembled a great army at Constantinople to punish the renegade princes. Thoros fled into the mountains of Armenia but Reynald, advised by the venerable Bishop Gerald of Lattakieh, concluded that Manuel's aims were political rather than military and that he intended to demonstrate his strength rather than to conquer Antioch. Therefore Reynald decided to submit willingly rather than try to resist the overwhelming might of the empire. First he offered to surrender Antioch to Manuel and accept a Byzantine garrison in the citadel. Informed that this was not enough, Reynald adopted the theatrical garb of the penitent and appeared before the Emperor barefoot, bare-headed, with a rope round his neck and his sword in his left hand; holding the tip of the weapon he offered the hilt to Manuel. He and his followers then prostrated themselves in the dust.[3] Minutes passed before the emperor deigned even to notice him but eventually Manuel offered him a pardon on humiliating terms: Reynald swore to hand over the citadel of Antioch to an imperial garrison when required, to provide troops for the imperial army and to appoint a Greek Patriarch of Antioch rather than a Latin one. In April 1159 Manuel made a ceremonial entry into Antioch, with Reynald walking by the side of his horse, holding the bridle. Reynald's discomfiture appeared to be complete.

Yet Reynald was not to profit from this object lesson in power politics. He was a man of action and never felt happier than when in the saddle and at the head of his knights. In November 1160 he was informed by his scouts that between Marash and Tulupa large herds of animals were being moved into winter pasture. Although the animals belonged to Syrian and Armenian Christians Reynald felt no compunction in deciding to seize them. Returning laden with the spoils of his raid Reynald was ambushed by the Governor of Aleppo, Majd al-Din, in a narrow defile near Commi. Although he fought bravely he was soon overpowered, bound in chains and sent (tied across the back of a camel) to Aleppo, where he remained a prisoner for 16 years. No one seemed in a hurry to ransom him: certainly not Manuel, nor Baldwin of Jerusalem, nor even his loyal subjects. In his absence Constance's son by her first marriage, Bohemond III, was declared the rightful prince of Antioch and for Reynald a chapter in his life had come to an end.

The period spent as a prisoner of Nur al-Din seems to have sharpened his appetite for adventure. When in 1175 the Vizier Gumushtekin released him as an act of gratitude to the Franks for their assistance against Saladin, the one-time Prince of Antioch found that he no longer had a wife or a home. Nevertheless, his reputation as a warrior of note and one of the leading knights of Outremer guaranteed that he would not lack for employment. Within months of his release he had married the heiress of Oultrejourdain, Stephanie de Milly, whose husband, Miles of Plancy, had been murdered in 1174. Thus Reynald gained the great castles of Montreal (ash-Shaubak) and Kerak, which overlooked the caravan routes from Egypt to Syria. Through his lands passed pilgrims, herdsmen and caravans loaded with the fruits and cereals of Moab, sugar-cane, sea salt, balsam and indigo. From the gloomy, reddish-black stone battlements of Kerak Reynald was able to look out in the secure knowledge that here he was master and need never again bend his knee to emperor or king. For the Muslims Reynald ceased to be a man of flesh and blood and became a figure of legend, a dark lord who preyed on passing pilgrims and dragged them back to his sombre fortress from which no-one escaped without ransom.

Raymond of Tripoli

The period before the fall of the kingdom of Jerusalem in 1187 was marked by internal dissension which damaged the unity of the realm. Royal authority had always been limited by the right of the barons to be consulted on important issues and they had never entirely surrendered their right to choose the king. In the *haut cour* the barons constituted the governing body of the realm and were able to control royal policy, in political, economic and military terms. Under strong kings like Baldwin III and Amalric I, the power of the barons was held in check by the personality of the king but with the accession of Baldwin IV in 1174, the disruptive tendencies of the magnates struck at the roots of the state.

Without a consistent guiding force at the centre, fragmentation was always likely, particularly as two distinct factions began to emerge among the barons. On one hand the newcomers to the Holy Land were often fired up by religious zeal or by a desire for adventure or land; their needs could only be satisfied by an aggressive military policy towards the Muslims. In this they were frequently supported by the military orders of the Templars and Hospitallers, who were unprepared to compromise with the enemies of their religion. In contrast, the native barons were often third- or fourth-generation inhabitants of Outremer, who had learned the benefits of peaceful co-existence with Muslim neighbours. They had adopted some eastern habits in food and clothing and the Westerners often accused them of becoming orientalised. In this the newcomers were shortsighted. The native barons had learned to adapt themselves to their environment, particularly in terms of military strategy. Their aims were defensive not offensive. From their great fortresses they ruled the land.

Foremost among the native barons was Count Raymond III of Tripoli. Born in about 1140, Raymond succeeded to Tripoli at the age of 12 when his father, Raymond II, was murdered by Assassins at the gates of his own capital. Raymond's mother, Hodierna, assumed the regency until her son came of age, while King Baldwin III of Jerusalem, as Raymond's closest male relative, took on the guardianship of the county. Raymond developed as a typical baron of the time: acquisitive, arrogant and headstrong. With the growing power of Nur al-Din of Aleppo in the north his county was constantly in the forefront of the border skirmishing. Without the support of either Byzantine troops or those of the kingdom of Jerusalem it is unlikely that his state would have survived. However, in 1164, with Amalric I campaigning in Egypt, Nur al-Din seized the opportunity to attack the Frankish principality of Antioch. Its ruler, Bohemond III, called on his friend, Raymond of Tripoli, to help him. At the battle of Artah, the impetuosity of Bohemond led to a total defeat for the Franks during which Raymond (among others) was captured. Along with Bohemond he was taken in chains to Aleppo, from which he was not released for ten years. As a vassal of the Byzantine empire Bohemond attained his release from Nur al-Din but for Raymond there was to be no escape. In his absence Raymond entrusted his Tripolitan lands to Amalric I of Jerusalem.

At the age of 24 Raymond could see that the best years of his life might be spent in a Muslim prison. However, he was unwilling to waste an opportunity to learn to understand his enemies and during his long captivity he learned Arabic, studied

Arab customs and laws, and forsook his youthful rashness. In 1174, just before the death of Nur al-Din, Raymond was at last ransomed for 80 000 gold pieces, significantly less than was later charged for the release of Reynald of Châtillon.[4] The money was raised partly by King Amalric himself and partly by the Hospitallers, to whom Raymond was frequently indebted throughout his career. On his release, however, Raymond found that the affairs of the Holy Land had changed significantly. Within weeks of each other the two great adversaries Nur al-Din and Amalric I died, throwing the whole situation into confusion.

Amalric I was succeeded as King of Jerusalem by his 13-year-old son Baldwin IV, who suffered from leprosy. It was clear that a regent would need to be appointed not only during his minority but also during the occasions when his illness prevented him from carrying out his tasks of state. During the early months of the new reign authority rested in the hands of the seneschal, Miles of Plancy, who had come to Outremer during Amalric's reign and had won the favour of the king and the fiefdom of Oultrejourdain. As a newcomer to the realm he was unpopular with the native barons who resented his easy acquisition of power and the way in which he conducted affairs without consulting them. Miles ruled for a while in an almost dictatorial style, believing himself to be so secure that when warned of a potential plot against him he replied that even if his enemies found him asleep they would be afraid to wake him.[5] It was into this situation that Raymond of Tripoli now came. Shortly after his release he married Eschiva of Bures, widow of Walter of Tiberias, and administered the lands of Galilee as a baron of the kingdom of Jerusalem, as well as remaining Count of Tripoli. His marriage to Eschiva was a happy one and although he had no children by her he loved the four sons she had by her first marriage. Indeed, it is significant how loyally the four stepsons supported Raymond even during the dark days after Hattin.

During 1174 Raymond appeared before the king and demanded that he should be made procurator, or regent, of the kingdom. He based his claim on being Baldwin's closest male relative, being (as ruler of Galilee) the realm's richest and most powerful magnate, and finally of having a special relationship with Amalric's family by which the late king had looked after his county during his captivity. Raymond was fortunate in the support of most of the great barons, including Humphrey of Toron, constable of the kingdom, Baldwin of Ramla, Balian of

Ibelin and Reynald of Sidon, besides many prominent churchmen. The situation was simplified when Miles of Plancy was murdered in the dark streets of Acre. His assassins were not discovered though his wife, Stephanie de Milly, blamed Raymond of Tripoli for her husband's murder. After her marriage to Reynald of Châtillon she was able to drive a wedge between the new Lord of Kerak and the Count of Tripoli which was to prove disastrous to the kingdom.

For two days the king considered Raymond's demands before agreeing to them and, amidst general acclamation, the count was invested in the chapel of the Church of the Holy Sepulchre with the entire government of the realm, subject only to the authority of Baldwin himself. William of Tyre, an eyewitness to these events, gives us a good description of the 34-year-old count. Raymond was slender of build and of medium height, with straight, dark hair and a swarthy complexion.[6] Temperate in both eating and drinking, life seems to have made him thoughtful and cautious. Proud but not foolhardy, he was regarded by his Muslim enemies as having the keenest intellect among the Frankish leaders.

Raymond retained the procuratorship until 1176 and during 1175 he led the forces of the kingdom and of his own county in raids into northern Syria to try to restrict the growing threat from Saladin. He helped prevent the Egyptian leader from capturing Aleppo and in return the Vizier Gumushtekin released prominent Christian prisoners, including Reynald of Châtillon and Joscelyn, titular Count of Edessa. However, when in 1176 the young Baldwin IV came of age, Raymond surrendered his authority. This not only reduced his own power but that of the faction of native barons which looked to him for leadership. Instead, the young king came increasingly under the influence of his mother, Agnes of Courtenay, and the clique which included her brother, Joscelyn. Agnes hated Raymond and had little difficulty in convincing her ailing son that the Count of Tripoli aspired to his crown. For two years after 1178 Raymond was concerned with the affairs of his county and, with his good friend Bohemond III of Antioch, he campaigned against the Saracens in northern Syria. However, these were years of disaster for the Christian cause culminating in the defeat in the valley of Marj ʿUyun on 10 June 1179, during which Raymond's stepson Hugh of Tiberias was captured as well as Baldwin of Ramla and Odo of Saint-Amand, Grand Master of the Templars. Raymond's own territory was ravaged by the Muslims so that he was eventually forced into signing a truce with Saladin in the spring of 1180.

The Patriarch Eraclius

In his history, William of Tyre recorded an ancient prophecy that as the 'True Cross' had been rescued by one Heraclius (namely the Byzantine emperor who regained it after his successful campaign against the Persians in 627) so it would be lost by another Heraclius. He was, of course, referring to the Patriarch Heraclius — or, more accurately, Eraclius — who had been his rival for the patriarchate of Jerusalem in 1180 on the death of Amalric of Nesle on 6 October. Through the writings of William of Tyre and Ernoul, historians have built up a picture of Eraclius as a thoroughly unworthy father of the church, who had risen to prominence through his good looks and his rather too close relationship with the king's mother, Agnes of Courtenay. Dismissed as a man of little learning, Eraclius is also accused of keeping a mistress in the person of Pasque de Riveri, a draper's wife from Nablus, who was maintained in luxury at the expense of the church and was vulgarly known as 'Madame la Patriarchesse'.[7]

It seems likely, however, that Eraclius has been the subject of character assassination. Certainly, as a member of the court faction of Agnes of Courtenay, he was unlikely to receive favourable treatment from either William of Tyre or Ernoul, squire to Balian of Ibelin, both ardent supporters of the rival faction headed by Raymond of Tripoli. In fact, far from being an unlettered man, Eraclius had been educated at the University of Bologna during the 1160s and had evidently become a *magister*.[8]

Eraclius was born in the Auvergne region of France about 1128 and after studying in Italy travelled to the Holy Land, appearing in two patriarchal documents of 1168 as *magister* Eraclius. Within a year he had been appointed Archdeacon of Jerusalem and in 1175 he became Archbishop of Caesarea. How much his rise was due to the favour of Agnes of Courtenay it is not easy to know but certainly when he was appointed to the patriarchate in 1180 in preference to his rival, Archbishop William of Tyre, the influence of the king's mother was decisive. William of Tyre never forgave Eraclius and tried to prevent his selection by spreading stories of his dissolute lifestyle. Not surprisingly Eraclius retaliated by aligning himself with William's opponents. From 1180 onwards there can be no doubt of the fact that his weight was solidly behind the party which grew up around the Courtenays and the Lusignans and which was instrumental in staging the *coup d'état* of 1186.

The Courtenays

Once the religious zeal of the early crusaders faded, the Latin kingdom of Jerusalem became a land of intrigue, corruption and feverish competition. During the reign of Baldwin IV the power of his maternal family, the Courtenays, grew at the expense of other baronial families like the Ibelins. With Agnes of Courtenay as mother of the king and her brother Joscelyn holding the major office of seneschal, the Courtenays composed a powerful court party to which newcomers to the realm like Gerard of Ridefort, Amalric de Lusignan and his brother, Guy, were attracted.

Although the Courtenays were an old native family they had little influence in the kingdom of Jerusalem itself. The first Joscelyn had come to the Holy Land with the Count of Nevers in 1102 and had been enfeoffed with land to the west of the Euphrates, centring on the town of Turbessel.[9] From these poor beginnings the Courtenays carved out the state of Edessa. However, under the assaults of the Muslim leader Zangi the county was lost between 1144 and 1150. With the imprisonment and blinding of her husband, Joscelyn II, in 1150, the Countess Beatrice sold the remaining lands of Edessa to the Byzantine Emperor Manuel, in return for a life pension for herself and her children. With the remaining Frankish population of Edessa she retired to Antioch. Before her marriage to Joscelyn II, Beatrice had been the wife of William of Saone, and she enjoyed dower rights in the Antiochene lands of Saone. The two children who left with her were Agnes and the young Joscelyn, now titular Count of Edessa (a county that no longer existed). Under these circumstances it was obvious that both young people would need to display unusual qualities if they were to survive such a pitiless childhood.

Agnes had been born in 1133 and by blood was related to the royal house of Jerusalem as well as the ruling families of Tripoli and Antioch. She was married early to Reynald of Marash, a powerful knight who was killed in 1149 at the battle of the Inab.

Her dower lands at Marash were conquered by the Muslims and apart from her share of her mother's pension from the Byzantines she remained poor and consequently unmarried for eight years. However, her physical attractions were such that she was unlikely to remain a widow for ever in spite of her poverty; indeed she soon acquired a reputation for sexual indiscretion which she was not to lose throughout her life.[10] Although she was betrothed to Hugh of Ibelin she attracted the attention of King Baldwin III's brother Amalric, Count of Jaffa, who became infatuated with her. Although she was his fourth cousin — within the degree of consanguinity forbidden by the Church — and, moreover, a woman of uncertain morals, Amalric insisted on marrying her in 1157. They had two children, Baldwin and Sibylla, before Baldwin III of Jerusalem died childless in 1162 and Amalric succeeded his brother as king. Agnes now found that the Patriarch of Jerusalem, Amalric of Nesle, and the foremost barons insisted that her marriage should be annulled before they would accept her husband as king. Amalric was forced to agree, though he insisted that the legitimacy of his two children should be accepted as well as their rights in line of succession. By special papal dispensation Agnes was absolved of any moral censure for her invalid marriage and was allowed to retain the title of countess, though her children were now removed from her custody. Undaunted, Agnes turned back to her original love and married Hugh of Ibelin, Lord of Ramla. Although he died in 1169, while on a pilgrimage to Compostella, Agnes enjoyed half the revenues of Ramla for life, even though the fief passed to Hugh's brother, Baldwin. In 1171, Agnes married for the fourth time, to the extremely ugly but shrewd Reynald of Sidon, soon to be the holder of one of the greatest baronies in the realm. Agnes had seen much suffering in her life and this may account for the bitterness which was apparent even in her pursuit of pleasures. By her middle years she had become a deeply cynical woman, determined to wrest as much from life as she could. At court her rival was Amalric's widow, the Byzantine Princess Maria Comnena, dowager queen during the reign of Baldwin IV, and mother of the young Princess Isabella.

In 1157 Joscelyn of Courtenay followed his sister to Jerusalem as a consequence of her marriage to Amalric and being a kinsman of King Baldwin III he was granted an income from harbour-dues at Acre and some land near that city. However, the native barons of Jerusalem were jealous of the favours shown to this

Edessan exile. Perhaps in response to the growth of opposition to Joscelyn, Baldwin took him north to Antioch in 1162 and appointed him to the fief of Harim, on the Muslim border. In 1164 he was captured and imprisoned at Aleppo where he stayed for 11 years, only to be released along with Reynald of Châtillon in 1175. At once he set about re-establishing his fortune. After the long years of his imprisonment he found that the powerful rule of Amalric I had been replaced by the minority of the young leper, Baldwin IV.

Although Amalric had married Maria Comnena (after his first marriage had been declared invalid) he had had just one daughter by her and therefore Agnes's son Baldwin was the heir to the throne. When Amalric died in 1174 Agnes attained a position of power as the new king's mother and she was determined to restore the family fortune by helping Joscelyn to achieve high rank in the kingdom. It was undoubtedly through her influence that Joscelyn was released in 1175 and then became seneschal in 1176, holding that office until 1193, during which time he enriched himself at the expense of the treasury. When the young king came of age in 1176 Raymond of Tripoli was obliged to surrender the regency and this opened the way for Agnes and Joscelyn to tighten their hold on Baldwin and through him on the government of the kingdom. Having begun the reign simply as the dowager Lady of Ramla, by the time of her death, in 1186, Agnes was the foremost lady in the land.

King Baldwin IV

In 1170 William of Tyre was appointed by King Amalric I as tutor to his nine-year-old son, Baldwin. William records that he instructed the young prince in liberal studies and tried to train him in the development of character as well as in the knowledge of letters. Baldwin gave every indication of becoming a splendid young man, being of a 'lovable disposition', 'comely of appearance' and eager to learn. Like his father he was a keen student of history and was always well disposed to follow good advice. However, William records an occasion when his suspicions were aroused that all was not well with the prince's health. During a rough and tumble between Baldwin and his companions William observed that when the other boys pinched him he showed no signs of pain. At first he attributed this to the prince's remarkable fortitude but on investigating it he discovered that Baldwin had lost feeling in his right arm and hand. In spite of the attentions of the best physicians it soon became apparent that he was suffering from leprosy, one of the most dreaded diseases of the Middle Ages.[11]

Leprosy was by no means an unusual disease in medieval times and was more common in the East than it was in Europe. As a result, laws had been made which covered the exclusion of the leper from all parts of social life. He lost all his rights and was regarded as an outcast, able to keep the company only of other lepers and usually confined to certain areas like the leper colony near the Postern of St Lazare in Jerusalem. The intention was naturally to prevent the spread of disease, but the outcome for the individual was to be condemned to an existence almost totally bereft of normal human relations. In such cases death, which usually came early, brought a welcome release to the sufferer.

Yet in spite of his grievous affliction Baldwin refused to regard himself as an invalid. At the age of fourteen he was already accompanying the Count of Tripoli and the constable, Humphrey of Toron, with the royal army, which he was later to lead in person with notable success. He was a born fighter and yet also had the patience to endure his suffering without complaint. A strong sense of duty burned in him more brightly than in any of the other great figures of the period. Had he lived longer he would have proved a worthy opponent of Saladin. Yet as he approached puberty the disease seemed to increase its grip, attacking his face and extremities, horrifying his courtiers and filling his people with grief and pity. Nevertheless, Baldwin's leprosy made one thing certain: he would never be allowed to marry and could not beget an heir to the throne. During 1175 the attention of the *haut cour* turned to his elder sister, Sibylla, who it was decided must marry a prince from the west and provide for the future security of the realm. It was decided to invite William Longsword, son of William of Montferrat and a relative of both the King of France and the Emperor of Germany, to come to the Holy Land. He arrived in October 1176 and within 40 days married Sibylla, receiving the county of Jaffa and Ascalon and a virtual guarantee of succession when Baldwin died. However, although William of Tyre describes William Longsword as being tall, handsome and courageous, the king's new brother-in-law survived only a matter of months before succumbing to malaria and dying at Ascalon early in 1177, leaving his wife pregnant with the future Baldwin V.

The hopes of the kingdom now rested on the shoulders of a grievously ill king and his new-born nephew. Clearly a new husband would have to be found for Sibylla and in the meantime one of the leading princes must act as regent. The arrival of Philip of Flanders, cousin of Baldwin IV, with a large following of knights from the West raised hopes that he would accept the regency of the kingdom. However, it soon became apparent that he had come not with the intention of fighting for the cross but in order to marry off the two sons of his cousin, Robert of Bethune, to Amalric's two daughters, the pregnant Sibylla and the seven-year-old Isabella. Balian of Ibelin was outraged that so powerful a knight with so great an army had come all that way just to talk about weddings. Had the kingdom sunk so low that its princesses should be bought and sold in such a way? What was needed was help from the West not this kind of 'carpetbagging'. If Philip refused to accept the regency then the matter was ended. Baldwin sadly rejected the proposed marriage agreement and instead Reynald of Châtillon was chosen to govern for the ailing king.

In spite of his illness and the fact that at times he could not walk and had to be carried in a litter, Baldwin showed great courage and resolution. In November 1177, he led the forces of the kingdom into battle and inflicted on Saladin the worst defeat of his career. At the end of October, the Count of Flanders (eventually persuaded to do something positive) had left Jerusalem and travelled north to join Raymond of Tripoli in an expedition against the town of Hama. With him went over 100 knights from the kingdom along with many Hospitallers. Saladin was in Egypt and his spies informed him that much of the Frankish strength had gone into northern Syria so he decided to strike into the kingdom from the south in an attempt either to force Raymond to pull back from his siege of Hama or else to win an easy victory over the depleted forces at Baldwin's disposal. As Saladin marched out of Egypt and began to cross the desert towards the Frankish lands, the Templars, who guarded the frontiers of the realm, pulled back their knights within the city of Gaza and prepared to defend it. However, the Egyptian army passed it by and moved towards Ascalon. Baldwin had only just recovered from a severe bout of illness but with 500 knights and with Aubert, Bishop of Bethlehem carrying the True Cross he moved swiftly to Ascalon, arriving only hours before Saladin's troops. At once he saw that his forces were badly outnumbered by the Saracens and so he declined to fight in front of the city and stayed within its walls. Saladin now made a serious miscalculation. Leaving only a covering force to mask the king's force in Ascalon, he continued his drive towards Jerusalem. Now no Christian troops remained between him and the Holy City and he appears to have become over-confident. In any case, the discipline of his troops slackened and they began to break up into marauding bands, pillaging the countryside. Ramla was burned and the city of Lydda besieged. In Jerusalem many people abandoned their homes and crowded into the tower of David, certain that the last days of the kingdom were at hand. At this crucial moment Baldwin's courage did not fail him. He sent messengers to the Templars at Gaza telling them to join him at Ascalon and when they arrived he left the city and headed up the coast to Ibelin, before moving inland. Saladin, on hearing of Baldwin's movements desperately tried to call in his scattered forces.

On 25 November the Saracen army was near the castle of Montgisard just east of Ramla, when Baldwin's army caught up with them. With the king was Odo of Saint-Amand (Grand Master of the Templars) with 80 of his knights, as well as Reynald of Châtillon, Reynald of Sidon, Joscelyn of Courtenay and the Ibelin brothers, Baldwin and Balian. Although heavily outnumbered the Franks had the advantage of surprise. Some of the Muslims were caught without their armour, while their baggage animals became intermixed with the cavalry. Saladin's army consisted of two advanced wings and a retired centre body, and as the Franks came into sight he ordered the wings to close in on the centre. In the confusion of the moment this may have resulted in the outer flanks masking the centre so that when the charge of the Christian knights struck it was unable to give way in the usual Muslim fashion, in order to form up again elsewhere; it was shattered by the sheer weight of the charge. Abu Shama described the Franks as 'agile as wolves and howling like dogs and full of fiery ardour'. Baldwin of Ramla had asked King Baldwin for the right to lead the assault as the battle was to be fought within his lands and permission was granted. With his brother Balian, the Lord of Ramla led his knights against the strongest part of the Muslim army, which was commanded by Taqi al-Din and broke it decisively. Saladin's army began to scatter and only the swift intervention of his personal guard saved him from the assault of three Frankish knights. Foremost among the king's knights (besides the Ibelin brothers) had been Count

Raymond's stepsons, Hugh of Tiberias and William of Galilee.[12]

According to William of Tyre, who seems to have been present at the battle, the Christians pursued the remnants of Saladin's army for 12 miles and reached the marshes of Cannetum Esturnellorum before night brought a halt to the action.[13] Baldwin certainly had no intention of following up this unexpected victory and returned in triumph to Ascalon. The next day the weather changed and rain and cold set in making the retreat of the Muslim army a desperate one. The Bedouin, that 'treacherous race', sold many captive Muslims to the Franks and attacked the stragglers as they tried to return to Egypt. Saladin was fatalistic both about the setback and his personal safety, insisting that 'again and again we were on the verge of destruction; nor would God have delivered us save for some future duty'.[14] But that duty was still some way off. In the second week of December Saladin reached Cairo with his reputation tarnished by this serious defeat.

For Baldwin IV the battle at Montgisard was to be the highpoint of his reign. When he returned to Jerusalem carrying high the True Cross it was regarded by a grateful populace as little short of a miracle. The kingdom had survived the greatest threat to its existence. However, resources were insufficient to reinforce the victory and in the two years that followed the Franks suffered a series of setbacks. Moreover, Baldwin's leprosy was now advancing swiftly, disfiguring his face, hands and feet, and threatening his eyesight. Never again would he lead his knights from his charger.

Gerard of Ridefort

Little is known of the early life of this knight other than that he came originally from Flanders and accompanied the Second Crusade, staying behind after the others returned and attempting to carve out a life for himself in Outremer. Apparently, in 1173 he travelled to Tripoli and served under Count Raymond after the count's release from imprisonment in Aleppo. He soon ingratiated himself into the favour of the count who promised him advancement by offering him the next suitable heiress in his county. Within months the wealthy Lord of Botron, Guillaume Dorel, died leaving behind a daugher, Cecile, and it fell to Raymond as liege lord to find her a husband. Naturally Gerard expected him to honour his promise and probably Raymond would have done so, with incalculable consequences for the future of the kingdom of Jerusalem, had not a wealthy merchant from Pisa, named Plivano (a dealer in perfumes, brocades and spices) offered Raymond the weight of the girl in gold if he could marry her and take Botron. This was a phenomenal offer and Raymond by accepting it probably did no more than other lords would have done. Plivano apparently paid him 10 000 besants for the girl, equivalent to Cecile's weight of ten stone![15] Raymond, no doubt, would have found another bride for Gerard; but the knight was so angered at this slight that he left Tripoli and joined the Order of the Templars. Upon entry to this Order he was supposed to swear forgiveness to his personal enemies but Gerard was a paranoic who made hatred of Raymond the governing principle of his life. As a Templar he rose high by his undoubted ability and achieved the rank of seneschal. What is more, he attracted the attention of Agnes of Courtenay and enjoyed the favour of the court party which formed around her and her brother. Fuelled by his anger, Gerard was determined to do everything in his power to thwart the designs of the Count of Tripoli. On the death of the Grand Master of the Templars, Arnold of Torroga, in 1185, it was expected that his successor would be the Commander and Treasurer of Jerusalem, the able Gilbert Erail. However, by a very narrow margin the conclave elected Gerard and when the new grand master attended the crowning of Guy and Sibylla in 1186 he is said to have declared in public, 'Cette couronne vaut bien la mariage de Boutron!' showing that he had never allowed his bitterness against Raymond to die.[16] However, in striking at the count he was also damaging the stability of the kingdom itself.

6

The Kingdom in Peril: 1180–86

If any event can be said to have sharpened the divisions within the kingdom of Jerusalem it was the marriage of Baldwin IV's sister Sibylla to Guy of Lusignan at Easter 1180. After the death of her first husband William Longsword, in 1177, there had been frantic effort to find Sibylla a new husband who might eventually succeed the ailing leper king. For a while it seemed that Hugh III of Burgundy would take up the offer, but when he decided to remain in France Sibylla took matters into her own hands by falling in love with Baldwin of Ramla, scion of the princely house of Ibelin and the finest knight in the kingdom. This was a popular choice among the native barons but when Baldwin was captured at the battle of Marj 'Uyun in 1179 the lady proved fickle. From his Muslim jail in Damascus Baldwin assured Sibylla of his love which she apparently returned. Nevertheless, she informed Baldwin that she could not marry him while he was in heavy debt for his ransom. Baldwin, who faced the enormous ransom of 150 000 gold pieces, a valuation which he was only prepared to accept after Saladin had ordered two of his teeth to be pulled out, had lost not only his looks but was in danger of losing his love as well. Consequently, he set out for Constantinople to beg the help of the Emperor Manuel Comnenus. Manuel, always generous and never more so than to so renowned a knight, chivalrously agreed to help.

With Baldwin of Ramla removed temporarily from the scene, the king's mother, Agnes of Courtenay, began to sway her daughter Sibylla with her own hatred of the Ibelin clan. Moreover, one of her own lovers, Amalric of Lusignan, told her that he had a younger brother, a handsome and gallant knight, who would suit Sibylla very well.[1] Amalric was a member of one of the foremost noble families of France. The Lusignans were Counts of La Marche and Poitou but as a younger son his prospects had not been good at home. However, making the most of his obvious advantages, his youthful good looks and strong sword arm, he came to the Holy Land as a soldier of fortune and within a few years had risen through good service both to the king and to his mother to the rank of constable. He had made a good marriage with the daughter of Baldwin of Ramla and had become Agnes's lover. As a newcomer to the kingdom he was not popular with the native barons and thought too much like a Frenchman to understand the real needs of the kingdom. His thirst for personal advancement was quite inappropriate in a situation where the realm was facing so great an external threat. Encouraged by Agnes, he told Sibylla about his handsome brother and when she showed interest he promptly agreed to return to France to bring Guy to meet her. Sibylla apparently found Guy as handsome as she had hoped and told the king that she wished to marry him. At first Baldwin IV was shocked by the idea. Guy was clearly not made of the stuff of kings and the reaction of the native barons was immediately hostile. They, who had hoped to see Baldwin of Ramla as their next king, were hardly going to welcome this weak boy.

Bad news travelled fast and in the spring of 1180 Bohemond of Antioch and Raymond of Tripoli, hearing of the proposed marriage of Sibylla and Guy of Lusignan, crossed into the kingdom at the head of their troops. It is likely that they intended to stop the marriage if possible and pressurise the king into choosing a more suitable candidate for his sister. However, in this they were to be thwarted. In fact, it seems that the king was persuaded that they intended to overthrow him by force and, in panic, arranged a hasty marriage for Sibylla and Guy. Such was his haste that against all precedent the marriage took place during Lent. Guy was thereupon given Jaffa and Ascalon as his fief which was a clear indication of his eventual succession to the throne. At the news of the marriage Bohemond and Raymond withdrew their troops in frustration and the latter did not return to the kingdom for a further two years.[2] He clearly was disgusted to see another newly arrived knight elevated without the consent of the barons. If Guy was eventually to be the King then Raymond felt the matter should have been debated before the *haut cour*. One cannot resist interpreting Raymond's own motives. Ousted from the regency in 1176 when Baldwin IV came of age, the Count of Tripoli had to stand by as Agnes of Courtenay increased her influence on the king. During Baldwin's bouts of illness the regency had not returned to Raymond but had gone instead to Reynald of Châtillon and now it appeared that the inexperienced Guy of Lusignan was to be elevated above them all.

Raymond was not the only baron to feel aggrieved. Baldwin of Ramla had expected to marry Sibylla and possibly in due course to succeed the leprous king. Having at last raised the money for his ransom through the good offices of the emperor and his own brother Balian, he returned to Jerusalem only to find that Sibylla had married Guy. The rift between the Courtenays and the Ibelins now grew greater. In a statesmanlike gesture Baldwin IV tried to prevent this division by betrothing his eight-year-old half-sister Isabella, daughter of Amalric I's second marriage to Maria Comnena, to Humphrey IV of Toron. The complicated marriages within the Levantine Frankish nobility meant that Balian of Ibelin's stepdaughter was being betrothed to Reynald of Châtillon's stepson. Yet, however much the king struggled to avoid the growing split in his kingdom his courage and strength were not enough.

The Courtenays further demonstrated their power in the selection of the new Patriarch of Jerusalem when the aged Amalric of Nesle died in October 1180. The canons of the Holy Sepulchre had the task of electing his successor and it was a traditional practice that in reaching their decision they received advice from prominent people, both clerical and lay. Agnes of Courtenay, the queen mother, was relentless in her support of Eraclius, Archbishop of Caesarea, who, it was rumoured, had been her lover and was in any case a prominent member of her political circle. William, Archbishop of Tyre, who had been the king's tutor and was the chancellor of the realm, advised the canons not to choose Eraclius but instead to seek a new patriarch in the West. By saying this William was disqualifying himself as well as Eraclius from the succession and one must conclude that the Archbishop of Tyre felt that a choice from within the kingdom would only intensify the dangerous divisions which had developed between the court party and the barons. A new cleric from France would be able to operate independently of either group. In the event, William's suggestion was rejected by the canons and two candidates were put forward for the king to make the final choice: Eraclius and William. The king might have been expected to favour his old tutor but under pressure from the Courtenays, who saw the political danger of allowing Raymond of Tripoli's friend to become patriarch he gave way and Eraclius was chosen instead. Not content with this success the court clique, which now clearly consisted of the Courtenays, the Lusignans, Reynald of Châtillon and the Patriarch Eraclius, chose a suitable moment in 1183, after Guy had been given the regency, to strike at William of Tyre, having him excommunicated on a trivial pretext. For all William's powerful support in the kingdom he was forced to carry his case to Rome where he died, though the details are obscure. Rumours that he was poisoned there by an agent of the Patriarch Eraclius have no corroborative evidence.[3]

The Courtenays correctly identified Raymond of Tripoli as the strongest of their opponents and the leader of the native barons. He was a man to whom the Ibelins looked for support and as the king's nearest male relative he had a strong claim to the regency which became ever more necessary as the king's health deteriorated. Consequently, they turned their attention to persuading Baldwin IV that Raymond coveted his throne. In the spring of 1182, Raymond set out on a journey from Tripoli to his wife's city of Tiberias but was stopped at Gibelet by the king's men who forbade him to enter the kingdom.[4] Raymond returned to Tripoli in confusion. However, the Courtenays had overreached themselves. With the king now almost wholly paralysed the native barons were unwilling to concede power totally to their opponents. They eventually prevailed upon the king not to believe ill of the count, and Baldwin relented and allowed Raymond to visit him at Jerusalem to confirm his innocence.

While these squabbles took place between the leading barons of the kingdom it was fortunate that the truce which had been signed with Saladin in 1180 held good. However, although for over a year both signatories to the truce scrupulously observed it, in the summer of 1181 Reynald of Châtillon found himself unable to resist the temptation of interfering with the passage of Muslim caravans past his castle of Kerak. Leading his own troops to Taima, on the desert road from Damascus to Mecca, he attacked a peaceful caravan close to the oasis. It seems that this was merely a part of his plans, for he had initially proposed to go as far as Medina. Saladin reacted promptly by sending troops under his nephew Farrukh-Shah to ravage Reynald's lands in Oultrejourdain. This served to bring Reynald hurrying back to defend his territory. Nevertheless, the damage was done. When Saladin complained to Baldwin IV about the truce violation and demanded compensation, the King admitted the justice of the claim but felt unable to force Reynald to disgorge his prisoners.[5]

Fate now offered the Egyptian leader a chance to put pressure on the Lord of Kerak. Just before Easter of 1182 a ship containing some 1500 Christian pilgrims was wrecked on the Egyptian coast at Damietta. In spite of the truce, Saladin immediately seized the survivors and imprisoned them, offering to free them and their property when Reynald agreed to release his prisoners. Again Baldwin was forced to endure the insult of receiving a direct refusal from his liegeman. For Saladin this meant that the truce was now at an end and he decided to invade the kingdom of Jerusalem to punish the truce-breakers.

Saladin planned to head for Damascus, pillaging and wrecking the Christian settlements as he passed. Leaving Cairo on 11 May 1182, he crossed the Sinai desert to 'Aqaba on the Red Sea before turning northwards and passing eastwards of the Christian army (which Reynald had persuaded the king to assemble at Petra in Oultrejourdain, with the view of catching the Eygptian army on the march). Raymond of Tripoli and the Ibelins had tried to convince Baldwin that to do this meant stripping the kingdom of garrison troops and leaving it open to incursions from both north and east. In the event they were right, for Saladin's troops passed by unchallenged, burning crops as they went. By the time he reached Damascus Saladin knew that Farrukh-Shah had already raided the land of Galilee, along with the Muslim rulers of Bostrum, Baalbek and Homs, seizing 20 000 cattle and 1000 prisoners. The Muslim forces had advanced as far as Tiberias and Acre. Many of the Christians, unaware that the truce was ended, were surprised and their settlements overrun. The town of Daburya, near the western slopes of Mount Tabor, was full of people who had come in to help with the harvest. Although they took refuge in a fortified tower the Muslims swiftly mined its walls and captured 500 of them. The cave fortress of Habis Jaldak, to the east of the Sea of Galilee, was made up of chambers hollowed out of a cliff face, overlooking the fertile land of Suhite. Its possession allowed the Franks to enjoy the lucrative grain revenues of the area. It had been garrisoned by Syrian Christian troops and the Franks attributed its fall to the cowardice of the garrison which surrendered after Farrukh-Shah's miners occupied the lowest chamber and began to tunnel through to the higher levels. In Damascus Saladin rested his troops before leading out a combined Egypto-Syrian force on 11 July, to invade Palestine to the south of the Sea of Galilee.

Realising that he had allowed his opponent to slip by him, Baldwin now turned northwards and advanced up the west bank of the River Jordan, accompanied by the Patriarch Eraclius bearing the True Cross. Near the fortress of Belvoir the two armies clashed in an inconclusive battle.[6] After a day's fighting (in terrible heat) both sides withdrew. Casualties were heavy on the Muslim side, with over 1000 killed or wounded, though it seems that as many men died of heat stroke as from their wounds. Saladin realised that the Franks were not prepared to renew the battle and that he would find it difficult to force them to do so. His army was, moreover, camped in an unhealthy area, infested by poisonous snakes and frogs, and with pestilential air. It is recorded that the doctors were particularly busy at that time dealing with the many minor wounds that refused to heal. A withdrawal to a healthier camp was vital.

Saladin's invasion had certainly been checked but he now transferred his attention from the Damascene border of the port of Beirut in the north. Saladin ordered his brother al-Adil to despatch the Egyptian fleet of 30 to 40 vessels to Beirut while Egyptian forces harried Gaza, Ascalon and Darum in the south of the kingdom of Jerusalem. With the crusaders stretched between pressure in both north and south simultaneously, Saladin marched, in August 1182, against Beirut in conjunction with his fleet. Baldwin IV, who had withdrawn his troops to Saffuriya after the inconclusive battle at Belvoir, now had to rush them north, ordering the 33 galleys he had collected at Tyre and Acre, with the help of the Italian maritime republics and freelance pirates, to try to break up the Muslim siege of Beirut. In the event, after a vigorous three-day assault on Beirut, Saladin pulled back his toops and ordered his ships to lift the blockade. He had made his point. He had never intended to capture Beirut, as his lack of heavy siege equipment showed, but he had managed to exploit the mobility given him by possession of both Egypt and Syria, and had demonstrated to the Franks the vulnerability of their frontiers.

From the early years of the crusader kingdoms the Franks had been concerned to establish strategic frontiers with their neighbours. Clearly the possession of the Levantine sea coast was most important, for otherwise they would have no means of supply or support from the Christian lands of the West. The land facing

Damascus was also of great importance to them and their failure to establish a permanently fortified border here meant that these frontier areas were the scenes of frequent *razzia* raids by Muslim troops. However, it was in the south that the greatest insecurity lay: in the vast areas of Transjordan, between Damascus and the Red Sea, the lack of manpower made active possession impossible. In the area south of the River Yarmuk the crusaders had erected mighty castles like Shaubak (in 1115) and Kerak (in 1142). They fortified 'Aqaba on the Red Sea coast and erected strongpoints along the main highway of Transjordan which led from Hijjaz through Ma'an to 'Aqaba and then through Sinai into Egypt. The crusader castles controlled the water supply in that barren wilderness and the Muslims had nothing to the east of this line which could have threatened the Frankish hold on the land.

However, after 1174, Saladin's desire to link his possessions in Egypt and Syria was thwarted by the Christian hold on the desert highway in Transjordan. For the Muslims this was the sorest point of their contact with the infidels. Saladin had already recaptured Eilat in 1171, after 55 years of crusader domination, but if he thought that this would liberate the desert road he was mistaken. The rise of Saladin had coincided with a novel aggressive strategy by the new Lord of Kerak, Reynald of Châtillon, who was determined to push crusader frontiers into Sinai and Arabia by establishing strongpoints there. To dismiss Reynald as a merely piratical baron is to do an injustice to a man who was more than a mere adventurer. Though he was associated with the court party of the Courtenays and Lusignans, Reynald was no mere *parvenu*. His 30 years experience of the Levant, 15 years of it in a Muslim prison, had taught him much. Where Raymond of Tripoli advocated a defensive strategy and a policy of co-existence with the Muslims, Reynald saw only security through strength. For him safety lay in creating a *cordon sanitaire* on the southern and south-western frontiers of the kingdom. Reynald was a man who had learned to understand his enemies not, like Raymond, so that he could live peaceably alongside them, but so that he could discover their weakness and use it against them. By 1175 when he emerged from the dungeons of Aleppo he knew Arabic, probably Turkish and could communicate with the desert Bedouin of Transjordan and Hijjaz. After his marriage to Stephanie de Milly and his acquisition of the great fief of Oultrejourdain he took up the role of defender of the most sensitive part of the crusader kingdom. He had not lost the energy or the brutality of his earlier years and occasionally played the part allotted to him by the Muslims of the human fiend, the *Brins Arnat* of the chroniclers, the robbing baron who descended on helpless caravans and dragged his prisoners into the sombre shadows of Kerak. However, this was not true to Reynald of Châtillon. He maintained his supremacy in the territory by charging tolls for passing traders and collecting protection money, even providing military escorts to Muslim caravans when the mood took him. Moreover, the spy system that he organised among the Bedouin in Transjordan and in the northern Hijjaz meant that he was frequently as well informed of movements in Muslim lands as Saladin himself.[7]

In the five years after 1177 Reynald continued to try to turn the Frankish strongpoints in Transjordan into bases from which he could control the desert routes. This meant that he needed to push deep into enemy territory, which accounts for the frequent expeditions and raids during this period. In 1177 a cavalry force set out from Shaubak and crossed Sinai, eventually reaching Faqus, between Tanis and Bilbais, on the eastern branch of the Nile. Clearly it was possible to penetrate the eastern defences of Egypt and to disrupt the Sinai caravans. However, water was vital to the desert routes and the oasis at al-ʿArish was particularly important. In 1182 crusaders raided the town, drove away the people, and cut down the palm trees to destroy the livelihood of the population. In the spring of the previous year Reynald, assisted by the local Bedouins, invaded northern Hijjaz and reached Taima, the main halting point on the route to Medina. Reynald made his intentions clear when he claimed Sianai as part of the kingdom of Jerusalem, within the territory of the Lord of Kerak. However, the loss of Eilat to Saladin in 1171 had created an obstacle to crusader expansion in the south and Reynald determined to remove it. Late in 1182 he set in motion his Red Sea expedition which served to awaken Islam from its complacency and earned Reynald Saladin's undying hatred.

Reynald had long been considering carrying the war against the Muslims into their heartland, where he planned to strike at the holy cities of Medina and Mecca and, some claimed, even to seize the body of the Prophet and take it back with him to Kerak, where he would charge pilgrims to see it.[8] For two years boats had been under construction on the Mediterranean coast, at Ascalon, which were then transported in sections on the back of camels to the coast at ʿAqaba.[9] The Red Sea was one of the great commercial arteries of the Islamic world, at the centre of a trade that stretched from Morocco in the West to India in the East, and from Madagascar in the South to China in the North-east. Nor was the Red Sea simply a commercial route; it was also the way by which millions of Muslim pilgrims came from North Africa to visit the holy cities of the Hijjaz. As such it was of inestimable value to the Islamic faith.

Reynald first led his troops overland to besiege the city of Eilat, which quickly fell to him but the fortress of Ile de Graye on a nearby island held out and he was forced to stay in person with two of his boats to blockade it. His plan was to cut off the garrison from its supply of drinking water: a spring on the mainland. Meanwhile the rest of the squadron — five boats duly painted black to make them less easily visible and manned by freebooters and Mediterranean pirates — set out to sail down the African coast of the Red Sea, helped by local pilots. As they proceeded they sacked the little Muslim towns they passed and eventually reached Aidhab, a bustling and prosperous port in Nubia, which they captured. Merchant vessels, heavily laden with the riches of the East and totally unarmed in that Muslim sea, easily fell victim to Reynald's raiders. From Aidhab the crusaders crossed to the Arabian coast, burned al-Haura and Yanbu, close to Medina, and even reached al-Rabigh, the port of Mecca. They intercepted and sank a pilgrim ship bound for Jedda, and destroyed a total of 16 Muslim vessels. In addition they landed on the Arabian coast, obtained horses from the Bedouin tribesmen, captured a caravan and advanced to within a day's journey of Medina itself. The effect of these actions on Arab opinion was astonishing. At first there seemed to be paralysis. It had never been considered possible that the Red Sea could be penetrated by the Franks and the people of Arabia had no knowledge of them as people or as fighters. Then there was a tremendous outburst of anger that the unbelievers could dare to threaten the holy places of Islam. Saladin, campaigning in northern Syria, could do no more than rely on prompt action by his brother al-Adil, ruler in Egypt. He was not to be disappointed.

Al-Adil faced the problem that Egypt maintained few warships in the Red Sea and the immediate need was to transfer boats from Fustat and Alexandria on the Mediterranean coast. In all this took six weeks, during which time Reynald's ships had the sea to themselves. However, nemesis was at hand in the shape of the

Egyptian admiral Lu'lu, an Armenian by birth and an admirable commander. At first the Egyptian fleet — consisting of dromons, either lateen-rigged, or heavily oared, some with two or three decks and others beaked for ramming — sailed into the Gulf of 'Aqaba and lifted the siege of Ile de Graye by destroying Reynald's two blockading ships and pursuing the crews into the desert where they were eventually tracked down by Bedouin. By this stage the Lord of Kerak himself had returned to his castle and was unable to witness the collapse of his expedition. Then Lu'lu sailed south to Aidhab, arriving too late to cut off the Frankish ships but following them relentlessly across to the Arabian coast. Here he trapped them at anchor and a fierce battle ensued. Both sides opened fire with arrows, stones and other missiles as the ships closed on each other and some of the heavier Egyptian warships fired pots of flour and powdered quicklime onto the Frankish ships to blind the defenders. Incendiaries fired from the Egyptian galleys, like fire-arrows and 'Greek fire', took the Franks by surprise for they had not had time to cover their ships' sides with hides and blankets soaked in vinegar (the usual defence in naval engagments). As the Egyptian ships forced the Franks towards the shore, boarding parties swung onto the decks and a fierce mêlée broke out in which the superior numbers of the Egyptians soon prevailed. There was no alternative for Reynald's men but to make for the shore. Here Lu'lu's marines relentlessly pursued them. The Franks were guided by Bedouin 'as impious as themselves' and it is said that Lu'lu's men pursued them for five days, with purses full of silver fixed to their lances in order to bribe the nomads to turn over the Christians. Eventually all the (170) crusaders were captured, having been promised quarter by al-Adil.[10]

However, when Saladin learned of his brother's offer he was furious for he had decided that not one of the infidels should live to tell of what he had seen of the weakness of Islam's defences.[11] The prisoners were eventually taken, shamefully mounted backwards on camels, to be executed in public, some at Alexandria, others at Cairo, Mecca and Medina. Saladin was determined that justice should be seen to be done and so their ritual decapitation was accompanied by as much public ceremony as possible. Saladin took pains to explain to his brother, al-Adil, why he was adamant that none of the Christians should live. It was more than their lives that were at stake; it was the sanctity of the Muslim holy places. If any of them ever returned

73

to tell of what they had done it might encourage others, perhaps in overwhelming numbers, to invade the Hijjaz so that 'tongues in the East and West would blame us'. Clearly Saladin was experiencing difficulty in convincing al-Adil that it was honourable for him to break his offer of quarter to the Christians. Saladin knew that in the interests of the greater Muslim world Reynald's men must die. But to al-Adil it was a much more personal problem. After all, it was his oath that would be broken, not Saladin's. Nevertheless, Saladin had been deeply shaken by the ease with which Reynald of Châtillon had been able to penetrate the southern defences of Islam. Moreover, the whole shameful episode had occurred when he, the acknowledged defender of Islam, was campaigning in northern Syria against his co-religionists. If he was not seen to be ruthless in his prosecution of the holy war in this instance then his whole standing in the Muslim world could suffer.

The growing power of Saladin posed the greatest threat that the kingdom of Jerusalem had faced since the early days after the First Crusade. In manpower and resources the Muslims far outweighed the Franks and in military strategy the options open to them were accordingly greater. However many victories the Franks won in the field the Muslim enemy would not go away. But if the Franks suffered one disastrous defeat then the whole kingdom could fall within a matter of weeks. This fear haunted the Christian leaders in the decade before Hattin. They knew that without substantial help from the West they could do no more than hold their own and attempt to discourage Saladin. In February 1183 an assembly of Barons at Jerusalem supported the idea of a general graduated tax levied on the entire population by four 'men of discretion' in each town and city, ranging from one raboin up to two besants on every hundred besants of wealth (based on land, rent and wages). The revenue was to be used to pay for mercenary troops in times of danger. The money collected from the Haifa–Jerusalem area was brought to the capital and placed in a chest with three locks and three keys in the possession of the Patriarch Eraclius and other worthies, while in the area north from Haifa to Beirut the money was to be kept at Acre under the supervision of the Archbishop of Tyre and the Seneschal Joscelyn of Courtenay.[12]

The news that Aleppo had fallen to Saladin confirmed the worst fears of the Franks. This new Muslim leader was stronger than any that the crusaders had faced before. With Aleppo he had completed a ring of steel around the crusader states. And Saladin did not rest to enjoy his triumph. On 10 August he marched out of Aleppo, reaching Damascus ten days later and immediately sending out orders for the mustering of his troops. By September he was ready to undertake a fresh invasion of Palestine, crossing the river Jordan opposite Baisan and entering the valley of Jezreel.

At this moment of danger the kingdom of Jerusalem was without effective leadership. While the Christian army waited at Saffuriya, a small town well supplied with water and provisions, King Baldwin IV was struck down by a fever and his incapacity from leprosy increased markedly. His appearance was a terrible reminder to his courtiers of the impermanence of human life and beauty, and around him there hung the stench of decay and corruption as if the grave had yielded him up to preside over the kingdom's last days. He had become totally blind and his hands and feet had withered to mere stumps. In his sufferings he became impatient of those around him, insisting on attending every session of his council and yet finding the endless squabbling and machinations of men with the hope of years before them frustrating when he knew his own days were numbered. Previously, during bouts of his illness, he had accepted the need for a regency but had always resisted the suggestion that he should surrender the kingship. However, on this occasion, the external danger was so great that he agreed to appoint Sibylla's husband, Guy of Lusignan, as regent and to retain only the royal dignity and the city of Jerusalem with an annual revenue of 10 000 gold pieces. Otherwise, the government of the kingdom was in the hands of Guy and the barons of the realm were called upon to swear to obey him. However, in his turn Guy had to swear not to aspire to the crown while Baldwin lived nor to take possession of any of the king's castles or cities. This last point was intended to counter rumours that Guy had promised such rewards to those in the kingdom who would help him to the throne.

Guy's rise had been meteoric but it had not been achieved without alienating many of the native barons. To them he had been promoted too fast and too far for one of his limited ability. In the space of three years he had married the king's sister, been acknowledged as heir to the throne and now appointed regent, with power over the whole kingdom. Compared with men like Baldwin of Ramla or Raymond of Tripoli, Guy cut a poor figure.

How could he, who knew so little about Levantine affairs, now lead the greatest army the kingdom had every raised, against Saladin? How could he assert his authority over such renowned warriors as the Ibelin brothers and Reynald of Châtillon, besides the visiting magnates from Europe, Godfrey III, Duke of Brabant, and Ralph de Mauleon?[13]

At this moment of crisis the crusaders had forgotten their prime aim: to defeat Saladin; and had become preoccupied with the power struggle within the kingdom. The native barons were determined to overthrow Guy and saw an opportunity in the Muslim invasion. If Guy's administration of the army was shown to be inadequate perhaps the king could be persuaded to dismiss him. From the outset therefore Guy was at the mercy of advisers who did not want him to succeed.

The Christian army at Saffuriya was the strongest raised by the kingdom of Jerusalem, probably even exceeding that which fought at Hattin. All of the great nobles were present with their entourages, including Raymond of Tripoli. In addition to over 1300 knights, there were 15 000 footsoldiers, including western contingents from Brabant and Aquitaine, and Italian sailors from Pisa, Genoa, Venice and Lombardy, who had left their ships at Tyre and Acre to march with the army. However, although Guy was in overall control, his voice was small compared to those of the experienced commanders who marched with him. The Westerners favoured an immediate attack on the Muslims. They pointed out that they had not travelled so far to sit and look at the foe; they longed to come to grips with the enemies of their religion. To this uproar was added the voices of Templars and Hospitallers. However, native barons like Baldwin of Ramla, Balian of Ibelin and Raymond of Tripoli pointed out the advantages of an active defence, which would tire out the Muslim army and eventually hasten its disintegration. More was to be gained from not fighting than from risking defeat in the field.

Eventually, Guy ordered the army to advance from Saffuriya to La Fève where it was within a mile of Saladin's camp at Ain Jalut. Although a skirmish took place neither side took the initiative and Guy withdrew to entrenched positions on the high ground. Saladin attempted to draw him out by destructive raids on the surrounding villages, by the provocation of his mounted archers and by feigned retreats, but the crusaders refused to move. Eventually, on 6 Ocrober 1183, Saladin withdrew, finding it impossible to maintain provisions for his army so deep in enemy country.

The crusaders had avoided defeat which had traditionally been the aim of their strategy when facing the numerically superior Muslim forces of Saladin and Nur al-Din. However, there was general dissatisfaction with Guy's leadership. The army had been the largest the kingdom could raise and if with that they dare not give battle what hope was there in the long run that a better opportunity would come? After all, they had been fortunate in having the troops of two visiting Western magnates in addition to the crews of the Italian fleet that had brought them. With such a substantial reinforcement was it impossible to meet the Saracens in the field? Moreover, while they had stayed within their entrenchments Saladin's troops had ravaged the countryside and inflicted grave damage on Christian settlements. Was it not the duty of a lord to protect his vassals and not sit back and watch him ruined by the enemy? Victory in the field, even though hard-earned, may have deterred Saladin from future incursions and at least have won breathing-space for the kingdom, during which time help might come from the West. Nevertheless, whatever Guy's feelings, the strategy of the native barons was forced upon him by his own lack of confidence and the awe in which he held Raymond of Tripoli and the Ibelins. It had been their advice which had prevailed in 1183.

Guy could not have succeeded in his first campaign. Blamed on one hand for not taking the offensive by those who wanted to attack, he was also denied the credit for the successful defence by those who advocated caution. In fact, the evidence strongly suggests that the native barons went out of their way to be as unhelpful as possible to the new regent. Then, having ensured that he failed, they advised the king that he was incompetent. Baldwin, was now apparently prepared to listen to the party of Raymond of Tripoli. He promptly turned against his new brother-in-law, stripping him of the regency when Guy refused to give the king the heavily fortified city of Tyre in exchange for Jerusalem.[14]

On 20 November 1183, Baldwin summoned his barons and declared that his heir was to be his nephew Baldwin, just five years of age, the (posthumous) son of William and Sibylla Longsword. His decision met with almost universal acclaim and the rift between the king and Guy was deepened when the latter was not even called on to swear allegiance to the boy. However, with the succession falling on a so young boy a new regent would be needed, and with the native barons in the ascendent that meant Raymond of Tripoli. For the moment the court party was in retreat with Guy of Lusignan disgraced. If the king could separate his sister Sibylla from her husband then perhaps she could be remarried to someone more acceptable to the baronial faction.

In 1184 Baldwin IV tried to annul Sibylla's marriage and the Patriarch Eraclius was instructed to demand from the couple the date when their marriage could be ended.[15] However, Guy and his friends were not content to see his rights so easily set aside. He sent word to Sibylla to leave Jerusalem before the King could prevent her and to join him at Ascalon. Baldwin, furious at what he saw as Guy's subterfuge, demanded that he appear in Jerusalem at once. Guy refused, pleading a convenient illness. Desperately ill himself and after several more refusals, Baldwin rode to Ascalon escorted by his knights. In full view of the citizens of that city the king beat on the gate in frustration but was refused entry by the count.[16] Baldwin then rode to Jaffa, second city of Guy's fief, and installed his own governor there. Saladin's spies were well aware of these tensions and constantly supplied their master with evidence that the moment was at hand to overthrow the Frankish kingdom.

Guy's behaviour was clearly treasonable but Baldwin's health was no longer strong enough for him to deal effectively with the rebel. Moreover, Guy had powerful friends, including the Seneschal Joscelyn, the Patriarch Eraclius and the Master of the Templars, Arnold of Torroga. In addition, for all his weakness, Sibylla stood by her husband and refused to be swayed into annulling her marriage as her brother demanded. When Guy ordered his troops to attack the camp of Arabs peacefully grazing their herds with the king's safe conduct near Darum, Baldwin could take no more of his brother-in-law's insolence. He convened a great assembly of the barons at Acre and assigned the administration of the kingdom to Raymond of Tripoli, with the general approval of those present. Raymond accepted the regency for ten years but insisted that the boy king should be assigned to the care of another in case, should he die before the ten years were up, it should be thought that the responsibility was his.[17] Joscelyn of Courtenay took upon himself the care of the young child.

As a last attempt to prevent Guy ever succeeding to the throne, Baldwin IV called upon the barons to swear to the provision that should his nephew die young, as seemed possible, then Raymond would continue to hold the regency until a committee made up of the Holy Roman Emperor, the kings of England and France, and the pope should decide the succession between Sibylla and Isabel, the two daughters of Amalric I.[18] Baldwin now ordered the immediate coronation of Baldwin V, which took place in the Church of the Holy Sepulchre in Jerusalem, with the boy held in the arms of Balian of Ibelin.

Since Reynald of Châtillon's raid into the Red Sea, Saladin had been determined to avenge himself on the Lord of Kerak. Aware of the divisions within the crusader ranks during his campaign of 1183 he promptly left Damascus in late October of that year and headed south for Transjordan, ordering his brother, al-Adil, to move up from Egypt to meet him at Kerak with his troops. Kerak had been since biblical times the capital of Moab and the castle of Kerak had been built by Pagan the Butler in 1142, alongside the ancient fortified settlement on the pilgrim route from Damascus to the Red Sea and Mecca. Stone from earlier buildings was used to supplement the reddish-brown volcanic tufa, which comprised most of the local stone. This was so hard that it was impossible to shape and was simply broken up and piled into the walls. The effect was to produce a grim and gloomy castle, which was separated from its township by a deep fosse, between 22 and 32 yards wide and over 32 yards deep. It had none of the architectural splendour of some of its northern counterparts and was more noted for its rude strength than for its craftsmanship. To Muslim pilgrims it was always a fearful place. They called it the wolf which fate had brought into the valley. With its sister castle of Shaubak it was spoken of as a lion that daily devours human flesh and drinks human blood.

The Lord of Kerak, Reynald of Châtillon, had apparently received warning of the attack and had increased his garrison accordingly. However, when Saladin began to besiege the castle on 1 November, Reynald made a tactical mistake by refusing to allow the townspeople of Kerak to move themselves and their chattels within the castle itself. He was convinced that he and his men could hold the fortified walls of the town. The land that slopes up to the plateau on which both castle and town stood was so steep that he felt the Muslims would be unable to mount a sustained assault. In this judgement he was wrong and his outnumbered men were soon forced back into the castle, abandoning the entire town to Saladin's troops. Only the heroism of a single knight, named Iven, prevented the Muslims from forcing their way into the castle itself. Like a latter-day Horatius he held off the enemy while behind him his comrades smashed down the bridge across the fosse. At last, riddled with arrows, he turned back to make his escape just as the bridge fell.

Not only did all Reynald's people lose their possessions but the township now gave Saladin a base from which to assault the castle itself. His engineers assembled eight great mangonels (a stone-throwing mechanism), which kept up a continuous bombardment, by night and by day, on the forbidding walls of the fortress, within which, ironically, a wedding was taking place. Kerak was crowded with hundreds of 'useless' people: non-combatant guests and entertainers who had come to celebrate the marriage of Humphrey IV of Toron, stepson of Reynald of Châtillon, to Isabella, stepsister to the king and stepdaughter of Balian of Ibelin. This marriage, which Baldwin IV had arranged in 1180, had been delayed for three years due to the extreme youth of the bride.

The chronicler Ernoul gives a remakable account of the noises caused by rocks hurled by the mangonels crashing into the walls of the castle while within the sounds of music and laughter and dancing attempted to shut them out.[19] A not entirely implausible story relates that during the siege Stephanie de Milly, mother of the bridegroom, personally prepared dishes from the bridal feast to send out to Saladin while he in return enquired in which tower the newly-weds were to sleep and thereupon instructed his men to cease bombarding that part of the castle.

Within the crowded citadel the villagers had the frustration of watching the Muslim troops in the village below, living in their houses, eating their food and taking their few possessions. Their animals were killed by the butchers who accompanied Saladin's armies and jointed as food for the army. Their houses became workshops and bakeries, while their supplies of grain, barley, wine and oil were soon consumed. In desperation the defenders of Kerak set up a mangonel of their own to try to strike back at the enemy but so heavy was the bombardment of rocks and boulders from Saladin's engines that none dared to service it. As the Muslims grew more confident they had themselves lowered into the fosse and attempted to fill it with enough rubble to enable a general assault to be launched against the castle itself.

During the 80 years or so of their occupation of the Holy Land, the crusaders had come to rely on the beacon as the most reliable and the swiftest form of communication between their isolated strongholds. In daylight a column of smoke would indicate danger while at night a beacon fire from a high hill or tower would do the same. Hearing of Saladin's approach the beacons at Kerak were lit and by means of a relay of beacon fires the news was relayed 50 miles to Jerusalem that Kerak was under the combined attack of Saladin from Damascus and al-Adil from Egypt. Baldwin IV insisted on leading the army to the relief of the castle, albeit in a litter. He had an answering beacon lit on the top of David's Tower in Jerusalem to tell Kerak that help was coming. In the vicinity of the Dead Sea Baldwin handed over command to Raymond of Tripoli. When informed of the approach of a relief force Saladin broke off the siege, abandoning and burning his siege engines. He had been far from encouraged by the ineffectiveness of these machines in breaching the walls of Kerak. On 4 December, Baldwin entered Kerak to the cheers of wedding guests and soldiers alike. Once again the heroic leper king had led his army to the relief of his vassals but this time it was in a curtained litter, carried by others rather than in the saddle and at the head of his knights. How strongly the life force seemed to flow in that ravaged body was astonishing to everyone. In his featureless face even the eyes were now dulled and sightless and yet the urge to live and to rule seemed undiminished. Imprisoned within the rotting shell of his body there was a young man in the prime of his life.

However, Saladin had not given up hope of taking Kerak and in the following summer he besieged it again in company with his nephew, Taqi al-Din. With a combination of Egyptian and Syrian troops he invested the castle, though this time the surrounding settlement was abandoned by the Christians. The Muslim troops found extreme difficulty in crossing the deep ravine that separated the houses from the hillside on which the castle stood. Saladin decided that only by filling in this chasm could his men actually reach the walls in order to scale them. Fascines, piles of earth and rubble, rocks and boulders, dead bodies, carcasses of horses and cattle, all served to fill the fosse. While this work was carried out his siege engines continued to assail the walls, though with little immediate effect. The defenders poured all kinds of missiles on the Muslim sappers beneath, including rocks, jars of naphtha, boiling oil, 'Greek fire' and burning faggots to ignite the fascines that the Saracens were using to fill the fosse. 'Greek fire' had been widely used in Levantine warfare since its development by the Byzantines in the

seventh century. One Christian chronicler described its effect like
this:

> In appearance the Greek fire was like a large barrel of
> verjuice, and its fiery tail was the length of a long lance. In
> coming it made a noise like heaven's thunder. It seemed like
> a dragon flying through the air. So great a light did it emit,
> because of the great abundance of fire that made the light,
> that one could see as clearly through the camp as if it had
> been day.[20]

Saladin responded by building trenches, covered in hide, for his
sappers to crawl through as they approached the fosse. Progress
in filling this ditch reached the point where a fettered Muslim
prisoner managed to break free and escape by leaping into the
fosse from the battlements of the citadel. However, the Franks
were again advancing from Jerusalem with a relief force under
Raymond of Tripoli. Saladin called off the siege at once, burned
his siege engines and marched out to meet it. The Franks had
camped at Al-wala and Saladin cautiously took up his position at
Hisban. However, he was outmanoeuvred by the Frankish
leaders who entered Kerak after a night march. Saladin had once
again suffered defeat in front of the walls of Kerak. Yet the relief
of Kerak had been an expensive success, for while the bulk of the
Frankish army was in Transjordan, Muslim raiding parties from
Syria crossed the River Jordan and attacked Nablus, Sebastiya
and Jenin.

The destructive raids on the border territories were having a
disastrous effect on Christians and Muslims alike and when these
coincided with a prolonged drought the outlook was bleak. So
seriously did Raymond of Tripoli consider the situation that he
assembled the barons as well as the military orders to ask their
advice on what should be done. It was clear that the Franks badly
needed a truce if they were to recover, and so an approach was
made to Saladin for a four-year cessation of hostilities. In fact,
Saladin was facing serious problems in Mesopotamia and was
only too willing to accept the truce, which was signed at the end
of 1184 and saved the kingdom from mass starvation.

Early in 1184 the mission to the kings of the West (which had
been mooted at the Council of Acre) was undertaken by the
Patriarch Eraclius and the two masters of the military orders.
The envoys sailed for Italy and for several months the future of

the kingdom of Jerusalem became the central issue of European attention. While at Verona the Master of the Templars, Arnold of Torroga, died, but this did not materially affect the embassy as most of the negotiations were carried out by the Patriarch Eraclius. He was granted audiences by the pope, Lucius III and the Holy Roman Emperor, Frederick Barbarossa, who promised to try to take the cross in 1186. Travelling on to Paris, the envoys offered the keys of the kingdom to Philip Augustus of France. However, this wily monarch was quite unprepared to make any offers until he had seen what the English would do. As a result he hurriedly arranged for Eraclius and his party to take ship for England, where they stayed from January 1185 to mid-April. At Reading the envoys met the ailing Henry II of England and, as they had with Philip Augustus, they offered him the keys of Jerusalem. Henry was in no hurry to accept this offer and called a great meeting of his nobility and clergy at Clerkenwell, where many took the cross. Undoubtedly Eraclius' pleas had a considerable emotional effect on the assembly but he was far less successful in convincing Henry to accept responsibility for the kingdom; nor would he agree to the partriarch's plea that he should send one of his sons. After all, had either Richard or John left in 1185, they would immediately have had access to his treasure in Jerusalem and this was by no means Henry's wish. The treasure was a tangible expression of his commitment to the crusades and as such it removed the need for him to go to the Holy Land in person. Eraclius found the English monarch frustrating in the extreme. Indeed, on one occasion he even knelt at Henry's feet and entreated him to come to rescue the Holy Land. When Henry replied that he would send money instead, the patriarch responded that it was a leader not money that they needed. Relations between the king and patriarch became so strained that Henry apparently commented sarcastically about 'clerics who can afford to call him boldly forth to battles, knowing well that they are not going to sustain a blow in them'.

Henry II of England had made many promises to take the cross during his reign but had always found convincing reasons to avoid doing so. As early as 1166 he had levied a crusading tax to aid the Franks of Outremer, but as his reign progressed strife between himself and his sons prevented him doing more than sending money. The murder of Archbishop Thomas à Becket in 1170 caused a breach between Henry and the Church which the king was eager to heal. In 1172, at Avranches, he promised massive aid to the defenders of Jerusalem, amounting to an offer to maintain as many as 200 knights. Although this force was apparently never raised, Henry sent annual payments to Jerusalem and thereby earned himself the title '*praecipius terrae Palestinae sustenator*'. The money he sent was put in the safe-keeping of the Templars and Hospitallers, apparently on the assumption that when Henry eventually came to Jerusalem he would find ample funds to finance his crusade. However, this meant that the money was unavailable to the crusaders during the crisis years of 1182–87. By 1187 it is estimated that Henry's treasure in Jerusalem consisted of 30 000 marks of silver, a prodigious sum. However, because Henry had specified that he alone could draw on the money his physical presence in Outremer was essential. Moreover, Henry had made it clear that if the Templars or Hospitallers drew on the money in their care, he would reimburse himself from their Order's assets in his lands.

The envoys had one final meeting with the kings of England and France at Vaudreuil on 1 May 1185 at which they were offered more money and men. However, Eraclius was clearly disappointed that he had failed to win any commitment from the West to come to the aid of the kingdom. Ironically, the English and French knights who had taken the cross in response to Eraclius' pleas arrived in Outremer during 1186 and found that Raymond of Tripoli had concluded the four-year truce with Saladin. Presuming their services were no longer needed, they returned to Europe after completing their pilgrimage to the holy places.

On 16 March 1185 Baldwin IV died in Jerusalem. He had shown great courage in the face of his illness, and in spite of the fact that he was so often unable to offer a lead in either war or diplomacy he was much more than a mere figurehead. To the very end he was one to whom both the contesting factions looked and whom they had to obey. The fate of Guy of Lusignan showed what might have happened had the realm been blessed with a healthy king: after the funeral of Baldwin IV, Raymond of Tripoli officially took over the government of the kingdom while Joscelyn of Courtenay looked after the welfare of the young Baldwin V. With the young king in the care of the seneschal there was a chance for the court party to regain its pre-eminence. In August 1186 the sickly child died, throwing open once again the question of succession. Baldwin IV had fortuitously anticipated this in his will (by leaving the choice between his sisters Sibylla and Isabel to a committee of Western rulers). However, Joscelyn of Courtenay now saw an opportunity to oust Raymond and become 'the power behind the throne' by crowning his niece Sibylla. He would need to act quickly before the assembly of the barons could insist on carrying out the will of Baldwin IV. Joscelyn therefore called on the regent to suggest that he retire to Tiberias to assemble the barons there, while he, the seneschal, would take the king's body to Jerusalem for burial, escorted on the journey by the Templars. In view of the numerous grounds that Raymond must have had for distrusting the Courtenays it is difficult to understand how he was so completely fooled by this story. Nevertheless, he did as Joscelyn suggested and retired to Tiberias where he summoned the barons to assemble.

Events now amounted to a palace revolution. It is clear that a number of prominent figures were privy to the plot: otherwise they could not have acted so quickly to support the seneschal. Joscelyn seized the castle of Acre and left a garrison there, before moving on to take Beirut — the city which had been given to Raymond to defray the costs of his regency. Having secured this he contacted Sibylla and told her to hurry to Jerusalem with all her knights, seize the citadel and arrange for her own coronation. Guy and Sibylla needed no urging and reached Jerusalem, where they were joined by their allies, the Patriarch Eraclius and Gerard of Ridefort, the new Master of the Templars. Once Reynald of Châtillon had been summoned from Kerak the conspiracy was complete and the only important opponent of the *coup* within Jerusalem was Roger of Moulins, Master of the Hospitallers, who insisted that they should all be bound by the oath that they swore to Baldwin IV to respect his will. Sibylla signalled her victory by summoning all the barons from Tiberias to attend her coronation at Jerusalem.

The baronial assembly at Tiberias never took place because news of the *coup* reached Raymond and he called an emergency meeting at Nablus, the stronghold of his friend Balian of Ibelin. All the native barons save Reynald of Châtillon and William of Montferrat, grandfather of the late king, met him there and were united in rejecting Sibylla's summons with scorn. They were determined to hold to the letter of the law, leaving Raymond as regent while the matter was referred to the monarchs of the West. They countered Joscelyn's actions by despatching two Cistercian monks to warn the conspirators that they were breaking their oaths to Baldwin IV. Eraclius and Gerard of Ridefort, confident in their hold on the capital, replied that they would not be bound by such an oath but intended to crown Sibylla. Moreover, to prevent violence they would bar the gates of Jerusalem to the barons until the coronation had taken place. Roger of Moulins was alone in dissociating himself from this message.

The crowns and coronation regalia of the kings and queens of Jerusalem were kept in coffers that needed three keys to open them.[21] The Patriarch of Jerusalem held one, while the other two were kept by the Masters of the military orders. Eraclius and Gerard promptly offered up their keys but Roger of Moulins refused on the grounds that such an action must not be taken without the consent of the *haut cour* of the barons. Stoically he resisted the pressure from those around him until eventually he cast the key out of the window of his house, symbolically washing his hands of the matter. He knew he could do no more. The coronation soon followed in which the Patriarch first crowned Sibylla and then called upon her to crown her royal consort. Guy knelt before her and had the crown placed on his head by her own hands. The proceedings were concluded when Reynald of Châtillon gave a powerful speech emphasising the legitimacy of the coronation and how Sibylla was the mother of the last king and the sister of his predecessor. Thus, he asserted, there could be no possible doubt about her right to succeed to the throne.[22]

When the barons at Nablus received the news that the gates of Jerusalem were barred against them by the Templars they realised that civil war was now a distinct possibility. Therefore, they sent a soldier (who knew the city well), into Jerusalem disguised as a monk. Having witnessed the coronation he returned to Nablus and told the barons what he had seen. They realised that they had been outwitted and that there was little that they could do but accept Guy's succession as a *fait accompli*. Baldwin of Ramla received the news with a show of bitterness. He had a personal reason to hate Guy of Lusignan, who had once robbed him of a wife and now had been elevated to a kingship which might have been his own. 'I'll wager he won't be king a year,' prophesied the great knight sadly. 'Lords, do the best you can, for the land is lost, and I shall leave the country for I do not wish to have reproach or blame for having any share in the loss of the land. For I know the present king to be such a fool and such a wicked man that he will do nothing by my advice or yours. Instead he will prefer to go astray on the advice of those who know nothing. For this reason I shall leave the country.'[23]

Raymond of Tripoli was not willing to give in so easily. He reminded the barons that as regent he still represented the law in the kingdom. Moreover, among their number was Humphrey of Toron, husband of Isabella (half-sister to Sibylla), who possessed at least an equal right to the throne. Moreover, it was also clear that the Hospitallers were not supporting the *coup* and with the Saracens tied by the truce signed in 1185 there was a chance to concentrate their attention on ousting Guy and the conspirators. Raymond suggested that they should crown Humphrey and Isabella and set up a rival monarchy. This would be tantamount to declaring war on the court party but the barons were confident in their strength. However, they had reckoned without the weakness of Humphrey himself. More of a scholar than a knight, he was unwilling to have greatness thrust upon him in this way. Under cover of night he fled to Jerusalem and confessed the barons' plan to Sibylla in order to obtain her pardon.

The defection of Humphrey of Toron meant the collapse of Raymond's plans and, with the exception of himself and Baldwin of Ramla, the other barons gave up the struggle and went to Jerusalem to accept Guy as their liege lord. For both Raymond and Baldwin this was a bitter moment. Since 1174 the Count of Tripoli had struggled to maintain his supremacy in the affairs of the kingdom. His enemies had often accused him of coveting the throne for himself and yet there is little evidence to suggest that this was true. With the support of most of the powerful barons there were times when he could have seized the throne in the name of national necessity. From 1180 onwards Baldwin IV had frequently been too ill to rule and after 1185 his five-year-old nephew was king in name only. Raymond would have had little difficulty in convincing his supporters that with the growing threat from Saladin there was need for a strong man on the throne. Yet he had taken no action to obstruct the rule of law, even when he was passed over as regent for the incompetent Guy of Lusignan in 1183. Now he was presented with the very worst scenario: Guy was no longer merely the regent but king, with Raymond's enemies standing at his shoulder, ready to misinterpret his every action. Moreover, with the exception of the proud Baldwin of Ramla, the other barons had swallowed their pride and had accepted Guy as their lord.

As the barons left Nablus they promised Baldwin of Ramla that they would present Guy with his request that his son Thomas should be given possession of his lands. However, Guy refused to do this unless Baldwin came in person and rendered homage. If he failed to do so Guy would declare his lands forfeit. This was a bitter fruit for Baldwin to swallow. Nevertheless, in the interests of his son he met Guy at Acre and rendered homage unwillingly to him, even refusing to kiss the king's hand. Having seen his son installed he left him under the care of his brother Balian and travelled northwards to Antioch with his knights and was granted lands by Bohemond III, who was overjoyed to receive so famous a knight. He knew as well as anyone how great a loss was Baldwin of Ramla to the kingdom of Jerusalem.[24]

Having successfully dealt with Baldwin, Guy now shifted his attention to the fount of opposition to his reign, the Count of Tripoli. He and Sibylla asked Raymond to account for the money he had spent during his regency, an act of such folly that from an abler pair one might have suspected that they wished to drive the count to an act of rebellion. Whatever their motives, Raymond was duly outraged at their rudeness and retired to Tiberias, refusing an oath of loyalty to the new king. Turning to Gerard of Ridefort for advice as to how to deal with Raymond, Guy was told to besiege him in Tiberias and force him to come to terms. Civil war now seemed certain. These developments were assiduously followed in the Muslim lands; truly, in the eyes of Saladin, 'whom the Gods wish to destroy they first make mad'. Surely Raymond of Tripoli was the Franks' wisest counsellor and a man worthy of the throne? And surely Baldwin of Ramla was the greatest knight of the realm, a man whose reputation was known throughout the Muslim lands? How could the Franks be stronger by the loss of such men?

At Tiberias Raymond found himself in a difficult situation. Legally he was still the ruler of the kingdom and yet now no one would stand by him if the king attacked. He owed no allegiance to Guy, who was in reality a usurper, and yet he had now been accepted by the barons of the realm. Did this confer legitimacy on Guy? Yet there was more at stake than merely a question of who ruled the kingdom: there was the future of the kingdom itself. The Franks were living on borrowed time, surrounded by a tight ring of Muslim states no longer quarrelling amongst themselves but now accepting a single ruler, Saladin, a man committed to the holy war and to the reconquest of Palestine.

The choice facing Raymond was whether to swallow his pride, offer allegiance to Guy and present a common front against the Muslims, or else to split the kingdom by resisting the king. For a man of Raymond's experience the choice was not as clear cut as this. He was a fourth-generation inhabitant of Outremer and no longer saw Christians and Muslims in black and white terms. Where Reynald of Châtillon or Gerard of Ridefort saw only fanatical enemies Raymond saw neighbours, fellow orientals with shared interests and problems. In times of drought or poor harvest both Christians and Muslims starved. There were issues which transcended religion and which joined people together however much their rulers or priests tried to hold them apart. There was nothing unusual in Christians and Muslims working together during the 90 year history of the kingdom. Treaties between Muslim states and the crusaders had been common and in view of the threat facing him from Guy of Lusignan Raymond felt compelled to seek support from probably the only source that could have helped him. However, in seeking help from Saladin Raymond was acting treasonably, in the spirit if not in the letter of the law. He must have known that Saladin was a committed exponent of *jihād* and would never compromise in the long run his life's aim to regain Jerusalem. This made him far more dangerous an ally than Guy of Lusignan was an enemy.

Raymond sent messengers to Damascus describing his predicament to Saladin, who responded by sending troops to Tiberias, as well as releasing those knights of Tripoli or Galilee that he was holding prisoner.[25] He promised Raymond that if he was attacked in the morning he would have Saracen support by evening. We will never know for certain what Raymond was hoping to achieve by this agreement with Saladin. A truce still existed between the Muslim leader and the kingdom of Jerusalem and so there was no absolute need for hostilities of any kind to take place. It is possible that Raymond's action was purely defensive, designed to deter Guy and the more impetuous among the Franks from taking precipitate action. Yet helping an apparent rebel against the 'lawful' government of the kingdom might be construed as breaking the truce on Saladin's part. Certainly he was not acting entirely altruistically whatever he might have claimed. He stood to benefit from the disintegration of the Frankish state and was willing to lend his assistance to this process short of actually initiating an attack.

In Jerusalem, men of good sense were attempting to counter the bad advice that Guy was receiving from Gerard and Reynald. Balian of Ibelin tried to reason with the king, pointing out the folly of military action against Tiberias. Only Saladin would benefit from Franks fighting Franks. Balian condemned Guy's advisors as rash. If the king would agree to disband his army Balian would visit Tiberias and try to reconcile Raymond to the new regime. In the face of such good sense Guy agreed to let Balian try. However, Raymond, now in a far stronger position with the weight of Saladin behind him, declared that he would only accept Guy if he was recompensed for his losses and had Beirut returned to him. When Balian returned with this message Guy refused to accept such terms. With the onset of winter matters rested until shortly after Easter 1187.

To Guy and his followers Saladin had already imperilled the truce by taking sides in the dispute between himself and one of his vassals. Consequently when Reynald of Châtillon broke the truce *de facto* by attacking a Muslim convoy early in 1187 he may only have been giving expression to a feeling prevalent among the members of the court party. Or perhaps this is being too charitable to Reynald. The Lord of Kerak had seen the disintegration of central authority in the kingdom of Jerusalem during the reigns of Baldwin IV and V, and now that he had helped so materially to place the weak Guy on the throne he was more than ever determined to follow his own course. Reynald had been building in Oultrejourdain a state within a state and the time was near when he would claim his independence of Jerusalem as a princely state like Tripoli or Antioch. To Saladin Reynald was a more real threat than any other posed by the Franks. Unlike Raymond of Tripoli or Bohemond of Antioch he was not content to co-exist with Muslims, his aims were expansionist and were directed at the heartland of the Arab world. His close relations with the Bedouin tribes of the southern desert enabled him to know all the details of the trade routes of the Hijjaz. In this way he could disrupt both trade and communications between Egypt, Hijjaz and Syria and thereby break the ring of steel with which Saladin had surrounded the crusader states on the Levantine coast. Fate had placed this most dynamic crusader at the weak hinge of Saladin's strategical system and the Muslim leader knew it. His frequent attempts to seize Kerak had all ended in failure and his prestige demanded that he overthrow Reynald, the 'Satan' of the Muslims, if possible killing him with his own hand. It is with this in mind that one must interpret Reynald's attack on the Muslim caravan in 1187 and Saladin's reaction to it.

It seems that stories relating that Saladin's sister was travelling with the caravan from Mecca to Damascus were untrue, although they may have been enough to have prompted Reynald's attack.[26] Nevertheless, when news of the attack reached Saladin he was furious and demanded that the Lord of Kerak release the prisoners immediately. When he received no satisfaction he applied to King Guy, who feebly asked Reynald to do as Saladin requested but was met with the response that, within his own lands, the Lord of Kerak was as much master as the king was within his. The irony of this response cannot have been lost on the man who had closed the gates of Ascalon on King Baldwin IV. Reynald was asserting his independence and opposing the king's will as completely as had Raymond of Tripoli. But Guy was dependent on the support of men like Reynald for his position and he felt far too weak to threaten them. With the failure of the crusaders to put their own house in order Saladin decided that he had no alternative now but to raise the banner of holy war against them.

The end of the truce now altered the situation between King Guy and Raymond of Tripoli. Both men were placed in invidious positions: Guy knew that he needed the help of the count in any war against the full might of the Muslim armies; Raymond now found that was allied to an enemy of his religion with war imminent. Personal rivalries needed to be ended in the interests of the state. At Easter 1187 Guy summoned his barons to an assembly at Jerusalem, where they expressed the unanimous wish that he come to terms with the Count of Tripoli. They pointed out that Guy had already lost his best knight, Baldwin of Ramla, and if he now lost his shrewdest one the kingdom itself would be lost. Guy was impressed with these arguments and agreed to make peace with Raymond if it could be done. Thereupon a peace mission was chosen to go to Tiberias to reason with the Count. Its members, however, were ill-chosen. With Balian of Ibelin went the Master of the Templars, Gerard of Ridefort, Raymond's bitterest enemy, the Master of the Hospital, Roger of Moulins, Archbishop Joscius of Tyre and Reynald of Sidon.[27] The choice of Gerard was a bad mistake and contributed to the disaster that was to follow.

Apart from Reynald of Sidon, who travelled by a different route, the members of the mission spent their first night at Balian's castle at Nablus. However, at this point fate took a hand. Balian decided to spend the following day at home with his wife and then agreed to catch the others up at La Fève, by riding through the following night. Balian's squire, Ernoul, is the only

Christian chronicler who describes the extraordinary series of events that followed.[28] On 30 April Raymond of Tripoli received an envoy from the Muslim commander at Banyas, al-Afdal, son of Saladin, requesting permission for a force of Mameluke cavalry to pass through the count's territory on a reconnaissance mission into Palestine. With a state of war existing between the kingdom of Jerusalem and Saladin, Raymond found himself in a difficult position. His agreement with Saladin had been made for his own protection from King Guy. But now that Saladin was at war with the kingdom he, as a baron of the kingdom, could hardly assist the enemy without being guilty of treason. However, to have denied help to his ally (Saladin) would have broken his agreement with the Muslims and might have brought down upon himself and his people the wrath of the sultan. Moreover, he could not necessarily rely on the support of King Guy, having denied allegiance to him and therefore being viewed as a rebel. In the event, Raymond tried to achieve a compromise by granting permission to the Muslims to pass through his territory but stipulating that no damage should be done to Christian possessions there. Moreover, they must cross the River Jordan at sunrise and leave his lands by sunset.[29] Raymond went further and sent out messengers to spread the word throughout his lands that the people were to stay in their houses and were not to interfere with the Muslim troops. Hearing news of the king's mission he also sent a messenger to the Templar castle of La Fève to warn the emissaries of the danger from the Muslim troops.

On the morning of 1 May Raymond was able to watch in the distance the Muslim Emir Keukburi leading a strong force of Mameluke cavalry, numbering perhaps 7000 men, through his territory. What he could not have known was the effect that his warning message had had on the king's emissaries at La Fève. On receiving news of the planned Muslim incursion on 30 April, Gerard of Ridefort summoned all the Templar support in the vicinity to meet him at the castle. The Marshal of the Temple, James of Mailly, was at Kakun, just five miles away, with 90 knights and he hurriedly brought these to La Fève, setting up tents around the castle where they spent the night. Next morning the Templar force rode to Nazareth, where they were met by 40 secular knights. Here the Archbishop of Tyre rested, while the two Masters and their tiny force rode towards the Springs of Cresson, where they found the huge Muslim force watering its horses. At once a dispute broke out with Roger of Moulins and

James of Mailly sensibly recommending retreat and Gerard of Ridefort refusing to hear of it. Gerard taunted his Marshal: 'You love your blond head too well to lose it.' Stung into action, James of Mailly replied that he would die in battle like a brave man but that Gerard would flee like a traitor.[30] With the 130 knights were some 300 to 400 infantry; but so eager was Gerard to attack the Muslims that he spurred his knights into action with no thought of waiting for the support of crossbowmen and archers. In the event it was a massacre more than a battle. The Frankish knights were completely engulfed by the Mamlukes and the infantry never even came into action. Both James of Mailly and Roger of Moulins were killed along with all of the Templars except Gerard and two others who made their escape. The secular knights were taken prisoner and held for ransom.

Balian, meanwhile, had left Nablus as promised and began to ride through the night but realising that 1 May was the Feast of St James and St Philip he stopped at Sebastiya to visit the bishop until Mass could be heard at dawn. He then continued his journey to La Fève which he found apparently deserted. Ernoul searched the castle and found just two soldiers sleeping in an upper gallery, too ill to tell anything of what had occurred. With heavy hearts Balian and Ernoul now left the castle and spurred their horses along the road to Nazareth. Here they met one of the wounded Templar knights who had survived the battle, from whom they learned of the disaster at Cresson and the heavy losses suffered by the Franks. Showing great urgency Balian sent a summons to his wife at Nablus to raise all the knights she could and send them to Nazareth. He continued his journey there and met Gerard of Ridefort and the few other survivors from whom he learned the full story.

Raymond's first intimation of disaster was the sight of the Mamluke cavalry returning to cross the Jordan in the waning light of evening with Templar heads on their lances. He was relieved to hear that Balian of Ibelin had not been in the battle and he sent 50 knights from Tiberias to escort the Archbishop of Tyre and Balian into his castle. Gerard found that his exertions of that day had removed any desire on his part to meet Raymond of Tripoli. For the count the battle at Cresson had been a personal disaster. He knew that had he withheld permission for the Muslims to cross into his lands the battle would never have taken place. Admittedly he had sent a warning to the king's mission and could hardly be held responsible for the impetuosity of the master of the Templars, yet he knew that many would hold him responsible for the losses particularly for the death of Roger of Moulins, a man who had stood aside from the palace revolution of 1186 and had supported Raymond. Moreover, Gerard of Ridefort's hatred of the Count would now be even greater. Raymond knew that there was no alternative but to come to terms with the king and to offer a united front against Saladin.

Raymond told the king's emissaries that he was now content to give up the quarrel with Guy. After dismissing the Muslim troops whom Saladin had sent to Tiberias as part of his agreement with Raymond, the count set out with Balian to meet the king at the Hospitaller castle of St Job. When they met, the two men embraced and Raymond dutifully bent his knee to his new liege lord. After staying briefly at Nablus the party returned to Jerusalem where, with due celebration, the Count of Tripoli paid homage to Guy and Sibylla. Yet, whatever outward manifestation of reconciliation there was, the bitterness of years could not so easily be removed. Gerard would not forgive Raymond for the heiress of Botron nor for the disaster at the Springs of Cresson. Reynald of Châtillon would not forgive Raymond for the part he was believed to have played in the murder of Miles of Plancy, and for his close relationship with Saladin. Between the barons bitterness remained intense, with the house of Courtenay (now linked to that of Lusignan by the marriage of Joscelyn's daughter to Amalric, Guy's brother) hating and resenting that of Ibelin. It was the internal rottenness of the state that threatened the kingdom even more severely than the danger from a united Islam.

7

The Armies Assemble

Saladin left Damascus on 13 March 1187 and established camp at Ra's al-Ma', which was to be the mustering ground for the northern and eastern contingents of his army. He knew that his reputation as leader in the holy war depended on his fighting a successful battle against the Franks because, as one of his emirs reminded him, 'the people of the East curse us and say: Saladin abandoned the fight against the infidels and came to attack the Muslims'.[1] Saladin knew that he could take no chances and so he assembled his forces slowly, sending his nephew, Taqi al-Din, north to watch the Armenians and the frontier with Antioch, and leaving his eldest son, al-Afdal, to command the camp at Ra's al-Ma'. He travelled south himself to Busra to protect the caravans of pilgrims returning to Syria from Mecca, particularly the one containing his sister and her son, from any further attacks by Reynald of Châtillon. Whilst there he took the opportunity of ravaging the lands around Kerak until late in May. He also travelled to al-Qaryatain to meet his Egyptian forces marching northwards to the general muster.

It seemed that much of the Muslim world was on the march. Into the camp at Ra's al-Ma' came troops from east of the Euphrates led by Muzaffar al-Din Keukburi, Aleppans under Badr al-Din Dildirim and Damascenes led by the Mameluke Emir Sarim al-Din Qaimatz. At the end of May 1187 Taqi al-Din made a truce with Bohemond of Antioch ensuring his neutrality. This enabled Taqi to move south to join the muster with his own feudal levies and the troops of Mardin, accompanied by the Mosulis under Fakhr al-Din ibn al-Za'farani. With the arrival of troops from Sinjar, Nisbin, Amid, Irbil and Diyar Bakr, the northern muster was complete. Only the arrival of Saladin himself, with his Mamluke regiments and the forces of Egypt, was now necessary to bring together the finest army that the Islamic world had been able to commit against the crusaders.

The force assembled by Saladin was a vastly complex organisation, containing soldiers of different colour, race, nationality, language and military tradition. United by religious zeal but little else, men who had only recently been enemies now found that they were fighting together under one leader. It needed great administrative skill to weld this composite force into a cohesive whole. In order to appreciate Saladin's achievement it is necessary to examine the nature of the weapon which he had forged for the service of his God.

The Ayyubid military system established by Saladin in Egypt was an extension of that developed by Nur al-Din in Syria. The main emirs and military officers received an *iqta*, which was not a personal estate but a payment in land revenues and could be transferred from one district to another. The fief-holder, or *muqta*, could be posted to other parts of Saladin's lands and was never in a position to enjoy the entire revenue of his *iqta*, being permitted only to levy specific sums in money or kind which comprised his pay. In return, his obligations to the state involved supervising the cultivation and watering of the land, as well as supervising personally the collection of the harvests. This imposed limitations on his military role, as during harvest time he would inevitably be unavailable for service. Within the *iqta* the emir allocated to his Mamelukes a *jamikiya*, which could be a share in the *iqta* itself or a fixed allocation of pay.[2]

The backbone of Saladin's armies, as under the Fatimids in Egypt, was the regiments of Mamelukes. These warriors were almost entirely white Turks, who had been purchased as slaves and were trained in the arts of war at their master's expense, thus guaranteeing their loyalty. When they had proved themselves to be good soldiers they were given their freedom with a part or possibly, in the case of an outstanding candidate, an entire *iqta* to themselves. Senior Mamlukes could hold the rank of emir and even command armies, while from their *iqtas* they were themselves expected to supply soldiers, generally Mamelukes. Saladin inherited from the Egyptian Fatimids a central corps of about 5000 Royal Mamelukes, with an élite 'Young Guard' of 500 chosen warriors. Significantly, no one of Egyptian or Arabic origin was allowed to become a Mameluke.

Mamlukes comprised the major part of the *Askars*, or the full-time professional forces which followed Saladin and the provincial emirs, but there were also Kurds (hill-people from the mountains of north-western Iran), Armenians, Arabs and Turks, all of whom were paid at different rates according to their standing in the military hierarchy. Turks, Kurds and Turkman tribesmen could usually expect to be paid at twice the rate of Egyptian troops.[3]

Although the military strength of Egypt was considerable — Saladin had 14 000 horsemen in 1171 — he was never able to use its entire strength in his Syrian campaigns. The threat of Frankish land and sea attacks had been ever present since the days of Amalric I and so half his Egyptian army was always at home on garrison duty. For his campaigns after 1177 Saladin was content to use 4000 to 6000 men, which gave him the advantage of being able to use them on a rota basis, thus maintaining a constant supply of fresh reserves and not hindering the collection of the harvest in Egypt.[4]

The quality of his Egyptian troops varied considerably. The Arab cavalry wore chain-mail rather like their Frankish opponents and fought with swords and wooden or cane lances. Some wore helmets under their turbans but others were content with the turban alone which was known to be able to turn even a heavy sword blow. These cavalrymen must not be confused with the Turkish horse-archers for they fought as shock-troops and never used the bow. Nevertheless, man for man they were no match for the Frankish knights. The Egyptian infantry were generally unarmoured and fought with the *mitrad* (or thrusting spear) and the *harbah* (the javelin or throwing spear). Some carried bows and most were equipped with the *tariqa* (a kite-shaped shield).[5] The black-skinned Sudanese foot archers, who had made up much of the infantry body of Fatimid armies, were found in fewer numbers in Saladin's armies. In addition to their bows they carried spears and maces for close fighting.

The élite troops of the Egyptian contingent were the sultan's own Mameluke regiment, resplendent in yellow uniforms, with the 'emirs of 100' dressed in outer coats of red satin embroidered in gold and trimmed with miniver fur, as well as fringed inner coats of yellow satin, with beaver cloaks overall. Beneath this finery they wore body armour of mail or lamellar, and wore knee-length Khuff boots. As well as the bow, the Mamelukes favoured the mace in close fighting, as well as the *ghaddara*, a sharp steel staff of some 30 inches in length, kept in their saddle cases, which could cut off an arm with a single blow.[6]

The troops assembling in the north at Ra's al-Ma' were very different in appearance and military style from the Egyptians. They had been the troops of Nur al-Din and on his death they had followed the emirs and princes who had squabbled over the succession to the Zangid lands. Although some had gone to Damascus, and others to Homs, Harran and Hama, as many as two-thirds had remained loyal to as-Salih at Aleppo. During his long campaigns against Aleppo and Mosul, Saladin had been inspired not merely by the desire to reunite the lands of Nur al-Din, nor to create a great Ayyubid state of Eygpt, Syria and Iraq. Above all this he knew that unity meant strength and that only by calling on the united power of the Muslim world could he assemble the troops necessary to bring the holy war to a successful conclusion. By 1187 the first part of his aim had been achieved. Into the camp at Ra's al-Ma' came 7000 horsemen, 1000 from Damascus, 1000 from Aleppo and northern Syria, and 5000 from Mosul, Jazira and Diyar Bakr. It was these men, ostensibly under the command of al-Afdal, who requested permission of Raymond of Tripoli to pass through his lands and who, at the Springs of Cresson, wiped out the meagre Templar force of Gerard of Ridefort.

The strength of Saladin's Syrian and Iraqi armies was undoubtedly their cavalry, even more so than in his Egyptian host. Yet even here there were differences to be noted, between the Syrian and the Turkish horsemen. The Syrians, mostly from Aleppo and Damascus, carried spears and swords but few carried bows. Some, like the Banu Munqidh from Shaizar, were knights of Arabic stock who fought in the Frankish fashion, wearing conical helmets, *baida*, often ornate and heavily gilded.[7] Most of them wore quilted tunics, *al-Qutuns*, generally of linen or wool, padded with cotton or old rags and strengthened with scales of lamellar armour.

The Turks emphasised mobility above all other virtues. They were horse-archers and each rider kept his bow-case slung to the left of his saddle, while to the right was at least one and possibly three quivers, each containing 60 arrows. The Turkish bow was short and powerful but with limited penetration of Frankish armour. From a long range the arrows could occasionally cause light flesh wounds through the mail but their most devastating effect was on the Christian knights' horses. In addition to their bows, the Turks also carried weapons for fighting at close quarters, including mace, sword, knife and a light thrusting lance made of reed and tipped with iron. In man-tó-man fighting with the Frankish knights they knew they were no match and only chose to come to close quarters when their enemy had been disrupted by their arrows. The swords that they carried varied from individual to individual and were by no means all curved like scimitars. Indian swords were much esteemed by the Turkish warriors, as were the swords captured from Frankish knights.

Few of the Turks wore body armour though some had lamellar corselets imported from India. The vast majority preferred to rely on the speed and manoeuvrability of their horses to get them out of trouble. Most wore long topcoats of brocade or silk, covered in bright geometric patterns or floral arabesque motifs on bright grounds. The hems, cuffs and collars were ornately embroidered. Around the upper arms they wore *tiraz* bands and on their heads turbans or fur-trimmed, mitre-shaped hats called *sharbush*. They wore tall boots and loose trousers. Their hair was worn long and gathered in three pigtails: one on each side and one at the back of the head. They often had long moustaches and tufted beards. By the standards of the Franks their concern with their appearance seemed almost unmanly and yet they dressed for comfort in a hostile environment.

In addition to these Syrian and Turkish Askaris, the northern contingent also contained auxiliary forces raised from the many peoples of Mesopotamia. Pre-eminent among these were the Turkman tribesmen, sometimes known as the *Ghuzz*, who were hired by Saladin as mercenaries. These, notably the Yaruqi, were lightly armed horse-archers, who fought with bow, sabre and javelin. Their concern was less with the success or otherwise of the holy war and more with loot. Many Kurds had followed the Ayyubid family into Egypt and were now already enrolled in regular askars, though other groups attached themselves to the army as auxiliaries. Bedouin tribesmen from both Syria and Egypt had also been recruited as auxiliaries, though these men were notably unreliable and were content to fall on the weaker side and pillage them. They generally wore a camel-wool tunic and turban but fought unarmoured as they believed that no one could die except upon the day appointed. A last (but not insignificant) group of auxiliaries fought with the army as footsoldiers. These *muttawia*, or Muslim fanatics, came to Ra's al-Ma' from throughout the Muslim world in order to take part in what they saw as a holy crusade.[8]

The ending of the truce with Saladin was a clear sign to the Franks that a renewal of fighting was imminent. King Guy hastily summoned his vassals to meet him at Saffuriya, as reports from Muslim sources indicated that Saladin was summoning a great army from all parts of his lands. Clearly he intended to make a determined attempt to overthrow the kingdom of Jerusalem and in response the crusaders could afford no half measures. Unlike his opponent, Guy was faced by the problem of shortage of manpower. From its earliest years the kingdom had survived only because it had been possible for the crusaders to hold down the land by building castles at strategic points. This technique made the most of their limited manpower. With the security of the kingdom often dependent on no more than 750 knights it had always been considered too risky to meet the Muslims in open field. This does not mean that it never happened, but that it was rarely worth the risk. Baldwin IV's victory at Montgisard was less a pointer to what could be achieved by a determined commander than an act of desperation when all else seemed lost. The losses incurred by Gerard of Ridefort's small force at Cresson showed what would happen if the Muslims were able to withstand the first onslaught of the Christian knights. On that occasion, Gerard's impetuosity had cost the kingdom 130 knights, nearly a tenth of the total available.

The main strength of Guy's army was made up of knights drawn from two sources: his vassals and the military orders of the Hospital and the Temple. It is doubtful if feudal knight service was more strictly applied anywhere in the world than in the kingdom of Jerusalem during the twelfth century. No time limit was set down for how long the king might call on his vassals and it was not unknown for service of a full year to be required. Within the kingdom every vassal under the age of 60 was expected to serve in person, fully armed and mounted, anywhere in the realm within 15 days of the king's summons. With him he would bring as many knights, sergeants, esquires or mercenaries as his enfeoffment required.

The command of the royal army was normally in the hands of the king, though in the latter days of the reign of Baldwin IV it frequently fell to his *bailli* (or regent) to command, and beneath him to the constable of the kingdom and his lieutenant, the marshal.[9] Each of these officers was responsible for an aspect of the army: the constable for the supplies, discipline and pay of the troops; the marshal for the command of the mercenary troops in the field. On the march, the constable's troops normally took the place of honour, in the vanguard, while the marshal's men came directly behind, with the king's 'battle' behind that.

It is difficult to think of another time in history when the individual warrior counted for so much. The Frankish knight was almost like a modern-day tank, capable of breaking through an enemy line by sheer strength alone and also operating as a rallying point around which the infantry could shelter. To the Muslims he was a veritable man of iron, quite impervious to arrows and all but the luckiest sword blow or lance thrust. Thus even at such a disastrous defeat as Hattin it was noticeable how few knights were actually killed in the fighting. Although they lacked the mobility of the Turkish horsemen the combined weight of even a handful of these knights was irresistible. The Muslims had discovered this fact early and no longer offered a fixed line for the Frankish knight to shatter. Instead, they gave way, dispersed and formed up again at a distance. In this way they were able to tire their heavily armed opponents and concentrate their fire at the Frankish horses.

A century of experience in Outremer, combined with the continual infusion of Western ideas which came with each new wave of crusaders and pilgrims alike, created in the native barons a kind of military hybrid. With the mail hauberk and conical helmet of the Western knight went the surcoat, worn over the armour, which copied the Saracen love of heraldry by displaying colourful devices in red, green, yellow and black, embroidered in gold thread. In the battle line with these knights of Outremer there were even Syrian and Maronite knights, dressed like Saracens, but showing the cross on their armour. This seemed alien to the newcomers from the West who felt uneasy at aping the customs of the East. Instead they generally fought in plain hauberks, with sleeves of mail to the wrist and hemispherical helmets bearing crusader crosses and equipped with face-guards. By 1187 it was even noted that some crusader helms bore crests of stag's antlers or bull's horns. Kite-shaped shields were being replaced by those with a flat top, over which the knight was more able to see clearly. In recognition both of the importance and the vulnerability of their horses, some knights were beginning to equip their steeds with coats of padded, quilted material, similar to the *al-Qutuns* worn by the infantry.

The historian is fortunate in having fairly precise evidence of the service of the feudal knight in the kingdom of Jerusalem at the time of the battle of Hattin. Jean d'Ibelin, writing about 1265, records the following figures for the reign of Baldwin IV.[10] The county of Jaffa and Ascalon, which Guy held himself, owed 100 knights to the king, comprising 25 from Jaffa, 25 from Ascalon, 40 from Ramla and Mirabel and ten from Ibelin. Raymond of Tripoli, representing the principality of Galilee for his wife, Eschiva, and her sons, owed 100 knights: 60 from the lands east of the River Jordan and 40 from the western lands. Reynald of Sidon, whose barony included Beaufort, Caesarea and Baisan, also owed 100 knights; while Reynald of Châtillon, as Lord of Kerak, owed 60 knights, 40 from Oultrejourdain and 20 from Hebron. The seneschal, Joscelyn of Courtenay owed 24 knights from his seignory, while from their lands the Bishop of Lydda owned ten and the Archbishop of Nazareth six. In addition, the cities of the kingdom owed knight service as follows: Jerusalem 41 knights, Nablus 85, Acre 80 and Tyre 28.

As well as this source of manpower, the kings of Jerusalem had come to rely heavily on the two military orders of knights. However, neither the Templars nor the Hospitallers owed compulsory service to the king and considered themselves answerable to the pope alone. The result was that the kings of Jerusalem had for half a century been forced to sacrifice their independence of military command when the knight-priests were present with the army, as was generally the case. In particular, the Grand Master of the Templars had a considerable influence on the military policy of the realm. Not only Gerard of Ridefort but his predecessors (Arnold of Torroga and Odo of Saint-Amand) also showed, on occasions, how unreliable their advice could be.

From the outset, and quite unlike the Hospitallers, the Templars had been military in outlook. Founded in 1115 by Hugh of Payens and Godfrey of Saint-Adhemar, their primary aim had been to protect pilgrims in the Holy Land. They were originally known as the Poor Knights of Christ and each brother swore the monastic oaths of poverty, obedience and chastity, owning no more than the clothes that were given them. Under the patronage of the kings of Jerusalem the Order grew stronger and was given accommodation near the site of the Temple of Solomon in Jerusalem, hence the derivation of their name. Under the influence of Bernard of Clairvaux, the Order was committed to a never-ending struggle with the enemies of Christ. In a pamphlet entitled *On the Praise of the New Knighthood*, Bernard applied the rules of the Cistercian Order to the Templars:

> The soldiers of Christ wage the battles of their Lord in safety. They fear not the sin of killing an enemy or the peril of their own death, inasmuch as death either inflicted or borne for Christ has no taint of crime and rather merits the greater glory. . . . First of all, there is discipline and unqualified obedience. Everybody comes and goes according to the will of the commander. Everybody wears the dresses given to him, and no one goes in search for food or garments according to his whims. They live in a community, soberly and in joy, without wife or children. . . . They cut their hair short because they know it is shameful for a man to wear it long. Never overdressed, they bathe rarely and are dirty and hirsute, tanned by the coat of mail and the sun.[11]

The Fabian tactics evolved by the early kings of Jerusalem and so clearly appreciated by the native barons like Raymond of Tripoli and the Ibelins were anathema to the Templars. They had vowed to fight to the death in the defence of the holy places of Christendom and never to refuse combat against the infidels, whatever the odds. In the words of Jacques de Vitry: 'When the Templars were called to arms they did not ask how many the enemy were, only where they were.'[12] Naturally, such an aggressive mentality made them the most dreaded of all Christian warriors by the Muslims. However, it also made them headstrong and unreliable as the disaster at Cresson so clearly demonstrated. As a result the military advice of their Grand Masters was questionable, particularly where the manpower of the Franks was so limited that no wastage could be afforded.

In comparison with the native barons of Outremer, many of whom had adopted the eastern customs of their enemies, being clean shaven and dressing in colourful garments and fine silks, the knights Templar emphasised their rejection of earthly riches by being ill-kempt, dirty and unwashed. With close-cropped hair and long, wild beards, smelling of sweat in the dusty heat, they were fanatics akin to the hermits who frequented the wild desert places in the early years of Christianity. In battle they wore a long, white surcoat (embroidered with a cross) over their armour and carried a white shield, also bearing a red cross. Senior brothers wore a black or brown surcoat, with an emblazoned red cross. Their regulation arms were lance, sword, dagger, mace and shield, issued from the general armoury.

The Hospitallers had not originally been a military order and their true function was to care for the sick and injured at the Hospital in Jerusalem. In 1070 a hospice had been set up in Jerusalem by Amalfian merchants as a place of rest for pilgrims. It was near the Church of the Holy Sepulchre and was known as the Hospice of St John the Almoner. Before the capture of the city during the First Crusade, the hospice was run by Benedictine monks under the command of one Brother Gerard. After Jerusalem fell to the Christians in 1099 Gerard extended his work by building a hospital, with the support of Godfrey of Bouillon, first ruler of the new kingdom. Eventually a series of hospices was established throughout the land. By papal bull the Hospitallers were recognised as an independent religious Order and their charter now included the instruction that in defence of their hospices the brothers were allowed to take up arms. By 1126 the Order was developing a military function and by the middle of the century the Hospitallers were given control of some of the most important fortresses in the realm, including Krak des Chevaliers.

While their Master was supreme within the Order, the military side came under the jurisdiction of the marshal and beneath him, the *gonfanonier* (the standard bearer). The Hospitaller knight wore a black hooded mantle, the *cappa causa*, with a white cross sewn to it (indicating the fact that the Hospitallers still followed the rule of the Benedictine and Augustinian orders). When not on campaign the knight would wear a black skull cap under a turban or wide-brimmed hat. However, his military efficiency was somewhat impeded by the voluminous mantle, which had to be worn over his armour, and undoubtedly restricted his movements. Nevertheless, like the Templars, the Hospitallers were a vital contingent in any army raised by the kings of Jerusalem. With the distinctive black apparel of the Hospitallers and the white surcoats of the Templars, the Muslims had no difficulty on the battlefield in locating the whereabouts of their most intransigent opponents.

The Christian host which assembled at Saffuriya needed more than merely the 1500 or so knights supplied by the feudal vassals and the military orders. However impressive these knights were individually they were heavily outnumbered by the 12 000 to

14 000 cavalry that Saladin could put into the field. Moreover, in order to protect their horses from the Muslim arrows, they needed the fire-power of crossbowmen and these were professional troops, not easily raised from feudal levies. As a result, King Guy had to raise the money to hire a large force of mercenary infantry. These 'sodeers' or soldiers could be hired on a monthly basis and were far more effective and more highly prized than their Muslim equivalents. Fortunately for King Guy, gifts from European rulers in lieu of direct military aid were available to help him to hire troops as well as the money raised by the Saladin Tax. In addition, and most significant of all, was the money paid by King Henry II to the Templars in expiation of his involvement in the murder of Archbishop Thomas à Becket. Henry, as head of the house of Plantagenet, was related to the royal family of Jerusalem. Although he often expressed the desire to lead a crusade to the Holy Land he could not risk leaving his extensive possessions in France at the mercy of the Capetian king of that country. As a result he was forced to limit his assistance to finance. This money was eventually used to enable Guy to hire thousands of extra men and these fought at Hattin wearing the lion emblem of England.

As well as the mercenaries from western Europe, there were many raised from amongst the native Christians of the kingdom. Of these the Syrians were not held in high regard by the Franks but the Maronites, often a prominent part in Raymond of Tripoli's armies, were excellent bowmen. Added to these were contingents of Italian sailors who, as in 1183, fought as allies of the Franks, less for religious reasons than to defend their financial interests in the coastal cities of Tyre, Sidon, Acre and Beirut. Swelling the numbers, though of limited military relevance, were freemen raised by the *arrière-ban*, as well as numbers of lightly armed pilgrims, usually equipped with no more than a staff or bow, who added to the cosmopolitan nature of the army with their coloured crosses, stitched on to their shoulders or right breasts: red for France, green for Flanders, white for England and yellow for Germany.[13]

The most important weapon of the infantry was undoubtedly the crossbow, which outranged the Turkish bow and carried far more hitting power. So fearful was this weapon for the Muslims that Saladin always killed crossbowmen when he captured them. For the Christians it served an important purpose. On the march the Frankish knights were surrounded by their own infantry, who were able to absorb the Muslim arrows in their *al-Qutuns* and yet keep the Saracen horse-archers at such a distance with their crossbows that the weaker Turkish bow proved ineffectual. The Muslim writer Ibn Shaddad wrote of the effectiveness of these infantry tactics: 'Clothed in a kind of thick felt, and mail corselets as ample as they were strong, which protected them against arrows, I have seen men with up to ten arrows stuck in their bodies marching no less easily for that.'[14] The garment referred to by Ibn Shaddad is sometimes called a 'pourpoint' or an 'aketon', and is a quilted corselet. Its sleeved version, known as a 'gambeson' was generally a leather, linen or woollen tunic, padded with wool, cotton or rags and quilted vertically or diagonally.

The towns and church lands of the kingdom had an obligation to the king to raise sergeants, of whom most were infantry, though some fought mounted behind the knights. Jean d'Ibelin calculates that there were some 5000 or more sergeants available at the time of Hattin.[15] Both of the military orders used mounted sergeants, who were non-knightly members of each order. Both also employed light cavalrymen known as Turcopoles. The name 'Turcopole', literally meaning 'son of Turks' was borrowed from the Byzantines, who used the term to describe their own Turkish mercenaries. However, in the context of the kingdom of Jerusalem, this can be misleading. Turcopoles were generally children of mixed marriages, often between an Orthodox Christian mother and a Turkish or Syrian father. The Franks also used the term for Turkish converts fighting in their own army. By 1187 the term had so far changed that it was sometimes applied to Syrian Franks (Poulains) or even European Franks, who fought in the Turkish style. Essentially they were light cavalry according to William of Tyre but it would be wrong to see them as horse-archers on the Turkish model. Crusader tactics emphasised strength and shock rather than mobility and they would have had little opportunity to employ Saracen tactics within the Frankish military system. They were much employed by the two military orders and were commanded by their own officers, known as Turcopoliers. They fought with bow, sword, lance and possibly mace, and were lightly armoured, generally wearing the *al-Qutun* of the footsoldier. Unlike the knights, who rode Syrian, Cypriot or Arabian stallions, the Turcopoles generally used the small, hardy ponies bred by the Turkman tribes.

With the two great armies assembling on either side of the River

Jordan it seemed at last that a decisive encounter must take place. Saladin knew that he could not rely on assembling his eastern levies so readily again if he failed to force a battle and so the onus was on him to draw the crusaders out from their defensive position at Saffuriya. This would not be easy for the crusader camp was well chosen. Saffuriya itself was a small, unwalled town on the low hills some three or four miles north-west of Nazareth and within the lands of Raymond of Tripoli. It had ample water for the large army assembled there provided by the Fountain of Saffuriya, a mile to the south of the town, in an open valley full of lush green gardens, and could supply provisions from neighbouring villages. It had served as the rallying point during Saladin's invasion of 1183 and if the crusaders planned to repeat their tactics on that occasion it was a most appropriate site. However, although the crusaders would find it possible, in the event of a defeat, to fall back from Saffuriya to the fortified coastal city of Acre, any advance towards Tiberias was bound to be fraught with difficulties due to the inhospitable and waterless land between. As a result King Guy was faced with a difficult strategical problem and needed the advice of his wisest councillors, above all the recently reconciled Raymond of Tripoli.

Raymond, meanwhile, returning from his meeting with Guy and Sibylla in Jerusalem, went straight to his wife's city of Tiberias in order to arrange for its defence in the event of the expected Saracen invasion. With King Guy's heavy demands for the field army at Saffuriya, Raymond knew that he could spare few men as a garrison for his wife's protection. No doubt he advised her that it would be wiser for her to retire in safety to the coast. Surprisingly, Eschiva, daughter of Hugh of Saint Omer, refused to abandon her perilous position and showed great personal courage in allowing her husband to take away not only her own troops but her four sons as well. In making this decision, Raymond placed great reliance on his recent close relations with Saladin. He knew that a man of Saladin's reputation would never have harmed so great a lady as Eschiva. For a man who valued honour as highly as did the great sultan to make war on a defenceless woman would neither advance his personal standing nor his fortunes in the holy war. Thoughts of this kind must have given Raymond the confidence to instruct Eschiva that in the event of an attack she should retire to the citadel and, if threatened there, should take to the lake by boat and await rescue. Accompanied by Eschiva's sons, Hugh of Tiberias,

William of Galilee, Ralph and Otto, Raymond now turned his horse away from Tiberias for the last time and rode back to meet the king at Saffuriya.

Meanwhile, Saladin's army was on the move. On 26 June it abandoned its base camp and advanced to the southern end of the Sea of Galilee. From there Saladin left his heavy baggage behind and climbed towards the ridge of Kafr Sabt, eight miles north-west of his new base camp. Here he was almost halfway between the city of Tiberias and the crusader camp at Saffuriya and was able to control communications between them. However, he knew that it would be difficult to draw the crusaders away from their supplies and water at Saffuriya and onto the waterless plateau below him.

The crusaders were in a strong defensive position. They did not need to win a victory in the field, for although there were hotheads (particularly in the military orders) who wanted to fight at all costs, crusader strategy was traditionally based on attrition, in which the Muslims would waste their greater numbers and resources in attempting to break down an impregnable defence. If Saladin besieged a castle or town it would be possible to send a relieving column as had happened on many occasions in the lands of Oultrejourdain. However, if he should choose to cross the waterless plateau and advance on Saffuriya itself, or divide his forces as he had in 1177, Guy knew that the moment for offensive action would have come. Otherwise a defensive strategy was obviously wiser. Time was on his side. He knew from experienced warriors like Raymond of Tripoli that the onset of winter could cause morale to slump among the Muslim troops and this would force Saladin to withdraw from the kingdom without a battle. The most the Christians could achieve by risking a battle was to drive him out, probably at heavy cost to themselves. Thus the risks involved in fighting a battle seemed unacceptable as careful defensive planning could achieve all that a victory could. With hindsight this may seem obvious but as commander Guy was subject to conflicting pressures, both personal and military. And these were functions of the situation within his kingdom, in which factionalism had caused fatal rifts at a time when unity was vital.

His defeat at Montgisard in 1177, at the hands of Baldwin IV had shown Saladin the dangers of splitting his army and yet now he had no real alternative if he was going to succeed in drawing the crusaders out from their defences. Everything he knew about

King Guy suggested that he was an uncertain leader who was unlikely to react with the energy of Baldwin. Therefore, on 2 July, Saladin personally led part of his force to attack the city of Tiberias. With him went a great force of engineers and sappers as well as his own guard, 'the burning coals of the Muslims', men inspired with a fanatical hatred of their enemies in the holy war.[16] The rest of the army under Taqi al-Din and Keukburi stayed at Kafr Sabt to await the Christian reaction. It was a calculated risk but it was to prove decisively successful.

The Muslim chroniclers suggest that Saladin's decision to attack Tiberias was at least partly taken as a result of his knowledge of crusader psychology. He knew from spies that Eschiva, Raymond's wife, was still within the city and with a very small garrison. What better way to put pressure on his opponent, Guy, than by attacking Tiberias and putting the lady in danger? This would challenge the honour of the Franks who, as Christian knights, could hardly resist the appeals of the courageous lady of Tiberias. Saladin gambled on the fact that the recklessness which had so often in the past ruined crusader strategy would do so again. Both the military orders and the contingents of Western knights contained impetuous men who would urge Guy to abandon his defensive position at Saffuriya and advance across the waterless plateau towards Tiberias.

When Saladin's forces appeared before the walls of Tiberias the citizens tried to come to terms with him. However, Saladin grimly refused their attempts to buy him off and ordered an immediate assault on one of the city towers. With remarkable speed the tower was undermined and brought down and within hours Saladin's troops had fought their way through the breach in the walls, killing or enslaving the people and capturing the entire city except for the citadel. Once it became obvious that Saladin was not to be turned from his purpose by offers of gold, Eschiva ordered the small garrison to take refuge within the citadel. Here she was protected by strong fortifications and a deep moat. For a while she was safe but unless help came quickly from Saffuriya the citadel itself was bound to fall. Messengers were sent out through the Muslim ranks to take her personal appeals for help to King Guy. Significantly, the Muslims made no attempt to stop them.

Guy was well aware of what was happening at Tiberias. His scouts on the hills would have told him that Saladin had divided his army and had taken part of it to besiege Tiberias. What they could not tell him, however, was how to react. For this information he needed the advice of his wisest councillors. On the evening of Thursday 2 July he called a war council in his camp at Saffuriya to test their opinions. For himself he knew that the passive defence that he had adopted in Saladin's invasion of 1183 would be difficult to justify, particularly in view of the fact that one of his vassals was under siege only a few miles away and had called on him for assistance. In the oldest version of the laws of Jerusalem it was stated that the king had an obligation to come to the aid of a vassal attacked by Muslims. Guy was by no means the first king of Jerusalem to be faced by this difficult choice. The situation was one where military expediency clashed with feudal obligation. If Guy failed to aid Eschiva then the lady was absolved of all obligations to the king as her liege lord.

The war council must have been a difficult meeting for Guy. Around him were gathered the great figures of the realm, many of whom were far more experienced that he in the ways of war and the customs of the East; men who, until Saladin offered himself as an external threat, had been content to fight and hate each other and who, only the greatest pressure could have forced to co-operate. Older heads there may have been than Guy's but those of Gerard of Ridefort and Reynald of Kerak were no wiser. Even a lifetime of fighting Muslims had not quelled Reynald's fiery spirit or helped him to see the present situation for what it was — an obvious trap. Amid the babble and confusion of the firelit meeting Guy called on Raymond of Tripoli, his erstwhile enemy, to speak first. After all, Eschiva was his wife and Tiberias his home. Who had a better right to speak?

Raymond's last meeting with his wife had shown that he already anticipated that her city would be attacked by the Muslims. In that event he had left her clear instructions on what to do. Had he feared for her personal safety it seemed certain that he would have overruled her decision to stay behind with so meagre a garrison and taken her to the coast to find safety behind the walls of Acre. The fact that he allowed her to remain seems to indicate that he had confidence that she need fear nothing at the hands of the Muslim leader.

Although the historian can never recapture the atmosphere of this meeting so pregnant with significance for the kingdom, or know the actual words spoken by Count Raymond, the chronicler Ernoul has recorded the main arguments he used. At first it appears that Raymond was almost unwilling to give his views so certain was he that they would be rejected as coming from a traitor. He knew that many in the assembly' of barons hated him, blaming him for the disaster at Cresson and accusing him of being a secret convert to Islam. Nevertheless, King Guy pressed him to speak and so Raymond eventually addressed the meeting. As an experienced soldier and the greatest landowner in the kingdom Raymond spoke with an authority that few but his bitterest enemies could deny. And so when he recommended that Tiberias should be abandoned he was revealing insights which he was uniquely equipped to do. He knew that Tiberias was simply being used by Saladin to bait a trap for the crusaders. Saladin could not keep the city for long for as the weather deteriorated he would have to withdraw across the Jordan in response to pressures within his own army. Saladin was no more a free agent than Guy. And if in taking the city he had destroyed the defensive walls and the citadel how would Saladin garrison the city to resist a Christian counter-attack? No, the matter was obvious: Tiberias must be given up. After all, it was his wife's city and if the walls were destroyed he could rebuild them at his leisure. If his wife or her people were taken then they could be ransomed. But if the entire military force of the kingdom risked a march in midsummer across the waterless plateau between Saffuriya and Tiberias then the whole kingdom could be the price of a military defeat. According to Ernoul, Raymond continued:

> Between here and Tiberias there is no water, only the little spring of Cresson [*sic*] and there is nothing for an army. And well do I know, that as soon as you move from here, in case you do go to the rescue of the city, you will have the Saracens in front of you and they will harass you the entire day, and draw you out until they hold you all day midway between here and Tiberias. They will make you camp despite yourselves, because you will not be able to fight on account of the heat, and because the sergeants will have nothing to drink but will die of thirst, and if you attack, the Saracens will open out and withdraw into the hills where you will not be able to penetrate without your sergeants. And if you have to camp there, what will your men and your horse drink? Are they going to remain without water? Such a course would be fatal, and the next day they will take us all, because they will have water and food and will all be fresh. We shall all be killed and captured. And so I

think it much better to let the town go than lose the whole land, for surely if you do go there, the land is lost.[17]

Naturally Ernoul was writing with the advantage of hindsight and it is clear that he has added details to Raymond's speech of which the count could hardly have been aware when he made it. Nevertheless, the tenor of Raymond's speech was clear to all the assembled barons. An advance to Tiberias would be fraught with danger and the better option was to remain at Saffuriya or possibly take up a defensive position in front of the walls of Acre and invite Saladin to take the initiative by attacking them. In the event of a Muslim defeat it is difficult to see how Saladin could have escaped across the inhospitable land between Acre and the Jordan.

Gerard of Ridefort responded with typical venom.[18] 'He has a wolf's skin,' he muttered, but for once he was alone in his views as the meeting had been swayed by the reasons that Raymond had advanced. Guy announced that the count's arguments had been sound ones and that matters should be conducted as he advised. There would be no immediate advance to relieve Tiberias. With this decision taken there was little further discussion and the barons retired to their tents towards midnight. As the king sat down at his table to receive late refreshments, he found that one man had remained — Gerard of Ridefort, the Master of the Templars, who was determined to overturn the king's decision to remain in the camp. He was convinced that Raymond was a traitor and that his advice to them that day had been aimed at allowing Saladin to ravage the country unopposed. Guy was never confident when confronting the forceful Templar. After all, he owed his crown to Gerard and much of what he heard now had the ring of truth. Certainly Raymond had behaved treasonably in allying himself with Saladin and permitting the sultan's Mamelukes to pass through Galilee. If he had not allowed Keukburi to enter his lands there need never have been a disaster at the Springs of Cresson. And why now was he so confident about leaving his wife and his city at the mercy of Saladin if he had not got prior knowledge that they would be safe? In any case, Gerard reminded Guy, was not this the same advice Raymond had given him when he was *bailli* in 1183? Inexperienced and new to the kingdom, Guy had looked to Raymond's experience to help him in his first command. Instead of help Raymond and the Ibelin brothers had left Guy to his own devices and had complained of his inactivity to the then king, Baldwin IV, which led to Guy's disgrace. Why now, said Gerard, should Guy believe that Raymond was acting from any better motives? Only recently crowned king, Guy would earn the scorn of all his people if he stood by feebly at the head of the greatest army seen in the kingdom for many years, and watched the Saracens destroying a city a mere ten miles away. This was his first campaign as king and there were many barons who needed to be convinced that he had the authority to rule the country.

Gerard's arguments were forceful ones and Guy undoubtedly wavered in support for Raymond's strategy. Yet Gerard had one final card to play: one that the king could hardly resist. According to Ernoul, Gerard told the king,

> And know well that . . . the Templars would put aside their white mantles, and sell and pawn them lest the humiliation the Saracens have caused me and all of them together be not avenged. Go, have it announced throughout the army that all should arm and every man go to his company and follow the standard of the Holy Cross.[19]

Gerard's concern was clearly to avenge his humiliating defeat at Cresson and, in doing so, to discredit the hated Count of Tripoli. He knew how much the king had depended on the templars in the *coup d'état* that brought him the crown. In fact, it had been they who had held Jerusalem for him and prevented the barons from interfering in his coronation. For Gerard to threaten to withdraw their military support was tantamount to abandoning him to his enemies, both within and without the kingdom. No royal army from the kingdom had fought without the support of both the military orders since the reign of Amalric I. Guy could not contemplate the loss of the Templars just as on a personal level he needed the support of their Master. Regardless of the sense of Raymond's arguments, Guy knew that he would have to do what Gerard wanted.

In fact, there may have been another pressing reason for Guy's change of mind. When Gerard had opened Henry II's treasure to help raise mercenary troops he had done so without consulting the English king. In one sense he was acting in the best interests of the kingdom but also he was placing Guy even further in his debt. The two men must have been aware that they were likely to incur the wrath of a king notable for his ungovernable temper.

Only a great military success could possibly justify them in using his treasure. A passive defence, as had been successful in 1183, would hardly pacify Henry. Only a military victory in which the mercenaries raised with his money fought under the English flag could salve his pride.[20] No doubt Gerard made this a part of his secret discussions with Guy, so much so that, without any further discussion, heralds were sent to rouse the camp. The army would march to Tiberias at first light after all.

Drowsy men, awakened by the calls to arms, could not understand what had happened to change the king's mind. Only a few hours earlier the decision to remain on the defensive had been overwhelmingly agreed by all present at the royal council. Now everywhere there was noise and confusion as men came out of their tents shouting for news of why they were to march at once. Had the situation changed? Were the Saracens advancing? Slowly the truth began to spread throughout the camp. To many it seemed impossible: the king had changed his mind, or had it changed for him. The barons and knights grouped together angrily. To advance across a waterless plateau in midsummer heat was madness. Everyone knew it was a trap and that Saladin already held all the high ground along the route of the march. In any case, what hope was there of saving Tiberias now? Almost certainly it was already a smoking ruin. While their horses were being saddled and their squires attended to their weapons and armour, they went to the King's tent and demanded to know who had changed the plans. But this time Guy was resolute and they had to obey him. As a later chronicler observed, 'Perhaps if they had not obeyed that command he gave them, it would have been better for Christendom.'[21]

It is easy to blame Guy for his fatal change of mind, to see him as a man of straw blown first one way and then the other, but his burden was a heavy one. Rarely has a single man borne the burden of a kingdom so completely on his shoulders. What did he hope to achieve by a military decision fraught with danger not only for himself but for the entire Christian presence in the Holy Land? The results of a century of fighting, of building and carving out a living by hundreds of thousands of nameless people, were now being risked on the turn of a single card. How did he dare to gamble with the legacy of a line of great warrior kings from Godfrey of Bouillon (who had first set foot on the walls of Jerusalem on 15 July some 88 years before and had crowned his triumph in Muslim blood) right up to Baldwin IV, the tragic leper king who had so heroically fought against his debilitating disease so that he could devote himself to resisting the growing power of Saladin? That night in his tent Guy must have felt the presence of the ghosts of those who had gone before him, of Fulk of Anjou, of three great Baldwins, of Amalric I, Saladin's first great antagonist. Was all that they had fought and suffered for to be gambled for the sake of a single city? Was Tiberias really that important to him?

As a new king the loss of any city to the enemy was hard to bear. Yet Guy could hardly believe that he could reach it before it fell to the Muslims; it had been virtually stripped of its garrison to equip the field army. In fact, as he probably guessed, it had fallen even before he set out. Was he responding chivalrously to the appeals of Eschiva, turning the rescue of the embattled lady of Tiberias into a symbolic quest designed to test his own worth as king and knight? Yet Saladin was no oppressor of people, women in particular. Far from it, the Muslim sultan was renowned for the treatment he accorded his prisoners. Saladin made no war on women. In his conversation with Guy only hours before, Gerard of Ridefort had detected the weakness in the inexperienced monarch. The loss of Tiberias, as Gerard pointed out, was a blow to the king's honour. As a knight of relatively distinguished origins, Guy's knightly honour was very dear to him. Native barons like Raymond of Tripoli had learned that in the lands of Outremer personal honour could sometimes be an inflexible master where flexibility was a vital element in diplomacy. Guy was being driven both by private and public concepts of honour. Privately he needed to convince himself of his own qualities as a leader of men and this could only be done in the heat of battle and not in a passive — even though successful — defence as in 1183. Publicly he needed to convince both his supporters and his opponents within the kingdom that he was a worthy successor to the fighting kings of Jerusalem, and this could hardly be achieved by inactivity, however masterly it might be. Just as Saladin needed a battle before his eastern levies were forced to leave his service, so Guy had come to believe that only a decisive victory would satisfy his honour and serve to quieten Henry of England's rage.

Moreover, the march to Tiberias was not without precedent. The Franks of Outremer were professional soldiers, trained by a system devised in the reign of Baldwin I, and honed to a fine edge by generations of battle experience. The co-operation of infantry and cavalry was vital to the Franks in their struggles with the mobile Saracen horse archers, and it depended on the maintenance of a high level of discipline. Every man was allocated a position in the column from which he was forbidden to move, and while the formation remained unbroken the safety of the army was assured. On numerous occasions in the 88 years since the kingdom was established, columns based on close co-operation between horse and foot had carried out successful marches even in the face of constant enemy harassment. One example was Baldwin III's march to Busra in 1147, which bears a marked similarity to Guy's march to Tiberias, though the outcome was very different. On his return march, which lasted 12 days, Baldwin's column was under constant attack from Saracen horse archers. The Franks, suffering from dust, heat and thirst were, like Guy's, subjected to the smoke from a dry scrub fire. The essential difference was that Baldwin's discipline held firm, while Guy's collapsed. Baldwin III was able to exert a tight control over his barons, while Guy was never able to impose his personality on an army which contained such men as Reynald of Châtillon, Gerard of Ridefort and Raymond of Tripoli. With suspicion and jealousy rife even before the march began Guy's army never had the unity on which success depended. Baldwin III had allowed no gaps to develop in the marching column and had concealed casualties by carrying the bodies of dead soldiers in the backs of carts. Conducted in the heat of a Syrian summer Baldwin's 12-day march had been a triumph of disciplined battle tactics. However, in 1187, few believed that Guy possessed the qualities necessary for such a campaign.

Meanwhile the sight of the barons arguing amongst themselves and showing so little confidence in the king worried the common soldiers. As they prepared themselves for the long march they exchanged stories of omens which boded ill for the campaign ahead. To provide spiritual aid to the crusaders, wood from the True Cross, won back from the hands of the Persians after the battle of Nineveh by the Emperor Heraclius in 627, was delivered to the army by the hand of his namesake, the Patriarch Eraclius, though he declined to accompany the army himself. Instead, the bishops of Lydda and Acre were entrusted with the care of the priceless relic, which was encased in gold and adorned with pearls and precious stones. If the motives of the leaders were occasionally cynical it should not be forgotten that in an age of simple belief there would be many in the host who were deeply moved by this holy fragment and who felt that this was a real link between themselves and he in whose name they were willing to lay down their lives. The maintenance of a high level of morale was vital in medieval warfare, particularly where as in this case the balance of strength between the respective armies was so fine.

Saladin's scouts on the hills around Saffuriya immediately rode back to tell their master that the Franks were on the move. Outside the ruined walls of Tiberias Saladin was at morning prayer when the breathless riders brought him the news for which he had been waiting. It is not difficult to imagine the elation he must have felt. His life's work seemed about to be fulfilled. Perhaps victory in the holy war would be won that day.

Leaving a small force to complete the capture of the citadel at Tiberias, Saladin gathered his élite troops around him and galloped back the six miles to Kafr Sabt, where Taqi al-Din and Keukburi were already sending out parties to harass the Frankish army, though no attempt was made to hinder seriously its progress. Saladin was overjoyed. Pointing down at the Christian army slowly moving beneath a dust cloud in the distance, he said, 'There is what we were waiting for. Our strength is now tremendous. Let us achieve their defeat and Tiberias with the coast lands will open before us. Nothing stands in the way of our conquest.'[22] Saladin had good reason to be confident for he had earlier reconnoitred the plain of Lubiya and had reached the conclusion that it would serve as an excellent site for a battle, with all the natural advantages resting with the Muslims.

8

The Battle of Hattin

The area between Saffuriya and Tiberias, across which the Christian army had to march, was a mountainous plateau, crossed by shallow valleys and wadis (rocky watercourse, dry except in rainy season; from Arabaic *wādī*). In the twelfth century the main road from the Mediterranean coast to Tiberias began at the city of Acre and proceeded south-east until it reached the southern end of the Valley of Beth Netofah close to the village of Khirbet al-Bedeiwiyah. Near here the road meets another leading to Saffuriya to the south. After this the main road proceeds in an east-south-easterly direction, entering the Wadi Rummanah near the foot of Mount Turan, which rises over 1000 feet above the plateau. From here the road runs through Wadi Jaraban until it divides. The north-east route runs towards the plain between Meskenah and Lubiya in the south, reaching Hajarat al-Nasara, west of Tiberias. The southerly route passes north of Shejerah and Kafr Sabt, following the course of Wadi Mu'allaqa, before turning north-east and reaching Tiberias.[1]

King Guy had a number of options open to him in choosing his route for the march to Tiberias. North of Mount Turan he could have moved down the Valley of Beth Netofah, using the mountain to mask him from Saladin's forces to the south. Nevertheless, once he emerged from the eastern end of the valley he could be cut off from Tiberias by the Saracens advancing from the south at Kafr Sabt. Instead he ordered an advance by a road to the south of Saffuriya, which led eastbound through a wadi to the village of Mash-had, before turning northwards towards the main Acre–Tiberias road. The chroniclers speak of one curious incident which deeply affected the rank and file. Before the march began a footsoldier captured a Saracen woman who, it was claimed, had been spying for Saladin. To add to her mystery it was also said that she was a witch and had cast a spell on the whole army. It was decided to burn her at the stake but the flames did not harm her. It was not until a footsoldier decapitated her with an axe that the army could set forth.[2] Nevertheless, when the army began its march in the early hours of Friday 3 July, just before sunrise, it was with a deep sense of foreboding. The morning was hot and airless as they left the green gardens of Saffuriya and set out towards the brown, sunbaked lands ahead.

The Christian army marched in three columns. In pride of place commanding the vanguard was Raymond of Tripoli (as the march was through his lands), while in the centre was King Guy, his personal guard and the bishops of Acre and Lydda with the True Cross. The rearguard, including both the Templars and the Hospitallers, was led by Balian of Ibelin. Years of hard fighting in the East had taught the Franks the importance of tight formation and superb discipline. In the centre of each column were the knights, so powerful in combat yet so vulnerable on the march to the arrows of the Saracens. While around them, offering the defence of their gambesons, marched the footsoldiers, pikemen, archers and crossbowmen. On the flanks of the columns rode Turcopoles to give early warning of impending attack and also hopefully keeping the Saracen horse-archers at full range. Although the knights depended on the protection of the missile-firing infantry they were hampered by the fact that the pace of the march was determined by the men on foot, thus making the horsemen even easier targets.

As the march continued the morning heat began to take its toll. The sun was relentless and there were no trees to offer shade on the limestone road on which they travelled. The heavily armoured knights, with coloured surcoats keeping their hauberks from baking the flesh within, wiped dusty sweat from their eyes and peered suspiciously ahead, waiting for the attack they knew would come. All around them lumbered the footsoldiers, exchanging crude jests to relieve the tension. Some were well armed mercenaries from Genoa or the Low Countries, armed with crossbows, who earned their living by following the likeliest paymasters. Others were townsmen from the coastal cities who had answered the call of the *arrière-ban* and were fired up by the feeling that they were fighting not only for their faith but for the families back home in Acre, Tyre and Beirut and for the livings their fathers and grandfathers had won from this inhospitable land. Most of these wore the aketons of quilted cloth or the gambesons of leather, which would resist the blow of a Saracen sword and deaden the impact of an arrow. Among them there were also numerous slingmen, skilled in the use of this simple weapon who added to the missile firing capacity of Guy's army. The air was filled with many of the languages and dialects of Europe; the Christian army was truly an international force, and this was made more so by the presence of pilgrims from the Western lands, as well as native Christians from all parts of Outremer.

In the early part of the march the crusaders were attacked by clouds of Muslim skirmishers who fired their arrows into the dense Christian ranks and then rode away before their enemies could reply. However, Saladin was saving his main effort until later when the crusaders would be drawn onto the waterless plain of Lubiya. There were no water carts with the column and the soldiers had to depend on the meagre ration they carried in their leather bottles. Soon this had been exhausted and there were now no opportunities to replenish them. Gradually the pressure increased. To a background of fierce battle cries and the barbarous beat of their drums the Saracen cavalry swept down from the high ground. The air was full of a cacophony of sound. In the front rank of each *tulb* rode men clanging with all their might on timbrels, rattles, gongs, cymbals and other instruments while others blew trumpets as if to wake the dead. These were the men whose duty it was to terrify the enemy with their noise and to inflame the passions of their own warriors. As the din grew ever more intense the Muslim warriors rode intently towards the Christian lines, fearlessly ignoring the deadly quarrels and arrows which burst out from the crusader's ranks. Above all, those Franks who survived the battle would remember the relentless beating of the *naqqāra* (kettle drums).

In the great sweep of colour that burst upon the Frankish column from the surrounding heights the yellow standards of the royal Mameluke regiments could be identified, each bearing the insignia of its commander. Other standards, red or jasmine in colour, were embroidered with rich devices like roses, birds or geometric patterns. Behind them came the horse-archers, fighting in the manner of the ancient Parthians, resplendent in silk tunics over their cuirasses, darting in and out, filling the air with their arrows which thudded into shields, ricocheted away from the Christian hauberks, or stuck in the gambesons of the foot soldiers. But the horses of the knights were the Saracens' main target and the screams of these animals, bucking and tipping their riders, mixed with the cries and curses of men and the infernal noise of *naqqāra*, horns and cymbals stretching the nerves and magnifying the danger in a cauldron of babel sounds.

The Frankish footsoldiers fought back as best they could with their crossbows, which outdistanced the Saracen bow and fired a deadly quarrel which could penetrate the Muslim lamellar armour and kill. Unfortunately the crossbow was heavy to carry and difficult to load so that, as soon as the covering fire relaxed for a moment, the Saracens raced into the attack again. The passage of Guy's army was marked by the corpses of horses. Few knights fell at this stage because the light Saracen bow could not penetrate leather or armour unless fired at close range. For the moment Saladin was content to let the sun work for him.

By about 10 a.m. the Frankish army had been marching for five to six hours and was obviously suffering already from thirst. They had turned eastwards into the Wadi Rummanah and had reached Mount Turan. Here, by the village of Turan, there was an important spring of water, some way from the main road. However, Guy chose not to halt there but to press on. This was a decisive moment in the day's events for now he could expect to reach no water on the direct route to Tiberias. Why he chose to march on is open to speculation. Certainly the flank attacks by Muslim horse-archers were having an effect on morale, but they were hardly more damaging to thirsty men than passing a spring of water. In any event the crusaders continued until about noon when the heat was at its most intense, by which time the vanguard had travelled about 11 miles from Saffuriya.

In the relatively unchallenged vanguard of the Christian army, Raymond of Tripoli could afford the luxury of strategic thinking, which was denied to those crusaders at the rear who were forced to fight for every step they took. He knew that time was the real enemy now, and that the longer the Christian army spent on that barren plateau the more certain was its defeat. Every effort must be made to maintain the momentum of the march and yet there was the ever present danger of the *arrière-garde* becoming detached and surrounded by the Saracens. As it was, the infantry at the rear were exhausted from having to march backwards, in their attempts to hold off the Muslim attacks from behind. In the heat of the midday sun more and more men and horses were falling from exhaustion so that at last Balian and Gerard of Ridefort sent a message forward to Guy saying that the rearguard would have to halt in order to relieve pressure by counter-attacking the Muslims. This was exactly what Saladin had been hoping would happen, for to halt in that barren place meant certain death.

When Raymond heard the dreadful news that the column had been brought to a halt, his vanguard was near the junction of the Meskenah and Lubiya roads. Realising now that the main part of the army would never reach the Sea of Galilee unless they found water, Raymond decided to make a charge in the direction of the march. Instead of taking the southern fork by Lubiya and Tell Ma'un, which was bound to bring them into contact with the main Muslim army (holding the heights at Kafr Sabt), he decided to head across the rising ground to the north in an attempt to reach the springs at Kafr Hattin. The significance of this change was not lost on the Christian chroniclers, who approved of Raymond's decision to head for the village of Hattin, where the army could camp for the night and resume the march to Tiberias in the morning. After all, a further five or six hours march eastwards without water and through increasingly heavy Saracen forces was almost certain to lead to disaster. From Raymond's position the springs of Hattin were no more than three or four miles away. Yet to turn an army of tired men in the face of an active enemy was no easy thing.

The Christian army began to turn north-eastwards near the village of Meskenah amidst great confusion and marched on with Mount Nimrin on their left and Qarn Hattin on their right. Ahead of them, in a deep gorge at the bottom of Qarn Hattin were the springs which alone could save them. However, the tight discipline of the Christian columns began to break up as they were ordered to turn northwards. The knights, eager to reach water and safety at Hattin, spurred on their horses and broke contact with the footsoldiers on whose missiles they depended for safety. The moment of crisis had come. Saladin's tactics so far had been attritional, designed to weaken the cohesion of the Christian army. He knew that thirst and heat were his main allies and that he need not commit his troops fully until they had done their work. But now he saw that, as a result of Raymond's change of direction, there was a chance that the knights would reach water at Hattin. If they were able to establish themselves there, only a few miles from Tiberias, they might yet be able to turn the campaign their way on the following day.

At once Saladin sent word to his nephew, Taqi al-Din and to Keukburi, to lead their forces around the Christian army and take command of the springs at Hattin. While Saladin held the ridge at Kafr Sabt with his Egyptian troops and royal Mamlukes, the two huge flanks of the Saracen army swept out taking the Christians both in the rear and flank. Regiments of Mamlukes, Syrian lancers and Turkman horse-archers moved at high speed down the slopes in a relentless wave of coloured banners and flashing steel. Many of the Christian survivors later expressed amazement at the Saracen numbers, which they had obviously underestimated. It was the Saracen right wing under Taqi al-Din which barred Raymond's advance towards Hattin and safety. But Raymond was not prepared to show caution. He knew that if the crusaders did not break through to Hattin then the battle and the kingdom was lost. He was obviously prepared to venture at whatever cost to break Taqi's stranglehold on the paths leading to Kafr Hattin. However, at this crucial moment, a message arrived from the king to say that the rearguard had been brought to a halt once again and could go on no more. The Templars had charged their adversaries but had been unsuccessful and needed time to reform. Guy now believed that they could not reach the springs of Hattin that day and they should make camp where they were. He thereupon set up his tent near Meskenah though the Muslim assaults did not stop until nightfall. Raymond gave way to despair and rode back to remonstrate with the king, declaring 'Alas! alas! Lord God, the war is over. We are betrayed to death and the land is lost.'[3]

While the Christian army spread out around Meskenah, Saladin moved the main part of his army from Kafr Sabt to camp at Kafr Lubiya. Here they surrounded the Christians so completely that it was said that not a cat could have passed through the Muslim lines. The two armies were so close together that soldiers from each were able to hold conversations. Even now in the darkness the Muslims continued to fire arrows high into the air to fall suddenly on unprotected heads and shoulders. Such a silent and unexpected danger added to the usual inconveniences of desert warfare (like sand within the knight's armour which caused constant chafing of the skin, and spiders and scorpions which occasionally found their way into clothing) to keep morale within the Christian camp at a low ebb. In most cases neither men nor horses had tasted water since shortly after they left Saffuriya and the heat and exertions of the day had made matters worse. How different was morale in the Muslim camp. There the soldiers knew that they had their enemy trapped and the next day were promised the greatest victory of the holy war. Surely it was impossible for any of the Christians to escape. As an additional torment Saladin ordered water to be tipped ostentatiously into the sand in full view of the thirsting crusaders, while throughout the night the cries of the righteous, 'Allah akbar' and 'la ilaha illa Allah' echoed among the nearby hills.[1]

However, for Saladin there was no time for premature celebration. He knew how much work still had to be done. Certainly the Christian army was in a serious position, yet it had not been beaten in the field as yet. Few knights had been killed and he knew that much hard fighting lay ahead before victory could be assured. Only the most careful preparations now could guarantee him this victory to which all his life so far had seemed but a preparation. Thus while others slept or celebrated Saladin concentrated his mind on preparing for the decisive encounter still to come. He knew that victory would be earned through a combination of water and arrows. There must be no shortages when the decisive moment came. So throughout the night of 3 July Saladin personally organised the convoys of camels bringing water-filled goatskins from the Sea of Galilee, which were emptied into cisterns hastily cut into the ground. Other camels brought up military equipment from Kafr Sabt, notably 400 loads of arrows which were distributed among the various parts of the army. The next day 70 dromedaries, loaded with reserves of arrows, were stationed at various points around the army. Saladin knew that if the arrows once ceased he could expect to feel the weight of the Christian knights.

Few could have slept in the Christian camp. Morale had slumped and even the presence of the king and the True Cross did little to reassure men who sensed that they were trapped. Heat and thirst had done their work and many of the city dwellers who had answered the *arrière-ban* and followed their king to fight under the True Cross had lost their will to fight; those happier with pen or plough, saw or saucepan, had lost hope and only the pride of the knights and the sheer professionalism of the mercenary foot soldiers kept a sense of order in the camp.

Nevertheless, Guy realised that it was now far too late to retreat. His only chance was to go on and try to reach the water at Hattin. As yet his losses in men had been relatively light but far more important was the fact that so many horses had been killed. Some hundred of his knights were now marching with the infantry as dismounted men-at-arms. Some, though unharmed, had armour so riddled with arrows that one Muslim observer commented that 'the lions had become hedgehogs'.[5]

Just before dawn the Christian army formed up. Raymond of Tripoli again led the vanguard, accompanied by Eschiva's four sons and Raymond of Antioch and his knights. This time it seems unlikely that Balian of Ibelin was with the rearguard, though again both the military orders were there under their masters. As the day before Saladin made no attempt to prevent the Christians leaving the camp and waited instead until the heat of the rising sun began to have an effect on the parched and tormented crusaders. The Christians were now marching directly towards the sun and the oppressive heat soon exacted a high price as men and horses fell by the wayside only to be massacred by the pursuing Saracens. In the poetic phrases of Abu Shama:

> The Dog Star shed its beams on the men clad in iron and the rage did not go down in their hearts. The burning sky sharpened their fury; the cavalry charged in wave after wave among the floating mists of the mirage and torments of thirst with fire in the wind and anxiety in their hearts. These dogs hung out their parched tongues and howled under the blows. They hoped to reach the water, but before them was hell with its flames and intolerable heat overcame them.[6]

To the horror of the Christians as they marched, several knights broke away from the column and sought sanctuary in the Muslim lines, renouncing their faith.

Once again the main Saracen attack was concentrated on the Christian *arrière-garde* in an attempt to separate it from the rest of the army. Gradually its forward momentum slowed and it was brought to a halt. In the bitter fighting that followed one of Saladin's favourite Mamelukes, Mangouras, rode alone into the massed ranks of the crusaders and fought there until he was slain, dying a martyr's death.[7] For a while the Franks rejoiced, believing they had killed one of the Sultan's sons and displaying his head on the top of a lance. From his elevated position Saladin saw all this with sorrow yet his eyes constantly sought out his bitterest enemies in the ranks of the rearguard: the white-robed Templars and the sombre, black-mantled Hospitallers. He knew that no battle was won until these men had been humbled. In an attempt to relieve pressure on his force and prevent it being surrounded, Gerard of Ridefort now ordered the Templars to make a series of desperate charges, seconded by the Hospitallers. But both men and horses were now exhausted and their charges failed to defeat the heavily armed Mameluke askaris. Many of them were surrounded or cut down. While the fighting at the rear of the army threatened to break up its cohesion, the vanguard was moving over rising ground between Nimrin and the Horns of Hattin, determined to force its way through the Muslim troops guarding the narrow paths leading to the gorge of Kafr Hattin.

The Christian army was still showing remarkable discipline, having resisted all the efforts of the Saracens to separate the infantry from the knights. The leaders — veterans of a generation of Levantine warfare — realised that while the infantry kept the Saracens at long range with their crossbows, little damage could be done to the knights. Moreover, if the Saracens were to close in to hand-to-hand fighting, the lances of the knights would still prove too strong for them. However, the entire system depended on the maintenace of a severe discipline which was now being tested under the most extreme conditions. At last, the morale of the Frankish infantry began to break and with a unity of purpose that only shared suffering could give them, the exhausted foot-soldiers began to run and stumble in their thousands up the black, rocky slopes of the Horns of Hattin until the whole hillside was covered. Faced with the collapse of his entire defensive system Guy had no option but to pitch his tent at the foot of Qarn Hattin to act as a rallying point for the army.[8] Around him gathered most of the knights from the central column but few infantry obeyed his urgent summonses to return to their duty. Even when the bishops called them back to defend the True Cross itself there was little response. They were calling to men who had abandoned themselves to death.

The situation of the Christian troops was made more desperate by the fact that the Muslim irregulars had started scrub and brushwood fires, taking advantage of the westerly wind blowing from the Beth Netofah valley to fill the air with flames and dense smoke.[9] To men literally dying of thirst this seemed the final blow. The Saracens were able to attack from behind a smoke screen, with the Christian defenders not even seeing their enemies' approach until they were almost upon them. Much of the Christian force was now cramped into an ever-decreasing area, where their dense masses provided the Saracens with unmissable targets.

Raymond of Tripoli and the knights of the vanguard now found themselves cut off from the rest of the army. It seemed certain that the day was lost and so Raymond ordered his knights and those of Antioch and Sidon, to try to break through the Muslim ranks to the north and head for the village of Hattin. Facing Raymond were the troops of Taqi al-Din, Saladin's nephew and a man with long experience of fighting the Franks. He knew that he could not resist the weight of a charge by Frankish knights, particularly as Raymond's force would be charging with the advantage of the steep slope leading down to Kafr Hattin. Taqi al-Din decided that his best option was to open ranks and allow the Christian knights to pass through.[10] As he later explained to his uncle, Saladin, the flight of Raymond of Tripoli made the defeat of King Guy even more certain. In the event, Raymond's escape combined with his earlier close relations with Saladin left him open to the charges of treason and cowardice. In fact, neither charge has any justification in view of the collapse of both the rearguard and the centre of the army. With the flight of the infantry there was no alternative for the knights but to try to escape. As Raymond's knights fled from the field, Taqi al-Din's troops closed ranks again. There was to be no escape for the rest of the crusader army.

The collapse of the infantry left Guy in an impossible position. Though his knights fought heroically around his red tent their numbers were constantly dwindling as the Saracen horse archers closed in to point-blank range and shot down their unprotected horses. Toppling to the ground these Frankish 'men of iron' staggered to their feet shouting defiance at their adversaries but no longer posing a real threat to the extraordinarily mobile Saracens. Yet they continued to fight resolutely around the True Cross. In the chaotic melée around the holy relic the Bishop of Acre was killed and it was taken up by the Bishop of Lydda instead. Taqi al-Din now ordered his askaris to put aside their bows and, wielding sword, mace and lance, to charge the ring of knights defending the bishop. By sheer weight of numbers they bore down the defenders and Taqi himself seized the relic and rode exultantly out of the fight. This was the final blow to many of the Christians, suffering from the extremes of thirst and exhaustion. Now it truly seemed that their God had forsaken them, while to the Muslims it was a tangible sign of Allah's triumph. The True Cross had been present in almost all the battles that the crusaders had fought since coming to Outremer in 1099. It had represented the holiest of all Christian aspirations and had been the worthy source of martyrdom for countless thousands of crusaders, content to give their lives for its preservation. Its loss symbolised the fall of the kingdom as no other event could. Meanwhile, on the hillside above, Muslim light troops were attacking the wretched Christian footsoldiers huddled together there, killing many by hurling them over the steep precipices or rounding them up in droves. Thirty or forty at a time were seen roped together, being led away by just a single Turkish soldier, to fill the slave markets of Damascus, Aleppo or Mosul.[11]

But Saladin was blind to such minor manifestations of victory. His eyes were fixed on the red tent of King Guy of Lusignan and to his banner that was planted alongside it. He knew that the battle was not won until the tent was overthrown. The tension that he was feeling was nowhere more graphically illustrated than by the account left by his 17-year-old son, al-Afdal, who was with him during the last stages of the battle. Unexpectedly, from between the twin peaks of the Horns of Hattin, those Frankish knights who were still mounted launched a desperate charge at the heart of the Muslim host, carrying the tide of battle towards where Saladin himself was situated. Whether these knights sought to escape (as had Raymond of Tripoli) or whether they hoped to seize victory from defeat by killing Saladin is impossible to tell. Al-Afdal records that his father's face turned ashen and he grasped his beard and tugged it violently in vexation. Soon the tide of battle turned against the Christian knights and they were driven back towards Guy's tent. However, after re-forming, the knights charged again, even more furiously. Again these desperate men almost cut their way through to the Muslim leader. Rushing forward Saladin shouted at his own troops, 'Give the devil the lie', and at this the Saracens recovered and drove the Christians back to Guy's tent. Al-Afdal apparently called out excitedly to his father that the Franks were beaten but Saladin grimly replied that they would only be beaten when the king's red tent was overthrown.[12] Almost as he spoke first the banner and then the tent were overthrown. At the sight of this Saladin stooped to kiss the ground and to thank Allah for the victory, then rode slowly back to his tent to await his prisoners.

In the last desperate moments of the fighting, Balian of Ibelin and a few others hacked their way free but King Guy and most of his knights were so exhausted that they simply sat on the ground and threw their swords away. So utterly overcome were they physically and emotionally that they scarcely noticed the Saracens who came to make them prisoners. As the barons and knights were led away they could see columns of the Christian infantry being marched away into slavery. 'There they were, the insolent ones, humiliated; the rebels, naked men who possessed thrones led into captivity. How many arrogant masters caught as though in a hunt, kings brought low and free men reduced to slavery, imposters delivered up to the true believers!'[13] So many indeed were captured that at the slave markets prices plummeted and one man was even sold for the price of a pair of sandals.

Captured with Guy were his brothers, Geoffrey and the Constable Amalric of Lusignan, the aged Marquis William of Montferrat, Reynald of Châtillon, Joscelyn of Courtenay, Humphrey of Toron, Gerard of Ridefort, the Bishop of Lydda, the Master of the Hospitallers, three of Raymond's foremost vassals, Hugh of Gibelet, Plivano of Botron and the Lord of Meraclea, along with hundreds of other knights of rank and distinction. Although few had been mounted at the end of the fighting not many knights had been killed and the Bishop of Acre was the most prominent casualty: a striking illustration of the effectiveness of medieval armour. Losses had been heaviest amongst the military orders, who had borne the brunt of the first day's fighting as the Saracens had tried to isolate the rearguard of the Christian army. On the second day both the Templars and the Hospitallers had made repeated charges from the rear of the column to try to break Saladin's grip and allow the Christians to reach the springs at Hattin.

In his tent, after the battle, Saladin treated his captives well. He personally served King Guy a goblet of iced water to quench his thirst, a sign among the Muslims that his life was safe. However, when Guy in turn passed the goblet to Reynald of Châtillon for him to drink, Saladin urgently pointed out that the water was no gift of his to the Lord of Kerak. In fact, Saladin was bound by a solemn oath to slay Reynald with his own hand for his numerous atrocities against the followers of Islam. Reynald can hardly have hoped for a better fate and yet he made no attempt to placate his mighty adversary. When Saladin formally charged him with breaking his word repeatedly, Reynald answered him with scorn, saying 'I did only what princes have always done. I followed the well-trodden path'.[14] In his early days at Antioch he had once knelt at the feet of an emperor but now in old age his knees were too stiff to bend to the enemy of his religion. Reynald's haughty refusal was all that was needed to steel Saladin to his task and he swung his sword and struck Reynald a blow on the shoulder which cut deeply into his neck. As the Lord of Kerak sank to his knees one of the sultan's guards completed the task by sweeping off his head with a great blow. Saladin stooped to rub some blood from the severed head on his face as a token of his vengeance. At this sudden and dreadful sight King Guy's courage seemed to fail him but Saladin hastily dismissed the matter, assuring him that kings did not kill each other. Reynald, he told Guy, had presumed too far and too often to be forgiven. But as for the other captives there was the matter of ransoms.

The fate of the captured Templars and Hospitallers was not so fortunate as that of their leaders. While Gerard of Ridefort was being richly entertained, the brethren of the orders were being rounded up at Saladin's command. Those who had been taken by individual Muslim soldiers or emirs were bought back by Saladin for 50 dinars each. Against the crusading military orders Saladin considered himself to be eternally at war and so he decided he could not spare their lives. As he said, 'I wish to purify the land of these two monstrous orders, whose practices are of no use, who will never renounce their hostility, and will render no service as slaves, but are all that is worst in the infidel race'.[15] In any case, he knew that these servants of the cross usually disdained ransom so there was really little point in keeping them alive. Once all the knights had been assembled they were each offered the chance of conversion to Islam, an offer which few accepted, and then turned over to be executed by the *sufis*, the Muslim men of piety.

The slaughter of the Templars and Hospitallers after Hattin has done much to taint Saladin's reputation as a generous and lenient war leader. It may even have justified in Christian minds the massacre of Muslim captives by Richard the Lionheart, after the capture of Acre. Nevertheless, Saladin was pragmatic enough to realise that while men such as the religious knights survived, the holy war could never be said to have been won. According to Imad al-Din, who was present,

> there were in the gathering a number of volunteers, people of pious and austere habits, holy men, *sufis*, men of law, savants, and initiates in asceticism and mystical intuition. Each of them drew his sword, rolled up his sleeve, and begged for the favour of executing one prisoner. The Sultan

was seated, and his smiling face contrasted with the surly bearing of the miscreants. . . . The swords of some cut and slashed miraculously, and these were congratulated. The swords of others remained refractory and blunt, and they were excused. Others were ridiculous and had to be replaced.[16]

The mixture of piety and cold-blooded murder in this scene lies uneasily with the view of Saladin that his apologists have presented: of the magnanimous ruler, compassionate to the weak and helpless. Yet, however much he may have enjoyed the spectacle of seeing his enemies cut down in this way there would always have been a political motive behind his actions. And if he saved it was often so that his deeds would go before him, unlocking doors far more certainly than even his engineers and sappers could, as was illustrated by the campaign which followed the battle of Hattin.

When the news of Saladin's victory reached Damascus the population were delighted. It was as if a great burden had been lifted from the soul of Islam. The shameful collapse of 1099 had been avenged and, in the words of one chronicler, 'Monotheism had triumphed over the doctrine of the trinity, and the Nazarene sect was in ruins'. To ordinary Muslims such high thoughts were soon translated into more easily understood symbols. An image of Christ crucified upside down was carried aloft into Damascus amidst the jeering and hooting of the excited mob. Christians' heads, it was said, were as numerous as water melons, and more arrived every day. With them came the living proof of the Christian collapse in the shape of thousands of prisoners, shambling through the crowded streets towards an uncertain future. Their blank faces showed that they had passed beyond the fear and suffering of the battlefield and their minds had found refuge in a dull acceptance of what fate might bring. They had become as passive and uncaring as the numerous oxen, sheep and goats that were driven into the city as part of the spoils. When the True Cross had fallen into the hands of the infidels their confidence and certainty had gone with it. No longer could they hope to find salvation in the Christian lands of Outremer.

With the crusader army scattered and broken, Saladin was now free to move against Tiberias which, having no further hope of relief, Eschiva surrendered without a struggle. In return Saladin allowed her to leave the city with all her retainers, with safe passage to her husband's county of Tripoli. So ended the great campaign of Hattin, from which fewer than 3000 Chrisians escaped, most of them from the vanguard when Raymond of Tripoli's knights broke through the Muslim lines near Hattin. For those knights who escaped from the final catastrophe there could be little satisfaction. As they fled they knew that they had witnessed the end of the kingdom. Their lives were safe but their lands and their property would soon be forfeit to the Saracen conquerors. Foremost among the survivors, as he had been during the march from Saffuriya, was Raymond. Carefully avoiding Tiberias, which he knew must now fall to Saladin, he headed for Tyre. Most of those who had escaped from Hattin joined him there, including Reynald of Sidon and his old friend Balian of Ibelin.

For a while Raymond acted with energy as if trying to blot out the memory of the fateful march to Tiberias. He pleaded with the Genoese and Pisan factors at Tyre not to allow the entire kingdom to fall to Saladin. In return for their military aid he promised them considerable economic advantages. However, it was the arrival of Conrad of Montferrat at Tyre on 14 July that transformed the situation for the Christian cause. Conrad was the brother of William Longsword, the first husband of Queen Sibylla, and was a formidable commander, noted for his severity and his dictatorial ways. Having broken his journey to the Holy Land at the invitation of the Byzantine Emperor Isaac Angelus, Conrad had fortunately arrived too late to play any part in the Hattin campaign. Arriving by sea, and completely unaware of the disasters that had occurred, he first tried to land at Acre. The city was by now in Muslim hands and he was lucky to escape capture when a Muslim customs boat came alongside him in the harbour. Explaining that he was merely a merchant he enquired of the fate of Acre, learning to his horror that the city had fallen to Saladin and that the Christian army had been destroyed.[17] Sailing away before he could be intercepted he headed for Tyre, arriving as Reynald of Sidon (despairing of any relief) negotiated with Saladin for the surrender of the city. He had even accepted two of Saladin's banners and was displaying them on the battlements as Conrad arrived with his ships. Conrad was welcomed with great enthusiasm by the Tyreans. He brought with him money and soldiers and was soon able to place the city under an effective defence, unceremoniously throwing Saladin's banners into the moat. Unanimously the barons recognised Conrad as guardian of

Tyre until an expedition could be organised by one of the powerful Western kings.

Saladin was naturally enraged at Conrad's arrogant defiance at Tyre and resorted to a tactic which would have brought him little credit had he ever intended it other than as a fairly transparent ruse. Facing the towering walls of Tyre he had the aged William of Montferrat, who had been taken at Hattin and held prisoner ever since, brought out in full view of his son Conrad, threatening to expose him in the front line of the fighting unless the city was surrendered.[18] Whatever feelings Conrad may have had at this moment he knew that no Christian knight could submit to such blackmail nor would his father have expected it. Replying that his father had lived long enough already and that he would shoot him himself if necessary, Conrad grimly stepped down from the walls, thus signifying that the parley was over. All that Saladin could now expect from Tyre were stones, arrows and burning naphtha. It is doubtful if Saladin ever really intended to kill Conrad's father in cold blood and after a short time the old man was released.

The leadership of the Frankish cause in Outremer had passed to younger hands and for Raymond of Tripoli the news from his country was grim indeed. Early in August he heard that Saladin had entered his lands and had occupied Gibelet. He therefore sailed from Tyre to Tripoli in the company of Raymond of Antioch, son of his old comrade-in-arms, Bohemond. On his arrival it was apparent to all that Raymond was dying, though we will never know whether the illness was a physical one or was the outcome of exhaustion following the trauma of defeat at Hattin. Although he was only 47 years old he had prematurely aged. Moreover, he had lived long enough to see all that he had worked for brought to ruin by the stupidity of men whom he despised like Guy of Lusignan and Gerard of Ridefort. It is likely that his will to resist the physical exhaustion was no longer enough. Perhaps he was tired of life. Recognising that he was dying, Raymond appealed to Bohemond of Antioch to allow his son Raymond to succeed him in Tripoli as he had no heir of his own. Although Bohemond could not accede to this request — reminding Raymond that his eldest son would soon have enough problems of his own — he sent his younger son, Bohemond, to take up the reins of government in Tripoli. Raymond was pleased to accept this arrangement and as far as we can tell was more peaceful in his mind when he died of pleurisy at the beginning of October

1187. To the chroniclers his death was attributed to the great grief he had suffered after the defeat at Hattin.[19]

The last decade of Raymond's life had been a bitter one for him as he saw the kingdom that he and his forbears had fought to create and sustain torn apart by the ambitions and rivalries of lesser men. The Muslim chroniclers were united in believing that Raymond had been the most able of the Franks and the one most deserving of the kingship. Instead of this he had contributed substantially to the collapse of the kingdom as leader of the baronial party and had ended his days in disgrace, accused both of treachery and cowardice. His hopes for friendship with the Muslims had been wrecked by the headstrong actions of men like Reynald of Châtillon and Gerard of Ridefort, who saw no further than their own ambitions. They accused Raymond of doing what they themselves would have done had they been in his place. They claimed that he wanted the throne for himself and yet had Raymond been as ambitious as they thought he would surely have seized one of his numerous opportunities to oust the ailing Baldwin IV or the child king, Baldwin V. With the support of the native barons, he would have encountered little criticism for taking the throne in the interests of the state. With the threat from Saladin being the most serious that the kingdom had yet faced there would have been numerous precedents. Instead, he allowed himself to be outmanoeuvred by a man both more ambitious and less scrupulous than himself. It was the kingdom's misfortune that the man who usurped the throne did not have the strength to keep it.

9

The Siege of Jerusalem

The urge to relax and enjoy the fruits of victory must have seemed very great to the Muslim army after Hattin, yet Saladin was well aware that there was much work to be done. After all, the strength of the Christian hold on the kingdom had been in their numerous castles and fortified towns. In order to equip the field army King Guy had removed the garrisons from these fortresses and it would now be a simple task for the Muslims to occupy them. However, if action was not taken immediately and a relief force were to arrive from Europe, there was a danger that the Christians might re-establish their hold on the land by re-garrisoning these strong places. Thus for the moment all that was needed was a sense of urgency. Saladin expected no organised opposition within the kingdom since, apart from the northern states of Tripoli and Antioch, the Frankish capacity to put an army into the field had been completely destroyed. In fact, his troops were everywhere greeted as liberators. There had been thousands of Muslim slaves in the kingdom and these were now freed. Moreover, the peasants themselves, both Muslim and Syrian Christians welcomed Saladin, for his generosity and love of justice was widely known.

Saladin concluded that any Christian relief force would almost certainly come by sea and as the Franks still held most of the coastline of the kingdom, including the ports of Ascalon, Acre, Tyre, Sidon and Beirut, this was undoubtedly his paramount problem. The inland castles, formidable though they might be, could now expect no relief and would certainly either surrender on the offer of good terms or could be starved out. Yet standing above all in terms of the holy war was Jerusalem itself. Although its value was symbolic rather than strategic it was impossible for

135

Saladin not to make its capture his top priority. All the Muslims who had doubted his sincerity, who had accused him of desiring only self-advancement or the establishment of an Ayyubid Empire, would be silenced by this gesture. In itself it was a city no greater than Acre or Tyre but in the world of the holy war it was Islam's third holiest city. The question was, would the Christians defend it, denied as they certainly were any chance of relief? Should he, moreover, take it by storm and turn it over to a sack as had Godfrey of Bouillon in 1099? Should he cleanse the city with the blood of the unbeliever? Was this the gesture by which he would want posterity to remember his victory?

These thoughts were undoubtedly in Saladin's mind as he moved from the battlefield at Hattin towards the city of Acre. Here the Muslims were amazed to find the walls manned by soldiers, with war banners fluttering from the battlements, indicating that the city intended to resist him. However, the inhabitants of Acre had no wish to see their city burned and themselves put to the sword. As the Muslim troops were drawn up by Saladin preparatory to an assault on the walls, the gates of the city opened and envoys were sent out to negotiate terms of surrender. Saladin was able to liberate some 4000 Muslim slaves and soon was celebrating prayers in the city's great mosque, which for 90 years had served as a Christian church. The spoils taken from the city were enormous and would have financed all of Saladin's future campaigns. Yet he showed his characteristic generosity in rewarding his followers instead and the opportunity was lost.[1]

With no threat of a Christian field army in the forseeable future, Saladin realised the advantages to be gained from splitting his army and allowing his emirs to take the outlying castles and towns of the kingdom. Muzaffer al-Din Keukburi led part of the army to capture Nazareth and found huge piles of stores in the Crusader camp at Saffuriya. He also took the Templar castle of La Fève as well as the towns of Daburiya, Tabor and Zar'in. Husam al-Din Muhammad captured Sebastiya and Nablus, while Badr al-Din Dildirim moved southwards from Acre, accepting the surrender of the cities of Haifa and Arsuf and storming Caesarea, after the garrison failed to yield. From Egypt, Saladin's brother, al-Adil moved northwards, taking Majdal Yaba and Jaffa, the latter after a particularly bloody assault. Alone of all the people of the kingdom the inhabitants of Jaffa were to suffer enslavement.[2]

It was in the north that Saladin made the mistake which was to cost him so dear. He sent his nephew, Taqi al-Din, to attack Tyre and Tibnin. However, the significance of the latter was small and the time that Taqi spent besieging this town, which was full (according to the Muslims), of 'heroes, fierce in their religion', could have been better spent at Tyre.[3] Every day the Christian position at this vital seaport became stronger. It was only after Taqi had made a number of appeals for reinforcements that Saladin stirred himself into action. He set off from Acre on Friday 17 July with a large force to support Taqi at Tibnin. Eventually, after some hard fighting, the garrison surrendered on generous terms. Incredibly, Saladin granted them five days to collect their possessions and then allowed them to go to Tyre, where they swelled the garrison.

Moving with a marked lack of urgency, Saladin now marched towards Sidon, on the Mediterranean coast 23 miles north of Tyre. Saladin observed that while Sidon surrendered immediately the capture of Tyre would require a determined siege. He therefore moved northwards again and besieged Beirut, which fell after a determined resistance. Seventeen days later Saladin is recorded to have been on the coast at Ascalon, 170 miles away to the south. Again he had passed Tyre by without attacking it. Certainly it formed the only source of Christian resistance to him apart from Jerusalem. Also, his soldiers were becoming tired and disgruntled. Even success was becoming boring. The campaigning season was drawing to a close and few of them, particularly his Eastern troops, relished another hard siege.

If the failure to capture Tyre was Saladin's only error in this great campaign it was to prove a costly one, which condemned him and his people to four years of almost unrelenting warfare. Yet perhaps the answer to this failure must be found within Saladin's own complex personality. As the leader in the holy war he had achieved the greatest triumph of any Muslim leader. His prestige was immense and yet only the capture of the Holy City of Jerusalem could give tangible expression to his achievements. A man like Saladin risked death every day that he spent on campaign. A fall from his horse, a poisoned cup, a chance arrow, any one of a hundred threats to his life, could see an end to his great purpose. Before him there had been men who had sought Muslim unity, great men like Zangi or Nur al-Din, yet ultimately it had been denied them and on their deaths all their works had been unravelled by those who were concerned only with self-advancement. Now, Saladin had within his grasp all that Muslims had yearned for since the Franks came from the West to seize Jerusalem. And yet should he die it might all crumble as greedy men split and rent his lands for their own gain. Without him, Saladin believed, Islam might lack the unity to take and ultimately hold Jerusalem.

Nor was Saladin alone in these thoughts. They are often found in the despatches sent by al-Adil from Egypt, urging Saladin to make the capture of Jerusalem, al-Quds, the Holy City, his immediate priority.[4] Al-Adil reminded his brother of his predisposition to attacks of colic and suggested that if he should die suddenly of such an attack Jerusalem would stay in the hands of the Franks. This reminder of his mortality outweighed all strategic considerations in Saladin's mind. However important the seaport at Tyre might be for the future security of his lands, the seizure of Jerusalem became a symbol for which everything else would be sacrificed. So, resolved, Saladin decided to remove the Christian enclaves at Ascalon, Gaza and Darum, before finally turning on the Holy City.

On Sunday 23 August, Saladin reached Ascalon, bringing with him two important prisoners, King Guy and Gerard of Ridefort, who had both been imprisoned in Damascus after the battle of Hattin. Saladin offered them their freedom in return for the surrender of Ascalon. Although Guy had been persuaded to send a letter to the garrison of the city recommending surrender, it was assumed that the king was acting under duress and his instructions were therefore ignored. The garrison now began a spirited resistance to Saladin's besiegers, in which two of his leading emirs were killed, until the outer defences fell and mangonels were able to batter the city walls from close range. It was only a matter of time now before the city fell, and Guy was able to approach the defenders again to convince them that this time there was no disgrace in surrendering after such a defence. According to Ibn al-Athir, Guy's reception by the citizens of Ascalon was far from friendly: 'The people of Ascalon answered him in the most disobliging manner, and said many things that were painful to hear'.[5] Eventually, the garrison surrendered and were allowed to leave the city with their families on 5 September. Showing remarkable restraint, Saladin ordered that they should be escorted into Egyptian territory and housed comfortably until they could be repatriated to Christian territory. While he had been involved in these siege operations, Saladin heard the news that his emirs had captured Gaza and Darum, leaving him clear now to turn his attentions to Jerusalem. The Master of the Templars was granted his freedom, in return for the surrender of the Templar castle of Latrun, but Guy was kept prisoner until the following year at Nablus and later Lattakieh.

Meanwhile, by a curious twist of fate, while Guy was kept a prisoner in the citadel at Nablus, its lord, Balian of Ibelin, became for a while the guardian and ruler of Guy's capital, Jerusalem. After Balian had managed to fight his way clear from the wreck of the Christian army at Hattin, he had made his way to Tyre where most of the other survivors had gathered. His own lands, he knew, would now fall to the Saracens and his mind turned instead to the safety of his wife and children. After the fall of Nablus, Balian's wife, Queen Maria Comnena, fled with her family to Jerusalem for safety and Balian determined to bring her now to Tyre. He knew that Saladin was a man of honour and so he petitioned the great sultan for a safe conduct to visit the Holy City and bring his wife away with him. Saladin was always prepared to grant such a request from a noble adversary as he knew Balian to be, but he stipulated that Balian should stay no more than one night in Jerusalem and should not bear arms against him. Balian swore to abide by these conditions and set out for Jerusalem, accompanied by a small following, including his squire, the chronicler Ernoul.[6]

However, when Balian arrived in Jerusalem he found a situation which he could not have anticipated. If the attitude of the people in Tyre was one of growing confidence and a determination to resist Saladin, emboldened by the knowledge that they could be reinforced from the sea, what Balian found in Jerusalem was little short of hysteria. The arrival of a single noted warrior was treated by a desperate populace as if it signalled a whole relief army. In spite of Balian's attempts to explain the conditions under which Saladin had sanctioned his visit, he was assailed from all sides with demands that he assume command of the city. The Patriarch Eraclius and the officials of the Templars and Hospitallers were preparing the city to endure a siege and they saw Balian as divine providence. Here was a leader whom the people would trust, whom the soldiers would obey and whom the Saracens would respect and fear. In the urgency of the moment Balian was probably the only man present in Jerusalem who realised the futility of what was being planned. Before the battle of Hattin 1500 knights had encamped at Saffuriya but where were they now? If they had not been enough to resist Saladin's army, how could he, alone, do so now?

Balian, as a man of honour, was faced with a cruel dilemma. He was bound by an oath to Saladin yet as a Christian he was bound to defend the Holy City against the infidels. The Patriarch Eraclius argued that his oath was not binding as it was made under duress and with an infidel. Moreover, Eraclius told him, 'Know that it will be a greater sin if you keep your oath, than if you break it; it will be a great shame upon you and your heirs if you desert the city in the hour of its peril, and you will be unable to recover your honour no matter where you turn'.[7] In spite of receiving the Patriarch's absolution, Balian was not satisfied. He knew how magnanimously Saladin had acted in granting him freedom to visit his wife. Could he now break his oath to such a man? Finally, he resolved to explain his dilemma to Saladin and was rewarded when the great sultan freed him from his oath and, moreover, sent an escort to take Queen Maria, with her children and young Thomas of Ibelin, son of Baldwin of Ramla, to Tripoli. He even entertained her in his own tent and gave the young members of the Ibelin family jewels and costly garments, apparently weeping with emotion as he saw the downfall of so great a family. While his enemy looked after the welfare of his family, Balian was free to devote himself to the defence of Jerusalem.

Saladin had already made an offer to the people of Jerusalem which seems almost incredibly lenient by the standards of his time. During the siege of Ascalon, Saladin had summoned a delegation of the prominent citizens of Jerusalem to discuss the question of surrendering the Holy City. Their visit coincided with a full eclipse of the sun which was thought to be an ill-omen by the Christians.[8] Back in 1099 while the Christians were preparing to besiege Jerusalem a lunar eclipse had frightened the soldiers until it was decided that this was not an ill-omen as only solar eclipses boded ill for Christians. The coincidence of an eclipse during the last days of the kingdom was not lost on many of the superstitious folk. Saladin was clearly concerned by the news of the concentration of refugees in Jerusalem and the possibility that he would have to fight to take the city. As he declared, 'I believe that Jerusalem is the House of God, as you also believe, and I will not willingly lay siege to the House of God or put it to the assault'.[9] Instead he offered to leave the inhabitants free to fortify the city and to cultivate the lands around to a distance of five leagues. He even offered them help with money and supplies. However, if no rescuing force had come by the following Feast of Pentecost they were to surrender the city to him without a struggle and he would then convey the inhabitants safely to Christian lands. In the future the Christian places of worship would be respected and any who wished to visit the city as pilgrims would be free to do so. To many of his Muslim friends this seemed to be taking things too far. The Christians had not shown themselves notably honourable in the past so why should they be trusted now, especially with something that mattered so much to them? However, Saladin's faith was never to be put to this test for the delegation from Jerusalem haughtily rejected his offer, saying they would never surrender the city where Jesus had died for them: 'Our honour lies here and our salvation with the salvation of the city . . . If we abandon her we shall surely and justly be branded with shame and contempt for here is the place of our Saviour's crucifixion . . . We shall die in the defence of our Lord's sepulchre, for how could we do otherwise?'[10] Saladin thereupon solemnly swore to take the city by assault as had Duke Godfrey of Lorraine in 1099, and summoned his troops from all points of Syria to converge on Jerusalem.

Balian of Ibelin was a man not only renowned for his military prowess. On several occasions in the kingdom's recent history his moderation and thoughtful diplomacy had been vital in defusing potentially explosive situations. Yet as a product of one of the kingdom's most prominent families he could not easily overlook the likely political consequences of his decision to accept responsibility for the defence of Jerusalem. Guy of Lusignan was still king even though he was currently a prisoner of the Muslims. Sibylla, sister of Baldwin IV and mother of the child king, Baldwin V, was still in the capital. If he accepted the lordship of Jerusalem would her writ still hold good? Balian knew that for a successful military defence one voice above all others was necessary; there could be no committees. As the patriarch and the leaders of the Templars and Hospitallers of Jerusalem had called upon him to defend the city he in turn must demand not only recognition as the military commander but also a feudal oath of loyalty, sworn by all, to him as Lord of Jerusalem. The Patriarch Eraclius might inspire the defenders with his spiritual message but it was fighting men who would throw the Muslims from the battlements, drag away their great rams before the walls were breached and scald their climbers with boiling oil until the air was filled with the smell of scorched flesh.

Nor could Balian easily forget how Guy and Sibylla had humiliated his brother, Baldwin of Ramla. As his feudal vassal Balian had served Guy at Hattin but he had not respected the man. Guy was a mere parvenu who had usurped the position which rightly belonged to native nobles like his own brother, Baldwin, and to Count Raymond of Tripoli. Indeed, but for Guy stealing Sibylla away from him while he was in a Muslim prison, Baldwin would now be her husband and the king by right. In truth he had little loyalty left for Guy of Lusignan. Yet by accepting the responsibility for defending the capital, Balian was placing himself in an unpromising position. If he should fail — and failure seemed very likely — then it would be his name which would live in the chronicles as the man who lost the Holy City. Yet if he should win by some miracle it would be only to restore the city to the undeserving Guy, the man who had done so much to lose it. The thought was unacceptable. If he were to take on the responsibility for the city then it should be with himself as lord. The oath that he would require all to swear to him would overthrow the old regime of Guy and Sibylla. Otherwise he would take his sword and fight in the forefront as always, a true knight and a Christian, and leave the politics to others.

He can have had few illusions about the task facing him. In the whole city there were just two other knights, also survivors from Hattin. Balian was forced to knight all noble boys over 15 as well as to promote 40 burgesses to knightly rank. Yet, it took more than a name to give a man the qualities which only a lifetime of training could give. These new knights could never replace those lost at Hattin, nor could they inspire the enemy with the fear and respect of men such as old Humphrey of Toron, Reynald of Kerak or Baldwin of Ramla. These men were now dead or imprisoned and the kingdom's defence rested on the swords of brave but inexperienced boys and merchants.

In addition to his doubts about the fighting qualities of his knights, Balian could not feel secure about the loyalties of the people within the walls. It was well known to all the Franks that the thousands of Greek Orthodox Christians in Jerusalem, known as Melkites, would actually welcome a Muslim conquest to liberate them from the domination of the church of Rome. When Jerusalem had fallen to the Franks in 1099 relations between Latin and local Christians had been good. However, it soon became obvious that the Latin clergy had come to dominate the local churches and in 1101 the Eastern Christians were expelled from the Church of the Holy Sepulchre. The outcome was that the 'Holy Fire' did not come down to light the candles on Easter eve as had been traditional. As the secret of the fire seemed to be known only to the local clergy the Latins had little alternative but to allow them back into the church. Neither Armenian, Greek nor Syrian Christians prospered under Frankish rule. These and similar groups would not lift a hand to help Balian in his hour of need and yet they would demand his protection. He knew that it would take a miracle for the city to survive. Perhaps a relief force from Europe might arrive in time to distract Saladin's attention, or perhaps the sultan might die and the Muslim forces break up among the emirs struggling to succeed him.

In the two months which had elapsed since the disaster at Hattin, the fall of Christian castles, towns and villages through-out the country had produced an enormous movement of refugees. Although some may have been driven from one refuge to another, most had flocked towards the places which seemed to offer the greatest hope of safety: Tyre, because of its position on the coast and its mighty fortifications; Jerusalem because of its sanctity. It is difficult to estimate the size of the population of Jerusalem by the time of Saladin's arrival on 20 September though the total may have reached over 60 000, including women and children. Of these no more than 20 000 could have borne arms and fewer than 6000 of them could have been considered to be soldiers. Nevertheless, what the garrison may have lacked in numbers and military experience, it more than made up in fanatical courage. There were those who were prepared to fight Saladin in open field but were prevailed upon by Balian to do no such thing. With scarcely any trained knights remaining in the city such action would have been suicidal.

With the city's population swollen to at least three times its normal size, Balian faced the awesome problem of keeping these people fed and watered during what might be a prolonged siege. Once Saladin closed in on the city it would be almost impossible for supplies to be brought in from the surrounding areas and therefore he ordered his men into the nearby villages with orders to bring in every consumable article. Gold and silver was stripped from the roofs of Jerusalem's churches, notably the Holy Sepulchre, to be melted down by the Royal Mint and turned into coinage to pay the footsoldiers. Every day rumours reached the city of Saladin's progress along the coast; of which cities had surrendered and which had defied him and fought until they were taken. Yet the news was always the same in the end — each city fell until none but Tyre remained. It became obvious when the Jerusalem delegates returned from Ascalon that Jerusalem's turn had arrived at last. The city fathers had defied the great sultan and he had vowed to take the city by force. But would the man who had offered such honourable terms to so many other cities take Jerusalem with fire and sword in vengeance for the Christian attack of 1099? After all, Jerusalem was his life's aim and the symbol of the holy war.

By the middle of September Saladin's forces were closing in on Jerusalem, taking the monasteries and villages on its outskirts. On 20 September Saladin arrived from Ascalon, marching up the coastal road and then striking inland from the West. With the main part of the army he camped outside the walls, between Tancred's Tower and the Tower of David. If he had entertained hopes that the Christians would not fight they were soon dispelled by a desperate sortie from within the city by fanatical warriors who sold their lives dearly in front of their own walls. The prospect of a lengthy and bloody siege obviously lay before Saladin, yet this may have given him a grim sense of satisfaction. He had spent his life moving towards this goal and now that the prize in the holy war lay within his grasp it would be wrong if it were too easily won. After his generous offers to the inhabitants of the city had been refused, no one could now blame him if he fought his enemies with the same fanatical dedication they had shown in resisting him.

As soon as his army had encamped on the western side of the city, Saladin began to search for weaknesses in the defences. With his senior engineers and military advisers he studied the walls for a suitable place to launch an assault and was not the first to make a serious error of judgement. No doubt he was advised that in the majority of fortified towns and cities the citadel was placed where the walls were at their weakest, in order to strengthen them. However, in the case of Jerusalem this was not so. As a result, rather as the crusaders had in 1099, Saladin made his initial assault on the western walls. For some five days the attacks continued but the Muslims found the approaches to the walls extremely difficult to climb and in spite of their numbers they were unable to make their superiority apparent. The approaches were dominated by the towers of David and Tancred, which enabled the defenders to pour an effective fire onto Saladin's soldiers below. Large catapults situated in the high towers commanded the approaches to the walls for a distance of several hundred yards. Nor were the Saracen siege engines effective, and Saladin cursed the fact that his mangonels made little impression on the strong western walls. Under the heavy fire from the defenders it was quite impossible for his sappers to get close enough to begin mining operations.

Inside the city hopes began to rise. The much-vaunted Muslim army had made little impression on the city's defence and the people began to believe that the city might be saved after all. Balian faced the continuing problem of finding the money to pay his soldiers to fight. It might be thought that they would have fought willingly enough in view of the fate that might be waiting if the city were taken. However, the situation was more complex than it appears. Of the 60 000 or so Christians within the city, not all felt themselves similarly threatened. Saladin had taken pains to try to neutralise opposition to him from the Syrian, Orthodox and Jacobite Christians, making it clear that his fight was with the Latin Franks. If the city fell it was they who had most to fear. When it is considered that many of the kingdom's footsoldiers had traditionally been recruited from the native Christians the importance of buying these men's services becomes apparent. If they had little to fear — and perhaps something to gain — from a Muslim conquest, then why should they put their lives at risk to save the ruling Latin church? Balian had the answer in the coins that were minted from the church's gold and silver, and the treasure handed over to him by the Hospitallers, which Henry II had paid in expiation of his sins.[11]

The five days' fighting had not been without success for the defenders. A daring sortie from the city by a cavalry squadron ambushed and defeated a Muslim column advancing along the road from Ramla to Jerusalem. Yet most of the fighting was at relatively long range; Muslim attempts to storm the walls had been uniformly unsuccessful. Each morning the Christian defenders attacked the Saracens camped outside the western walls because the latter were hampered by the powerful rays of the sun rising in the East. However, by the afternoon the situation was reversed and the Muslims were able to launch their own assaults in the knowledge that this time the sun was their ally and was dazzling the eyes of the defenders as it sank in the West. In addition, the Saracens made use of the wind, notably refreshing in more peaceful times, which blew from the West each afternoon. By filling their siege catapults with piles of sand and dust they were able to hurl it into the wind so that it blew like a sandstorm into the eyes of the Christian defenders.[12] Under the cover of this sand-screen the Muslims tried in vain to assault the walls.

At the end of the first week of the siege Saladin made an important change of plan. He ordered his camp to be broken and his whole army to move away from the West round to a position on the northern walls, stretching from the Postern of St Lazarus, near the leper colony, past St Stephen's Gate and the Postern of St Magdalene, round the north-east corner of the city to the Gate of Jehosophat on the eastern walls. For a few blissful hours the Christian defenders believed that Saladin was raising the siege and marching away. In fact, he had come to the same conclusion as the crusaders of 1099. The likeliest area for a breach in the walls was in the north-east corner between the Postern of St Magdalene and the Barbican, which was where Godfrey of Bouillon had first entered the city in 1099 and where, to commemorate this epic event, a great cross had been raised above the city wall.

On the morning of 26 September the Christian defenders awoke to the news that the Muslims were now on the Mount of Olives. The joyous hopes of the previous night were dust in their mouths. Now the siege was intensified. Forty mangonels were erected on the northern side and these began a tremendous barrage of rocks and 'Greek fire' against the city walls. For the first time since the siege began the defenders were helpless to intervene. Meanwhile, Saladin prepared to combat the deep fosse which had so hindered him on the western side. Engineers and sappers from Aleppo and Khorasan began to assemble behind the front lines in the Muslim camp. When they were ready they advanced towards the fosse, preceded by shield bearers who covered them from the Christian arrows, stones and other missiles and Muslim archers who put up such a heavy fire themselves that soon the defenders were forced to shelter behind the battlements. As the defensive fire diminished the Muslim sappers were able to begin their work of destruction, covered now by a roof of shields. First they dragged at the stones and loosened the mortar with picks and levers, then they began to dig shafts under the main walls, propping up the foundations with wooden beams. They concentrated on constructing a shaft some 100 feet long under the Barbican and when it was completed they burned away the struts which had been supporting the wall above. With a great crash a whole section of wall on the north-east corner of the city collapsed, bringing down with it the great ceremonial cross.[13] By an irony the Muslims were to force the defences at exactly the same point. While a huge force of some 10 000 horsemen stood ready opposite the St Stephen's Gate to prevent a possible sortie by the city garrison, the sappers and engineers completed their work.

With their defences breached it seemed only a matter of time now before the city fell. The hard-pressed professional troops were unable to hold the walls while the Jerusalem militiamen fled from the area of the collapsed Barbican. Even though the city fathers asked for volunteers to man the breach, even offering each man a hundred bezants to do so, none were found who would take on such an apparently suicidal task.[14] While processions of the clergy continued to circle the walls, constantly interrupted by flights of arrows from the Saracen archers, Balian was faced with his most difficult decision. Should he surrender the city or should he allow it to be taken by assault? The consequences of the latter were horrible to contemplate. The city was crowded with thousands of helpless women and children. Should the Muslims force an entrance there would be a massacre to rival the bloody events of 1099.

Yet the morale of the garrison was unbroken. Many of Balian's best soldiers seem to have been elevated by the presence of the fragment of the True Cross which remained in the city in the possession of the Syrian Christians. In order to replace the Latin relic lost at Hattin, the clergy carried the relic in solemn procession around the city, intoning psalms and promising the defenders that their lives were sanctified and those who died in Jerusalem fighting for their religion were assured of salvation. Meanwhile Balian was in urgent discussion with the Patriarch Eraclius. Although many of Balian's men wished to fight to the death, even opening the gates and sallying forth to fight the Saracens, Eraclius hastened to remind them that they had responsibilities to the helpless women and children who, once their defenders had died gloriously, would suffer rape, slavery and forcible conversion to Islam.[15] Surely there was still time to negotiate. But this time was running out quickly. If the Muslims forced an entrance Saladin would be powerless to prevent his soldiers from carrying out a general sack.

Balian was eventually prevailed upon to open discussions with

Saladin for the surrender of the city. Even as the fighting raged around the breach in the northern wall, Balian sought out Saladin's camp in the valley of the Brook Kedron. Twice he was refused an audience by Saladin, who had been enraged by the severity of the siege and the heavy losses he had incurred. On the third occasion, the sultan told him that he intended to take the city by force and avenge the dreadful massacre of 1099. During these discussions furious fighting was taking place on the north-eastern walls of the city. As he gazed upwards Saladin noted that Muslim banners were flying from the walls and that the area seemed to be under Muslim control. He turned to Balian and said to him scornfully, 'Why are you offering to surrender the city when it is already in our hands?' However, at precisely that moment the Christian defenders launched a sharp counter-attack, driving the Saracens back and hurling their banners from the battlements. Saladin had been answered and he knew that there were forces at work at that moment beyond his control. The ways of Allah were not knowable to so humble a servant as he; and he knew that he should not presume to dictate the way that the Holy City would be delivered again into the hands of the true believers. He called a halt to his negotiations with Balian and asked if the Lord of Nablus would return the next day. Balian had won a further day of grace but what would the morrow bring?

Saladin may have taken a solemn oath to take Jerusalem by the sword but his emirs were keen to see a peaceful take-over of Jerusalem. Oaths were very important in the Muslim world, and Saladin above all men made their observation an article of faith. Nevertheless, oaths did not in themselves advance the cause of Islam. Saladin's success had been firmly based on his ability to pay and equip large armies and this was a supremely expensive business. Already the sultan's generosity had cost his treasury dear when, after the fall of Acre, he had distributed the city treasure among his friends and supporters. This must not be allowed to happen again. If Jerusalem should be taken by storm much treasure would be destroyed and many valuable prisoners massacred by the common soldiery. Moreover, Saladin's soldiers would consider it their right to loot a city taken by storm and he would have found it difficult to hold back his fanatical warriors once they were within the city. Yet Saladin was not a man to turn lightly from his task or to be swayed by such materialist arguments.

Within the city the people knew that their fate now rested on the word of the Muslim sultan. Brave as had been their defence, their walls were breached and it was only a matter of time before the city was overrun by Muslim warriors who had little reason to love the Christians who had enslaved their brothers, stolen their Holy City and defiled their holiest shrines. All that night the air was filled with the sounds of prayers and lamentations. At the Church of the Holy Sepulchre, women brought their daughters to bathe them naked in the water and cut off their hair as an act of penance, or to render them less attractive to the Muslim soldiery if the city were taken by storm. While the sounds of hysteria were but scarcely concealed, a wave of religious fervour lifted the people to acts of contrition. Barefoot and bareheaded many followed the priests and monks who carried the *Corpus Domini* and the Syrian True Cross, in holy procession around the walls of the beleaguered city. Round the northern and eastern sides of Jerusalem Muslim campfires littered the earth with specks of light as numerous as the stars that filled the sky. To the imprisoned Christians it was if they were alone in space, cut off from everything that had linked them with earthly existence. It was a night for fanatics to see visions and for the faithful to reassure themselves that they were not forgotten after all and that a miracle would still save them. God who had allowed his only begotten son to die in this city to save fallen mankind would not now let his city fall under the sway of the infidel. With such reassurance some were able to find contentment and sleep.

The next morning brought no relief to the man who bore responsibility for the Christian population of Jerusalem. Balian of Ibelin had lived much of his life as a warrior. He knew how to give hard blows and to take them. He knew how to look after himself and his family but now he was burdened by the greatest prize of all, the Holy City itself. He had done all he could to defend the city walls, the stone, the bricks, the mortar, but surely Jerusalem was more than just these tangible things. Surely Jerusalem was an idea as well as a city. He could do nothing now about saving the outward manifestation of the city but what of the people within the walls, the 60 000 who had flooded into Jerusalem as a place of sanctuary. It was surely in their hearts that God was to be found, as truly as in the Church of the Holy Sepulchre itself. Outside the walls sat a dread Prince of Islam who held all their lives within the palm of his hand. Balian knew him as a great prince and a magnanimous ruler, yet he was also the leader of Islam in the *jihād*. In the struggle between Christian and Muslim there had been no room for weakness. What mercy had the fierce crusaders of Godfrey of Bouillon, of Tancred, of Raymond of St Gilles and the others, shown to the population of Jerusalem in 1099? What could he expect from Saladin now, particularly as he had sworn to take the city by storm, and he was a man noted for keeping his word? Balian had never felt more alone as he went out to meet Saladin again, nor had he ever borne so great a responsibility.

Soldiers and citizens crowded the walls of the city, willing Balian to succeed in his negotiations with Saladin, while the streets and bazaars were crowded with women and old people. This time Balian had no difficulty reaching Saladin's tent, where he was greeted with sombre propriety. At once the sultan reminded Balian of the offer that he had made to the envoys from the Holy City during his siege of Ascalon. It had been so generous an offer that it had earned him criticism from his own people. Why had the Christians proved so proud and intransigent in rejecting it? They did not have the power to deal with him so. In consequence he had vowed that he would take Jerusalem by storm and now he was about to accomplish that task. What had Balian to say that could possibly turn him from his purpose?

Balian had concluded that nothing which hinted at the weakness of the Christian position would impress the Muslims. All that he and his warriors had left was their lives and these he would have to throw into the balance now if the scales were not to weigh heavily against him. He therefore replied to Saladin that if fair terms of surrender were not granted to the people of Jerusalem he would order them to fight to the death and to destroy much of the city before the Muslims could occupy it. Although it is likely that the chroniclers have embellished his great speech on that day the power and effectiveness of it are not to be doubted. Again he addressed Saladin and his emirs:

> O Sultan, know that we soldiers in this city are in the midst of God knows how many people, who are slackening the fight in the hope of thy grace, believing that thou wilt grant it them as thou hast granted it to the other cities — for they abhor death and desire life. But for ourselves, when we see that death must needs be, by God we will slaughter our sons and our women, we will burn our wealth and our possessions, and leave you neither sequin nor stiver to loot, nor a man or a woman to enslave; and when we have

finished that, we will demolish the Rock and the Mosque al-Aqsa, and the other holy places, we will slay the Muslim slaves who are in our hands — there are 5000 such — and slaughter every beast and mount we have; and then we will sally out in a body to you, and we will fight you for our lives: not a man of us will fall before he has slain his likes; thus shall we die gloriously or conquer like gentlemen.[16]

Everything the Muslims had seen so far of Christian fanaticism convinced them that Balian's threat was no idle one. Before they could force an entry into the city his soldiers would have time to desecrate the Muslim holy places and to massacre the prisoners-of-war. The picture Balian painted was of a holocaust which would equal or even surpass the horrors of 1099.

Saladin was forced to reconsider his threats. He had sworn to take the city by force but it would be a tragic end to the holy war if he became master of a ruined city, with the holy sites desecrated and laid low. Would a voluntary surrender by the defenders violate his oath? Surely the siege had been bloody enough already. He had forced the garrison to the point whereby they were willing to die rather than surrender on unacceptable terms and this was surely enough. After all, it had been the generous terms on which he had allowed other cities to surrender which had facilitated the Muslim take-over of the kingdom. If his terms had been harsh and every garrison had fought to the death, as Jerusalem's threatened to do, his conquest of the kingdom would have taken much longer and been far more damaging to his own forces. Moreover, if a relief force had arrived from Europe, it would have found numerous Christian enclaves throughout the land which the Muslims had lacked time to capture. Thus Saladin concluded again that generosity was his most potent weapon.

After lengthy discussions between Saladin and Balian the terms of the surrender were settled and the ransoms to be paid by the inhabitants were fixed at the following levels: every man was to pay ten dinars, every woman five, and every child one. In return for a ransom of 30 000 bezants some 7000 poor people were also to be freed.[17] Saladin graciously allowed the Christians 40 days to assemble the ransoms after which anyone found within the city was to be enslaved. The Christians were allowed to take with them any moveable property but they were encouraged to sell as much as possible to the Muslims in order to help them raise their own ransoms. Meanwhile, Balian obtained from the Hospitallers the remainder of the gold which Henry II of England had entrusted to them. With this he was able to ransom the 7000 poor people, who were selected on a street by street basis from among those who had no means of their own to meet Saladin's charge. On the other hand, those who had sufficient funds to meet their ransoms departed from the Jaffa Gate, after receiving safe conducts from Saladin's officials.

The behaviour of the Muslims in Jerusalem was impeccable. In contrast to the rabble who had accompanied Duke Godfrey in 1099, they looted no building and harmed no civilian. Saladin's guards patrolled the streets maintaining order and, had the Christians but known it, these men were maintaining more than that, for where the sultan's word of honour was at stake it would have gone hard on any of his men who had imperilled it. While Balian had succeeded in persuading the Hospitallers to part with the King of England's treasure, he was less successful in convincing the military orders to use any of their own wealth to ransom the poor of the city. Nor indeed was the Latin church willing to play the part of protector of the poor. The patriarch and his priests were prepared to offer just the 10 dinars each which secured their own safety. It is clear that many thousands were condemned to spend their lives as the slaves of Muslim masters through the indifference and parsimony of the church.

As the 40 days elapsed it became clear that there were still many unfortunates within the city who had no way of raising sufficient funds. Saladin had already shown great compassion on the Christian poor, feeding the widows and orphans of those who had fallen at Hattin. Now he made a further gesture by freeing many more poor people without ransom. In stark contrast to his generosity was the example set by many of the richer Jerusalemites, who seem to have followed the poor example set by their patriarch. Rather than using the considerable wealth of the church to help those unable to raise their own ransoms, he prepared to leave the city with a caravan of carts loaded with treasures and fine tapestries and carpets, as if he were a conqueror carrying the spoils of his victories, rather than the last patriarch fleeing in disgrace from God's Holy City. Saladin's emirs were disgusted and pressed their leader to confiscate this treasure but he insisted that he would not break his pledge to the Christians, even for this unholy man. Nor was Eraclius alone in his greed and selfishness. With the kingdom ended and Jerusalem fallen, Christian charity seemed to take a second place to selfishness. The more wealthy citizens of the Holy City seemed concerned only that they should survive in the condition to which they had grown accustomed. In spite of the fact that there was ample money in private hands to ransom the remaining 15 000 poor people, at the end of the 40 days these unfortunates were assembled and taken in columns to fill the slave markets of Damascus.[18]

Those who had succeeded in paying their ransoms were taken under escort towards the remaining Christian lands. Under the separate leadership of the Templars, the Hospitallers and of Balian himself, three columns of Christian refugees left Jerusalem for the last time. With them rode an escort of Muslim soldiers to prevent the desert Bedouin tribes from harassing them. Even now the Christian chroniclers could not help but contrast the kindness shown by their captors to the callousness of their own kind. Muslim warriors, it is recorded, touched by the suffering of the erstwhile enemies, gave up their horses to the aged refugees or carried the young children in their arms or perched on their saddles. It seemed that in the face of such suffering religious differences meant less than shared humanity. However, the reaction of the refugees' Christian brethren was anything but charitable. At Tyre only fighting men were admitted; while near Botron a renegade knight known as Raymond of Niphin promptly attacked the column of refugees and robbed them of what little remained to them. At Tripoli few found comfort: the authorities closed the gates on them, claiming that the city was already over-crowded by earlier refugees and food was growing short. It was only when they reached Antioch that many of the Jerusalemites found rest and a less hostile reaction. Those who had headed southwards towards Egypt fared slightly better. Although the Italian sea captains refused at first to take the beggarly refugees to Europe without a substantial fee, the Muslim authorities of Egypt quickly came to the aid of the Jerusalemites by telling the Italians that unless they transported the refugees free of charge then their boats would be impounded and forbidden to leave Egyptian ports.[19]

By taking Jerusalem Saladin had, in the eyes of his supporters, succeeded in 'releasing the brother shrine of Mecca from captivity'.[20] However, he was less certain that the caliph of the Abbasids would necessarily see it the same way. After all, since 1174 most of his efforts had been given to wars against his

Muslim brethren and for this he had suffered much criticism. He had always countered this by saying that he was only acting in this way so that his ultimate purpose, namely victory in the holy war, could be achieved more readily, and now in the reconquest of Jerusalem was the tangible proof of the fact that he had not lied. To reinforce this point it seems that Saladin dictated some 70 letters to his secretary, Imad al-Din, and had them sent to Muslim leaders throughout the East. He was determined not to lose a moment in exploiting the propaganda value of his victory.

On 9 October Saladin planned a great service of celebration in Jerusalem and many religious leaders competed for the honour of delivering the first sermon in the city for nearly 90 years. Eventually, the Qwadi of Aleppo, Muhi al-Din Muhammad, was chosen and when he mounted the pulpit in the al-Aqsa Mosque, garbed in a magnificent black robe, there was no disguising the deep emotion in his voice. Beginning softly with the conventional prayers to God for the triumph of the faith and the restoration of the Holy City he began an eulogy to Saladin, son of Ayyub, in a voice growing more powerful by the second:

> And prolong, O Almighty God, the reign of thy servant, humbly reverent, for thy favour thankful, grateful for thy gifts, thy sharp sword and shining torch, the champion of thy faith and defender of thy Holy Land, the firmly resisting, the great al-Malik al-Nasir, the unifier of the true religion, the vanquisher of the worshippers of the Cross, Salah al-Dunya wa al-Din. Saladin, Sultan of Islam and of the Muslims, purifier of the holy temple, Abu al-Muzaffar Yusuf, son of Ayyub, reviver of the empire of the Commander of the Faithful. Grant, O God, that his empire may spread all over the earth, and that the angels may ever surround his standards, preserve him for the good of Islam; protect him for the profit of the faith; and extend his dominion over the regions of the East and of the West.[21]

Saladin next turned his attention to returning the Muslim shrines to their original use as well as deciding what should be done with the Christian holy places. Although some of his advisers wanted to destroy them — particularly the Church of the Holy Sepulchre — hoping thereby to end Christian interest in Jerusalem, wiser voices pointed out that it was not the bricks and mortar that mattered, but the spirit and sanctity of the place where Jesus had lain in his tomb that attracted the Christians. Their great forerunner Umar, who had captured the city in 638, had taken no such action against the holy places of any religion. He realised that you cannot erase the holy places of the heart. Saladin wisely followed this example and even allowed a few Eastern Christians to stay at the Church of the Holy Sepulchre. Again Saladin's wisdom can be seen to have a political motive. The Eastern and Orthodox Christians who remained in Jerusalem had every intention of remaining loyal subjects of his and it would have been foolish for him to have extended his persecution to these, particularly as he valued his friendly relations with the Byzantine Emperor Isaac Angelus, who had congratulated him on his victory over the Franks. The Emperor asked Saladin to allow the Christian holy places to revert to Orthodox control and the Sultan willingly complied. He could see the value of driving a wedge between the followers of Rome and Constantinople.

The task of cleansing the city was a joyful one for Saladin's soldiers and was not tainted with the horrors that had accompanied the Christian cleansing of Jerusalem in 1099. The golden cross which had dominated the Dome of the Rock was taken down and broken up and Christian furnishings within the al-Aqsa Mosque were removed. To the Muslims the Rock was the holiest part of Jerusalem, for from here Mohammed had ascended into heaven. They were therefore horrified to find that the Christians had erected a chapel on the site and the footprint of the Prophet had been covered with marble depicting where Christ had stood before his Crucifixion. Saladin promptly ordered that the marble be cut away and the holy site revealed again. The entire area of the Temple, including the al-Aqsa Mosque, had been within the confines of Templar rule, and the Muslims were angered to find signs of living quarters and a latrine by the entrance to the mosque. These were cleared and the mosque restored with beautiful carpeting on the floor, illuminated texts from the Koran on the walls and rich candelabra hung from the ceiling. As an act of piety Saladin had installed in the mosque of Umar, the *minbar* (carved pulpit) that his master Nur al-Din had prepared to take with him to Jerusalem, should it have fallen during his lifetime. He may have felt that at least part of his debt was paid.

10

Aftermath

Saladin was beginning to realise that the capture of Jerusalem was not destined to be the final act of the holy war as he had hoped. The problems of victory were just as numerous, if sweeter, than those of defeat. The first was that the lengthy campaign of 1187 had stretched his finances to breaking point. His own liberality was proving a stumbling block. While his emirs had done well out of the numerous sieges and capitulations, the state treasury had seen little return. And with the threat from the Franks by no means completely extinguished there was the possibility that there was still a period of hard fighting ahead.

Even before the final ransoms had been paid in Jerusalem Saladin was facing a new crisis. His emirs, many of whom were more astute military thinkers than he was, were demanding that he should strike at Tyre, 'the only arrow left in the quiver of the infidels'.[1] Already he had given the garrison there far too much time to organise themselves. Moreover, refugees from a score of towns and castles had found their way there to seek protection behind the city's powerful walls. There could be no doubt now that Tyre would provide the greatest challenge the Muslims had faced since Hattin. Not only was Saladin facing the remnants of the kingdom's military forces, but also Western knights under a fresh and determined commander, Conrad of Montferrat. He was not tainted by defeat as were the Palestinian knights who had escaped from Hattin, but had the energy and pride of youth. In answer to repeated warnings from his commanders in the captured cities of the coast, Saladin at last turned his somewhat weary attention to the submission of Tyre.

Saladin had good reason to feel that perhaps the fates were now turning against him. If he had been chosen to take Jerusalem from the Franks after 88 years, then perhaps Conrad was the chosen one who would hold Tyre against him and undermine all his achievements. Certainly the young Crusader had inspired the Frankish population of the coastal city with the feeling that all was not lost and that their gallant defence against the Muslims might serve as a springboard from which the kings of the West could reconquer the Holy Land. While Saladin was completing the capture of Ascalon and Jerusalem, Conrad was feverishly strengthening the city defences of Tyre and digging a deep ditch across the neck of the causeway that Alexander the Great had built out to the city during his siege 1400 years before. It was said that Tyre was now 'like a hand spread upon the sea, attached only by the wrist'.[2] It had become an island which could only be approached by a narrow causeway, easily defended by relatively small forces.

Saladin marched from Acre on 8 November 1187 and moved northwards towards Tyre, but it was no longer with the enthusiasm that had marked the triumphal procession in the weeks following Hattin. His own generosity was now to be turned against him. His habit of liberating the garrisons of captured towns and castles had meant that what remained of Frankish military strength was assembled in Tyre, which was the only Christian-held town of any importance in the kingdom. It is true that his generosity to the defeated Christians had helped to accelerate the conquest of the kingdom, yet now he would have to face the consequences in front of the strongest defences yet. At the moment when his own capacity to attack was at its weakest, when his siege engines were in need of repair and his troops disheartened by the length of the campaign, he was about to face the sternest test since the battle of Hattin.

Among the leadership of the Muslim armies there was a strong feeling that enough was enough and that the season for campaigning was over. Muzaffar al-Din Keukburi was eager to undertake a pilgrimage, while al-Adil stayed in Jerusalem, al-Afdal in Acre, and others were spread around the country either besieging isolated pockets of resistance or garrisoning castles. Even Saladin did not reach Tyre until some two weeks after the fighting had begun. He was dissatisfied with the size and condition of his mangonels and it was not until 25 November that he moved up to Nahr al-Mansura, some one and a half miles to the east of the city walls. Eventually he was able to assemble 17 mangonels which were kept firing day and night throughout the siege. However, in places the walls of Tyre were 20 feet thick and the great catapults achieved limited success. With the arrival of fresh troops from Aleppo, under al-Zahir, Saladin was able to begin a general assault along the causeway. His men immediately suffered from missiles fired from Frankish *barbotes*: warships fitted with shields along their sides, from behind which archers and crossbowmen were able to enfilade any Muslims advancing along the spit. These barges controlled the seas on either side of the causeway. There was no alternative but to call up Muslim warships to try to drive the Frankish ships into harbour and keep them there. Eventually ten ships from Jubail and Beirut arrived and soon gained control of the seas around the causeway. Thus seapower became Saladin's most potent weapon against Tyre, by which he hoped to cut off the garrison from any relief. However, the Franks were not prepared to adopt merely a passive defence. Conrad was too active a commander to allow the Muslims to advance down the causeway unchallenged. At the first indication of an assault special parties of knights would sally out from the gates of Tyre led by a Spanish knight, known to both friend and foe as 'the knight in green'. In addition to his green shield and surcoat, this heroic figure bore a pair of stag's horns on his helmet and according to Ernoul he inspired even Saladin to admiration for his great exploits.[3]

At the beginning of December, al-Afdal reached Tyre from Acre and was soon followed by al-Adil. By this time the weather was of as much concern to the Muslims as the sallies from the Tyrean garrison. Heavy and continuous rain flooded the tents and turned the ground into a muddy quagmire; snow was in the air and lay thinly on the hills. Moreover, there was sickness in the camps (though whether this was just the physical manifestation of an underlying malaise is difficult to be certain). The Byzantines had always noted how wet weather and wintry conditions had a severe effect on the morale of Saracen troops and it is to Saladin's credit that he managed to sustain the siege of Tyre for as long as he did. The cold weather was merely a reminder to Saladin's soldiers that they were fighting out of season and that by rights they should have been home with their families months before. Imad al-Din writes that they had been forced to abandon the life of easy living and instead of living off the riches of their plunder they had to scavenge for food and pull their belts tighter to quell the pangs of hunger.[4] They had become too accustomed to easy victories. Saladin's name and generous nature had been enough, like Joshua's horn, to make walls crumble and defenders abandon themselves to his mercy. But here in front of Tyre they were facing a new and determined resistance. Perhaps the balance in the holy war was changing. Here they were fighting knights from the West who had little respect for the Saracens as warriors or for Saladin as their commander.

It was at this time, when Saladin most needed the support of all Islam, that he received the response of the Caliph of Baghdad to his letters communicating the news of the fall of Jerusalem. How bitter must have been the feelings of the victor in the holy war to realise that not all of his enemies, nor even the most dangerous, had faced him at Hattin, or Jerusalem, or Tyre. Politically the fall of the crusader kingdom had been unwelcome to the Abbasids. Saladin's concept of a pan-Islamic empire might have seemed merely a pipe-dream while the Franks remained such a potent threat to Islam, but now they had collapsed, there was nothing to prevent Saladin swallowing the whole of Iraq including Baghdad. What then would prevent him replacing the Abbasids with a dynasty of his own, deriving from his Kurdish father, Ayyub? The caliph and his advisers were intensely anxious to find out Saladin's true intentions and therefore sent Imad al-Din's brother, Taj al-Din, with their reply to Saladin's despatches and with instructions to find out as much as possible about what the sultan intended in the long run.

Saladin must have been surprised by the letter he received from Baghdad, in which were a series of criticisms of his behaviour, and very little recognition of the greatness of his achievement in liberating Jerusalem. Among many petty grievances was the accusation that Saladin had usurped the title '*al-Nasir*', which only the caliph was entitled to use.[5] Anyone who had knowledge of Saladin would have realised the foolishness of this charge. He was not a man who placed great store on wealth or empty titles. However, the most serious charge, which was kept until the end, was that Saladin had encouraged Turkman and Kurdish tribes within the lands of Iraq to question their allegiance to the caliph. This was clearly at the heart of the dispute between Damascus and Baghdad. Saladin, it was believed, had predatory intentions towards the caliph's lands in Iraq, and no amount of success against Christian enemies could compensate for the damage he was believed to be doing within the Muslim world. In conclusion, the caliph reminded Saladin,

'As to your jubilation over the capture of Jerusalem: had she not been conquered by the troops of the caliph, under the banners of the caliph?'[6] Saladin would have been more than human had he not felt deep bitterness at such an ungrateful response. Indeed, his foremost supporters, like his nephew Taqi al-Din and his brother al-Adil, advised him to show open resentment to the caliph. However, Saladin rejected such a petty response and insisted to the caliph's emissary, Taj al-Din, that he did not believe his master could have written such harsh words. He therefore replied in a conciliatory fashion to Baghdad that the accusations were false and that his only aim ever had been to act as the 'Commander of the Faithful' in the holy war against the infidels.

As if to emphasise that the tide was beginning to run against him, progress in the siege of Tyre received a severe setback. Within the city it was quite clear to Conrad that Muslim control of the sea was the likeliest way of forcing the city to surrender. It was already preventing relief forces and supplies arriving from Europe and must be broken. Therefore, he planned a secret operation for 30 December, in which a number of Frankish ships, (possibly 17 galleys and ten small craft) broke out just before dawn to attack the Muslim squadron which was blockading the city. Although the Muslim commander, 'Abd as-Salam al-Maghribi, had been very careful to guard against such a surprise attack, the timing of the raid at just before dawn caught the Muslims unawares. In their panic many crewmen jumped overboard and swam to the shore but others were captured. Chaos reigned with some of the Muslim ships being taken; others ran themselves aground to avoid capture. In the space of a few minutes the entire balance of the siege had been altered.[7]

Although the Muslim losses had been small there could be no disguising the fact that Saladin had suffered a tactical defeat, his first since Hattin. The ships which had been beached were broken up to prevent capture but it was obvious now that for the immediate future the Frankish ships held sway at sea. Moreover, this setback was enough to convince some of the army leaders that the siege should be suspended. They argued now as feudal retainers not as soldiers of Allah. For them the campaigning season had been maintained too long and their effectiveness was waning. In spite of every attempt to exhort them to greater efforts Saladin faced the fact that his army was disintegrating and chances of taking Tyre receded with every day spent in the rain and snow of a Levantine winter. Saladin distributed money amongst the soldiers to try to buy their enthusiasm but he was pursuing a lost cause. Even mercenaries were not easy to find at this time of the year. Eventually, Saladin appealed to his commanders for one last general assault after which, should it fail, the siege would be lifted.

On 31 December the final assault took place. There was little subtlety in the tactics employed nor was there any great hope that they would succeed. The entire army attacked in waves down the causeway but the outcome was predictable and by the end of the day the issue was no longer in doubt. On 1 January 1188 Saladin withdrew from Tyre and the army was allowed to disperse. Saladin had tasted defeat before at Montgisard but he had always tried to learn from it. Now at Tyre he was making the greatest mistake of his career. He had many critics who pointed out how much his previous policy had contributed to his failure but the greater error was that he had not tackled the thorny problem of the island-fortress after he had taken Acre and at a time when the garrison would quite possibly have surrendered or at best offered limited resistance. The weeks he spent at Ascalon and Jerusalem would have been better spent reducing Tyre.

Saladin's long years of campaigning must have sapped his mental as well as his physical reserves. The decision to leave Tyre was not sound either militarily or politically. Whatever minor successes might be ahead, Tyre was a defeat and one that he could not afford. His own troops knew him well as a man who lacked the staying power necessary to complete a long siege. Many times in his life had he called off sieges rather than prosecute them *à outrance*. Now, at Tyre, he had faced a determined resistance on the part of the Franks under Conrad of Montferrat that was beyond his powers to overcome. It is true that his troops were tired, ill-disciplined, and fighting now more in the hope of booty than for the holy war, but it was his duty as Commander of the Faithful to complete the work he had begun at Hattin. Jerusalem was the prize that he had plucked from the Christians but unless he occupied both Acre and Tyre he could never be certain that he could hold it. To have left Tyre in Christian hands was tantamount to inviting the Christian kings of the West to use it as an entry point into the Holy Land. No losses should have been spared in capturing Tyre for who could tell how much heavier the losses would be if the Western Christians broke out from the city?

At the end of 1187 Saladin must have felt the frustration of a commander who had captured the target on which he had set his heart, only to find that it was merely the first in a series of targets which stretched out of his sight and would require a seemingly limitless effort. News had already reached him that Pope Gregory had exhorted the kings of the West to lead their armies to the Holy Land to counter-attack the Muslims. Philip Augustus of France and Richard, son of Henry II of England, had begun their preparations, while the Holy Roman Emperor, Frederick I Barbarossa, had already written to Saladin threatening him with the direst consequences should he touch Jerusalem. In spite of his age (64), the emperor warned the sultan that, 'you will assuredly be taught how our own right hand, which you suppose to be enfeebled by old age, can still wield the sword on that day of reverence and gladness which has been appointed for the triumph of Christ's cause'.[8] This letter may have puzzled Saladin but he responded boldly to it, telling the emperor of the Germans that, 'We will not be satisfied with the land of the seacoast, but we will cross over with God's good pleasure and take from you all your lands in the strength of the Lord.'[9] Nevertheless, he had to face the fact that whoever Frederick Barbarossa was and whatever his power, a strong counter-attack from the West was certain.

Meanwhile, Saladin was benefiting from his close friendship with the Byzantine Emperor, Isaac Angelus. As news of Western preparations reached Constantinople it was immediately communicated to Saladin, while a closer military alliance was signed between the Greeks and the Saracens. Apparently, among the many gifts he sent the emperor Saladin included two early forms of 'chemical warfare': one was a great silver vessel of poisoned wine, capable of slaying at one sniff; the other was a large supply of poisoned flour and grain, to be distributed to Frankish crusaders as they passed through Byzantine territory.[10] In the event, however, the alliance with the Byzantines was of little real value to Saladin. Frederick Barbarossa was able to defeat the forces Isaac sent to bar his way and eventually the Germans ravaged the province of Thrace, taking Adrianople by storm and forcing the Byzantines into a humiliating treaty.

Ironically, at the very moment that Saladin had triumphed in the holy war forces within the Islamic world were threatening to shatter the unity he had created. Relations between Saladin and the Abbasids at Baghdad had never been worse. Early in February 1188 the tensions between Saladin's Syrian supporters and the caliph's Iraqis flared into open fighting at Arafat near Mecca, where two pilgrim caravans met. The caravan from Damascus, an unusually large one, was led by Ibn al-Muqaddam, one of Saladin's oldest comrades. He insisted that his caravan should enter Mecca first, thereby indicating the supremacy of his master over the Iraqis. The Iraqi leader, Tash-Tekin, refused to concede priority to the Syrians and when Ibn al-Muqaddam raised Saladin's banner in defiance Tash-Tekin ordered it to be thrown down. The Syrians resisted and a general melee ensued in which lives were lost and Ibn al-Muqaddam killed. Saladin was deeply shocked by this latest demonstration of Muslim hostility to him as the champion of Islam. He knew that his motives were always open to misinterpretation because his own family and his closest friends did not share his moral standards and demonstrated again and again their own ambitions, even when these ran counter to his own. While the Franks had posed a serious threat Muslims had been willing to grant Saladin their support but now that he had apparently removed the danger some Islamic leaders felt free to criticise his leadership. Saladin alone seemed to be aware that in taking Jerusalem, the holiest city of the Christian religion, he was issuing a challenge to the Christian kings of western Europe. Indeed everything indicated that they were eager to take up the challenge and undertake a great crusade to regain the Holy Land. Now, more than ever, Saladin needed to hold Islam united in the face of the greatest threat since the First Crusade some 90 years before.

If Saladin cannot fairly be accused of underestimating the threat from the West, a lifetime of experience with men did not prevent him from badly misjudging the captive Guy of Lusignan. Since coming to Outremer in 1180 Guy had done little to suggest that he was anything more than an unintelligent though fairly brave knight, who had been promoted beyond his abilities. As king he had allowed himself to be manipulated by stronger characters and had gambled his entire kingdom on a single battle. In defeat he had lost not only an army but the fruits of nearly a century of Christian settlement in Outremer. As a result he had few admirers among either Christians or Muslims. While Saladin had kept Guy imprisoned, he was inundated by requests from Queen Sibylla for his release. Eventually, he decided that to release so demonstrably incapable a soldier and ineffectual a ruler could do no possible harm to the Muslims but might in fact cause further confusion among the Franks. There was undoubtedly a political motive behind Saladin's generosity. While he might have liked it to be thought that he was graciously granting the request of a lady and a queen, the real reason for releasing Guy was so that a new factor would be introduced into the tangled skein of affairs which centred on Tyre. The arrival of the ambitious Conrad of Montferrat suggested that he would be most unlikely to accept Guy as his king, nor would most of the Tyrean population who had taken Conrad as their lord. This showed Saladin's prescience, for when Sibylla and Guy travelled together to Tyre they were refused entrance by Conrad, just as Guy had once refused Baldwin IV entry into Ascalon. Moreover, Balian of Ibelin while in Jerusalem, had thrown off his allegiance to Guy and most of the remaining native barons had followed suit. It seemed that Guy was a spent force and that Saladin had been right to discount him from his calculations. However, in one of history's more surprising ironies, Guy accumulated a small army of new arrivals from France and native troops and with just a few hundred knights and men at arms he set out to besiege the great fortress of Acre. When he heard the news Saladin was inclined to regard it as some kind of joke. Fatally he hesitated and by the time he stirred himself to make a military response Guy's small army had dug itself into an impregnable defensive position, able both to maintain the siege of Acre and yet to prevent Saladin's army from bringing relief. From such a small and unconsidered beginning Guy's camp became the launching pad for the Third Crusade. While Saladin could only watch and curse his own misjudgement the camp became the centre for the greatest colonial expedition of the Middle Ages.

Notes

Introduction

1. J. de Vitry, *History of Jerusalem*, Eng. trans. A. Stewart (London, 1896), pp. 64f.
2. H. E. Mayer, *The Crusades*, Eng. trans. J. Gillingham (Oxford, 1972), p. 85.
3. Usamah ibn Munqidh, *Memoirs;* Eng. trans. and ed. P. K. Hitti *An Arab-Syrian Gentlemen and Warrior* (Beirut, 1964), p. 169.
4. H. A. R. Gibb, 'The Achievements of Saladin', *Studies on the Civilization of Islam*, ed. S. J. Shaw and W. R. Polk (London, 1962), p. 100.
5. W. Montgomery Watt, 'Islamic Conception of the Holy War', *The Holy War*, ed. T. P. Murphy (Columbus, OH, 1976), p. 146.
6. Ibid., pp. 152f.

Jerusalem the Golden

1. See L. A. M. Sumberg, 'The Tafurs and the First Crusade', *Medieval Studies*, xxi (1959), pp. 224ff.
2. William of Tyre, *Historia rerum in partibus transmarinis gestarum*, Receuil des Historiens des Croisades: Historiens Occidentaux, vol. 1 (Paris, 1844), p. 354.
3. F. Gabrieli, *Arab Historians of the Crusades* (London, 1969), p. 12.

Saladin's Early Life

1. M. C. Lyons and D. E. P. Jackson, *Saladin: the Politics of the Holy War* (Cambridge, 1982), p. 2.
2. Ibid., p. 3.
3. William of Tyre, *Historia rerum*, pp. 884–8.
4. Lyons and Jackson, *Saladin*, p. 7.
5. S. Runciman, *A History of the Crusades* (Cambridge, 1952), II, p. 370.
6. Ibid., p. 380.
7. Ibid., p. 383.
8. Ibn al-Athir, *Al-kamil fi'l-tarikh*, vol. 2 (Beirut, 1965), p. 138.
9. Ibn Shaddad, *Sirat Salah al-Din* (Cairo, 1962), p. 40.
10. Abu Shama, *Kitab al-raudatain*, Receuil des Historiens, vols 4, 5 (Paris, 1898–1906), p. 524.
11. William of Tyre, *Historia rerum*, p. 1000.

Saladin in Syria

1. 'Imad al-Din, *Sana al-barq al-shami*, abridged by al-Bundari, ed. R. Sesen (Beirut, 1971), p. 179.
2. Lyons and Jackson, *Saladin*, p. 87.
3. Ibn al-Athir, *Al-kamil*, p. 421.
4. Lyons and Jackson, *Saladin*, p. 104.
5. 'Imad al-Din, *Sana*, p. 204.
6. S. Lane-Poole, *Saladin and the Fall of the Kingdom of Jerusalem* (Beirut, 1964), p. 150.
7. William of Tyre, *Historia rerum*, p. 1050.
8. Ibn al-Athir, *Al-kamil*, p. 635.
9. Lane-Poole, *Saladin*, p. 158.
10. Lyons and Jackson, *Saladin*, p. 143.
11. Lane-Poole, *Saladin*, p. 167.
12. Ibid., p. 172.
13. Lyons and Jackson, *Saladin*, p. 192.
14. Ibn al-Athir, *Al-kamil*, p. 497.

The Kingdom of Jerusalem

1. William the Tyre, *Historia rerun*, pp. 816f.
2. Runciman, *Crusades*, II, p. 348.
3. Ibid., p. 352.
4. William of Tyre, *Historia rerum*, p. 995.
5. P. Aube, *Baudouin IV de Jerusalem* (Paris, 1981), p. 95.
6. William of Tyre, *Historia rerum*, p. 1012.
7. Runciman, *Crusades*, II, p. 425; see also B. Z. Kedar, 'The Patriarch Eraclius', *Outremer: Studies in the History of the Crusading Kingdom of Jerusalem*, ed. B. Z. Kedar, H. E. Mayer and R. C. Smail (Jerusalem, 1982), pp. 177–204.
8. Kedar, 'Eraclius', p. 181.
9. Runciman, *Crusades*, II, p. 38.
10. Ibid., p. 362; see also B. Hamilton, 'The Titular Nobility of the Latin East: the Case of Agnes of Courtenay', *Crusade and Settlement*, ed. P. W. Edbury (Cardiff, 1985), pp. 197–201.
11. William of Tyre, *Historia rerum*, pp. 1004f.
12. Ibid., pp. 1037–47.
13. Ibid., p. 1043.
14. Lane-Poole, *Saladin*, pp. 155f.
15. Ernoul, *Chronique d'Ernoul et de Bernard le Tresorier*, ed. L. de Mas-Latrie (Paris, 1971), p. 114.
16. *L'estoire d'Eracles empereur et la conqueste de la terre d'outremer*, Receuil des Historiens des Croisades: Historiens Occidentaux, vol. 2 (Paris, 1859), p. 29.

The Kingdom in Peril

1. Ernoul, *Chronique*, pp. 56ff.
2. William of Tyre, *Historia rerum*, p. 1077.
3. Kedar, 'Eraclius', pp. 182f.
4. William of Tyre, *Historia rerum*, p. 1077.
5. Ibid., p. 1087.
6. Ibid., pp. 1087–95.
7. J. Prawer, 'Crusader Security and the Red Sea', *Crusader Institutions* (Oxford, 1980), pp. 481ff.
8. Ibn Jubair, *The Travels of Ibn Jubayr* [*sic*], ed. W. Wright (Leiden, 1907), p. 59.
9. G. Schlumberger, *Renaud de Châtillon: Prince d'Antioche* (Paris, 1923), p. 203.
10. Abu Shama, *Kitab al-raudatain*, vol. 4, pp. 230ff; Ibn al-Athir, *Al-kamil*, pp. 658ff.
11. Lyons and Jackson, *Saladin*, p. 187.
12. Kedar, 'Eraclius', p. 190.
13. R. L. Nicholson, *Joscelyn III and the Fall of the Crusader States: 1134–1199* (Leiden, 1973), p. 114.
14. William of Tyre, *Historia rerum*, pp. 1127f.
15. Ibid., p. 1133.
16. Ibid., see also *L'estoire d'Eracles*, p. 1f.
17. M. W. Baldwin, *Raymond III of Tripoli and the Fall of Jerusalem: 1140–1187* (Princeton, NJ, 1936), p. 58.
18. Ernoul, *Chronique*, p. 117.
19. Ibid., pp. 102–6.
20. Joinville, *Histoire de Saint Louis*, ed. N. de Wailly (Paris, 1883), para. 206.
21. Ernoul, *Chronique*, pp. 133f.
22. Shlumberger, *Renaud*, pp. 247–9.
23. Baldwin, *Raymond*, p. 78.
24. Ernoul, *Chronique*, pp. 137–9.
25. Ibid., p. 141.
26. *L'estoire d'Eracles*, vol. 2, p. 34.
27. Baldwin, *Raymond*, pp. 87f.
28. Ernoul, *Chronique*, pp. 148–52.
29. Ibid., pp. 144f.
30. Runciman, *Crusades*, II, p. 453.

The Armies Assemble

1. F. Gabrieli, *Arab Historians of the Crusades*, (London, 1979), p. 119.
2. H. A. R. Gibb, 'The Armies of Saladin', *Studies on the Civilization of Islam*, ed. S. J. Shaw and W. R. Polk (London, 1962), p. 75.
3. Ibid., p. 76.
4. Ibid., p. 78.

5. I. Heath, *The Armies and Enemies of the Crusades: 1096–1291* (London, 1978), p. 79.

6. Ibid., p. 92.

7. Ibid., p. 83.

8. Gibb, 'Armies of Saladin', p. 83.

9. Heath, *Armies and Enemies*, pp. 5f.

10. Ibid., p. 112f.

11. T. Wise, *The Knights of Christ* (London, 1984), pp. 5f.

12. Heath, *Armies and Enemies*, p. 13.

13. Ibid., p. 67.

14. Ibid., p. 71.

15. Ibid., p. 115.

16. Lyons and Jackson, *Saladin*, p. 257.

17. Ernoul, *Chronique*, pp. 159ff.

18. *L'estoire d'Eracles*, vol. 2, p. 50.

19. Ernoul, *Chronique*, pp. 161f.

20. See H. E. Mayer, 'Henry II of England and the Holy Land', *English Historical Review*, ccclxxxv (1982), pp. 737ff.

21. *L'estoire d'Eracles*, vol. 2, p. 53.

22. Abu Shama, *Kitab al-raudatain*, vol. 4, p. 265.

Battle of Hattin

1. J. Prawer, 'The Battle of Hattin', *Crusader Institutions* (Oxford, 1980), pp. 488ff.

2. *L'estoire d'Eracles*, pp. 54ff; Ernoul, *Chronique*, pp. 163ff.

3. *De expugnatione terrae sanctae per Saladinum libellus*, ed. W. Stubbs (London, 1875), p. 223.

4. Ernoul, *Chronique*, p. 168.

5. 'Imad al-Din, *Kitab al-fath al-qussi fi'l-fath al-Qudsi*, ed. Landsberg (Leiden, 1888), p. 24.

6. Abu Shama, *Kitab al-raudatain*, vol. 4, p. 266.

7. Ibid.

8. *De expugnatione terrae sanctae*, pp. 224f.

9. Lyons, *Saladin*, p. 262.

10. For a discussion of Raymond of Tripoli's motives see Baldwin, *Raymond*, pp. 125f.

11. Ibid., p. 129.

12. Ibn al-Athir, *Al-kamil*, p. 536.

13. Abu Shama, *Kitab al-raudatain*, vol. 4, pp. 272ff.

14. Ibid., p. 275.

15. Z. Oldenbourg, *The Crusades*, Eng. trans. A. Carter (London, 1966), p. 422.

16. Ibid.

17. Ibn al-Athir, *Al-kamil*, vol. 11, pp. 358f.

18. Runciman, *Crusades*, II, p. 472.

19. *L'estoire d'Eracles*, vol. 2, pp. 72f; Ernoul, *Chronique*, p. 178.

The Siege of Jerusalem

1. 'Imad al-Din, *Sana*, p. 353.
2. Ibn al-Athir, *Al-kamil*, vol. 2, p. 541.
3. Ibn Shaddad, *Sirat Salah al-Din*, p. 80.
4. 'Imad al-Din, *Sana*, p. 361.
5. Ibn al-Athir, *Al-kamil*, vol. 1, p. 696.
6. Ernoul, *Chronique*, pp. 174f. 185–7.
7. Ibid., pp. 174–6.
8. Ibid., p. 185.
9. Ibid., pp. 185f.
10. G. Hindley, *Saladin* (London, 1976). p. 2.
11. J. Prawer, *Histoire du Rayaume Latin de Jerusalem* (Paris, 1969), vol. 2, pp. 672f.
12. Ibid., p. 673.
13. Ibid., p. 674.
14. *De expugnatione terrae sanctae*, p. 245.
15. Ernoul, *Chronique*, pp. 14f.
16. Ibn al-Athir, *Al-kamil*, vol. 1, pp. 700f.
17. Lane-Poole, *Saladin*, pp. 228f.
18. 'Imad al-Din, *Kitab al-fath*, pp. 60f.
19. Ernoul, *Chronique*, pp. 320–4.
20. Lyons and Jackson, *Saladin*, p. 275.
21. Lane-Poole, *Saladin*, p. 237.

Aftermath

1. 'Imad al-Din, *Sana*, pp. 374f.
2. Lane-Poole, *Saladin*, p. 239.
3. Ernoul, *Chronique*, pp. 237f.
4. 'Imad al-Din, *Sana*, p. 379.
5. Lyons and Jackson, *Saladin*, pp. 280ff.
6. A. S. Ehrenkreutz, *Saladin* (New York, 1972), p. 209.
7. 'Imad al-Din, *Kitab al-fath*, pp. 80f.
8. J. F. Michaud, *Bibliothèque des Croisades* (Paris, 1829), vol. 2, p. 664.
9. Ibid., p. 665.
10. Ehrenkreutz, *Saladin*, p. 212.

Select Bibliography

Primary Sources

Latin and French historians

L'estoire d'Eracles empereur et la conqueste de la terre d'outremer: la continuation de l'estoire de Guillaume arcevesque de Sur, Recueil des Historiens des Croisades: Historiens Occidentaux, vols. 1, 2 (Paris, 1859)

Ernoul, *Chronique d'Ernoul et de Bernard le Tresorier*, ed. L. de Mas-Latrie (Paris, 1971)

Fulcher of Chartres, *Historia Hierosolymitana: Gesta Francorum Iherusalem Peregrinantium*, ed. H. Hagenmeyer (Heidelberg, 1913)

De expugnatione terrae sanctae per Salidinum Libellus, ed. W. Stubbs (London, 1875)

Joinville, *Histoire de Saint Louis*, ed. N. de Wailly (Paris, 1883)

Raymond of Aguilers, *Historia Francorum qui ceperunt Jerusalem*, Recueil des Historiens des Croisades: Historiens Occidentaux, vol. 3 (Paris, 1866)

Jacques de Vitry, *History of Jerusalem*, Eng. trans. A. Stewart (London, 1896)

William of Tyre, *Historia rerum in partibus transmarinis gestarum*, Recueil des Historiens des Croisades: Historiens Occidentaux, vol. 1 (Paris, 1844)

Oriental historians

Abu Shama ['Abd al-Rahman ibn Ishma'il], *Kitab al-raudatain*, vols. 1, 2 (Cairo, 1956–62); vols. 4, 5 in Recueil des Historiens des Croisades: Historiens Orientaux (Paris, 1898 and 1906) [except if otherwise stated references are to the RHCOr edn]

Ibn al-Athir, *Al-kamil fi'l-tarikh* (Beirut, 1965) [12 vols]

Ibn Jubair, *The Travels of Ibn Jubayr [sic]*, ed. W. Wright, Gibb Memorial Series (Leiden, 1907)

'Imad al-Din al-Isfahani, *Al-barq al-shami*, Sec 3; MS, Bruce 11, Sec 5; MS, Marsh 425 Bodleian Libary, Oxford

——, *Sana al-barq al-shami*, abridged by al-Bundari, Fath b. Ali, pt. 1, ed. R. Sesen (Beirut, 1971)

——, *Kitab al-fath al-qussi fi'l-fath al-Qudsi*, ed. Landsberg (Leiden, 1888)

Ibn Shaddad, Baha al-Din, *Sirat Salah al-Din*, ed. J. al-Shayyal (Cairo, 1962)

Usamah ibn Munqidh, *Memoirs*; ed. and trans. P. K. Hitti as *Memoirs of an Arab-Syrian Gentleman* (Khayats: Beirut, 1964)

Secondary Sources

A. S. Atiya, *Crusade, Commerce and Culture* (Bloomington: London, 1962)

P. Aube, *Badouin IV de Jerusalem* (Tallandier: Paris, 1981)

M. W. Baldwin, *Raymond III of Tripolis and the Fall of Jerusalem: 1140–1187* (Princeton University Press: Princeton, NJ, 1936)

J. H. Beeler, *Warfare in Feudal Europe: 730–1200* (Cornell University Press: London, 1972)

M. Benvenisti, *The Crusaders in the Holy Land* (Macmillan: New York and London, 1970)

M. Bloch, *Feudal Society*, Eng. trans. L. A. Manyon (Routledge and Kegan Paul: London, 1961)

T. S. R. Boase, *Kingdoms and Strongholds of the Crusaders* (Thames and Hudson: London, 1971)

C. M. Brand, 'The Byzantines and Saladin, 1185–1192: Opponents of the Third Crusade': *Speculum*, xxxvii (1962), pp. 167–81.

——, *Byzantium Confronts the West 1180–1204* (Harvard University Press: Cambridge, 1968)

A. Bridge, *The Crusades* (Granada: London, 1980)

J. A. Brundage, *The Crusades: a Documentary Survey* (Marquette University Press: Milwaukee, 1962)

P. Contamine, *War in the Middle Ages*, Eng. trans. M. Jones (Blackwell: Oxford, 1984)

N. Daniel, *The Arabs and Medieval Europe* (Longman: Beirut, 1975)

H. Delbruck, *Geschichte des Kriegskunst im Rahmen der Politische Geschichte*, vol. 3 (Berlin, 2/1923)

P. Deschamps, *Au Temps des Croisades* (Hachette: Paris, 1972)

P. W. Edbury and J. G. Rowe, 'William of Tyre and the Patriarchal Election of 1180', *English Historical Review*, ccclxvi (1978) pp. 1–25

A. S. Ehrenkreutz, *Saladin* (New York University Press: New York, 1972)

F. Gabrieli, *Arab Historians of the Crusades* (Routledge and Kegan Paul: London, 1969)

H. A. R. Gibb, 'The Arabic Sources for the Life of Saladin', *Speculum*, xxv (1950), pp. 58–72.

——, *Studies on the Civilization of Islam* (Princeton University Press: Princeton, NJ, 1962)

——, *The Life of Saladin from the Works of Imad ad-Din and Baha ad-Din* (Clarendon Press: Oxford, 1971)

J. Gray, *A History of Jerusalem* (R. Hale: London, 1969)

F. Groh, *Der Zusammenbruch des Reiches Jerusalem: 1187–89* (Jena, 1909)

R. Grousset, *Histoire des Croisades et du Royaume franc de Jerusalem* (Plon: Paris, 1934) [3 vols]

B. Hamilton, 'The Titular Nobility of the Latin East: the Case of Agnes of Courtenay', *Crusade and Settlement*, ed. P. W. Edbury (University College Cardiff Press: Cardiff, 1985), pp. 197–201.

I. Heath, *Armies and Enemies of the Crusades: 1096–1291* (Wargames Research Group: London, 1978)

——, *A Wargamers' Guide to the Crusades* (Patrick Stephens: Cambridge, 1980)

P. Herde, 'Die Kampfe bei den Hornern von Hittin und der Untergang des Kreuzritterheeres (3. und 4. Juli 1187)', Romische Quartals-chrift fur Christliche Alterumskunde und Kirtschengeschichte, lxi (1966).

G. F. Hill, *A History of Cyprus* (Cambridge University Press: Cambridge, 1940–52) [4 vols]

G. Hindley, *Saladin* (Constable: London, 1976)

J. E. Hult, *Bohemond III: Prince of Antioch* (unpubd. thesis, New York University, 1974)

B. Z. Kedar, 'The General Tax of 1183 in the Crusading Kingdom of Jerusalem: Innovation or Adaptation?', *English Historical Review*, lxxxix (1974), pp. 339–45.

——, 'The Patriarch Eraclius', *Outremer: Studies in the History of the Crusading Kingdom of Jerusalem*, ed. B. Z. Kedar, H. E. Mayer and R. C. Smail (Yad Izhak ben Zvi Institute: Jerusalem, 1982), pp. 177–204

J. E. King, *The Knights Hospitallers in the Holy Land* (Methuen: London, 1931)

A. Krey, 'William of Tyre: the Making of an Historian in the Middle Ages', *Speculum*, xvi (1941), pp. 149–66

J. L. La Monte *Feudal Monarchy in the Latin Kingdom of Jerusalem: 1100–1291* (The Medieval Academy of America: Cambridge, 1932)

S. Lane-Poole, *Saladin and the Fall of the Kingdom of Jerusalem* (Khayats: Beirut, 1964)

T. E. Lawrence, *Crusader Castles* (Golden Cockerel Press: London, 1936) [2 vols]

F. Lot, *L'Arte Militaire au Moyen Age en Europe et dans le Proche Orient* (Paris, 1946) [2 vols]

M. C. Lyons and J. Riley-Smith, *Saladin: the Politics of the Holy War* (Cambridge University Press: Cambridge, 1982)

A. Maalouf, *The Crusades through Arab Eyes*, Eng. trans. J. Rothschild (Al Saqi: London, 1984)

H. E. Mayer, *The Crusades*, Eng. trans. J. Gillingham (Oxford University Press: Oxford, 1972)

——, 'Henry II and the Holy Land', *English Historical Review*, ccclxxxv (1982), pp. 721–39.

J. F. Michaud, *Bibliothèque des Croisades* (Ducollet: Paris, 1829) [4 vols]

W. Muller-Weiner, *Castles of the Crusaders* (McGraw-Hill: New York, 1966)

D. C. Munro, *The Kingdom of the Crusaders* (Kennikat Press: Port Washington, 1966)

R. L. Nicholson, *Joscelyn III and the Fall of the Crusader States: 1134–1199* (Brill: Leiden, 1973)

Z. Oldenbourg, *The Crusades*, Eng. trans. A. Carter (Weidenfeld and Nicolson: London, 1966)

C. W. C. Oman, *A History of the Art of Warfare in the Middle Ages*, vol. 1 (Methuen: London, 1924)

G. Ostrogorsky, *History of the Byzantine State* (Blackwell: Oxford, 1956)

R. Payne, *The Dream and the Tomb: a History of the Crusades* (Robert Hale: London, 1986)

R. Pernoud, *The Crusaders*, Eng. trans. E. Grant (Oliver and Boyd: London, 1963)

J. Prawer, *Histoire du Royaume Latin de Jerusalem* (Editions du Centre National de la Recherche Scientifique: Paris, 1969)

——, *The Crusaders' Kingdom* (Praeger: New York, 1972)

——, *The World of the Crusaders* (Weidenfeld and Nicolson: London, 1972)

——, *Crusader Institutions* (Clarendon Press: Oxford, 1980)

——, 'The Jerusalem the Crusaders Captured: a Contribution to the Medieval Topography of the City', *Crusade and Settlement*, ed. P. W. Edbury (University College Cardiff Press: Cardiff, 1985)

J. Richard, *Le Royaume Latin de Jerusalem* (Presses Universitaires de France: Paris, 1953)

J. Riley-Smith, *The Feudal Nobility and the Kingdom of Jerusalem: 1174–1277* (Shoe String Press: Hamden, Conn., 1973)

R. Rohricht, *Geschichte des Königsreichs Jerusalem* (Innsbruck, 1898)

——, ed., *Regesta Regni Hierosolmitania* (Innsbruck, 1893–1904)

C. J. Rosebault, *Saladin: Prince of Chivalry* (Cassell: London, 1930)

S. Runciman, *A History of the Crusades* (Cambridge University Press: Cambridge, 1951–54) [3 vols]

——, *The Families of Outremer: the Feudal Nobility of the Crusader Kingdom of Jerusalem* (London, 1959)

H. Russell Robinson, *Oriental Armour* (H. Jenkins: London, 1967)

G. Schlumberger, *Campagnes du Roi Amaurey 1er de Jerusalem* (Plon: Paris, 1905)

——, *Renaud de Châtillon: Prince d'Antioche* (Plon: Paris, 1923)

K. M. Setton, ed., *A History of the Crusades* (University of Wisconsin Press: Madison, 1969) [4 vols]

D. Seward, *The Monks of War: The Military Religious Orders* (Eyre Methuen: London, 1972)

E. Simon, *The Piebald Standard: a Biography of the Knights Templars* (Cassell: London, 1959)

R. C. Smail, *Crusading Warfare: 1097–1193* (Cambridge University Press: Cambridge, 1956)

——, *The Crusaders in Syria and the Holy Land* (Praeger: New York, 1973)

——, 'The Predicaments of Guy of Lusignan, 1183–1187', *Outremer: Studies in the History of the Crusading Kingdom of Jerusalem*, ed. B. Z. Kedar, H. E. Mayer and R. C. Smail (Yad Izhak Ben-Zvi Institute: Jerusalem, 1982), pp. 157–76

W. B. Stevenson, *The Crusaders in the East* (Cambridge University Press: Cambridge, 1907)

L. A. M. Sumberg, 'The Tafurs and the First Crusade', *Medieval Studies*, xxi (1959), pp. 224ff

C. Thubron, *Jerusalem* (Heinemann: London, 1969)

A. A. Vasiliev, *A History of the Byzantine Empire* (University of Wisconsin Press: Madison, 1961)

J. F. Verbruggen, *The Art of Warfare in Western Europe during the Middle Ages* (Amsterdam and New York, 1976)

W. M. Watt, 'Islamic Conceptions of the Holy War', *The Holy War*, ed. T. P. Murphy (Ohio State University Press: Columbus, OH, 1976)

T. Wise, *Armies of the Crusades* (Osprey: London, 1978)

——, *The Knights of Christ* (Osprey: London, 1984)

Index

Maps

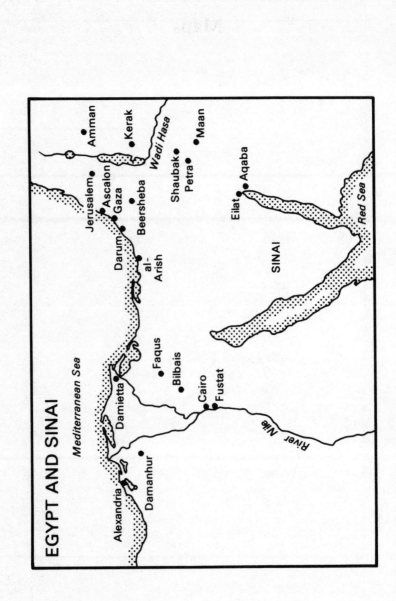

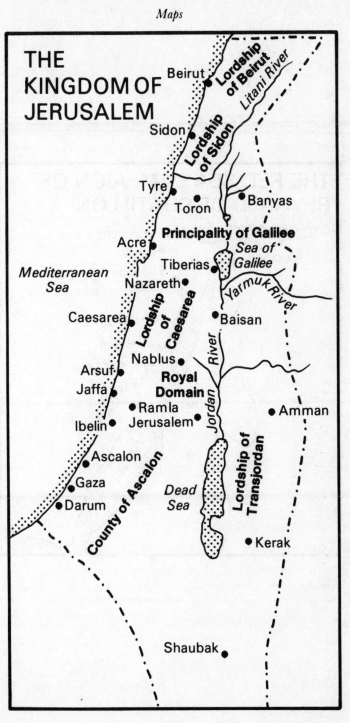

THE KINGDOM OF JERUSALEM

Beirut

Lordship of Beirut

Litani River

Sidon

Lordship of Sidon

Tyre

Toron

Banyas

Principality of Galilee

Acre

Tiberias

Sea of Galilee

Mediterranean Sea

Nazareth

Yarmuk River

Caesarea

Lordship of Caesarea

Baisan

Nablus

Jordan River

Royal Domain

Arsuf

Jaffa

Ramla

Ibelin

Jerusalem

Amman

Ascalon

County of Ascalon

Lordship of Transjordan

Gaza

Darum

Dead Sea

Kerak

Shaubak

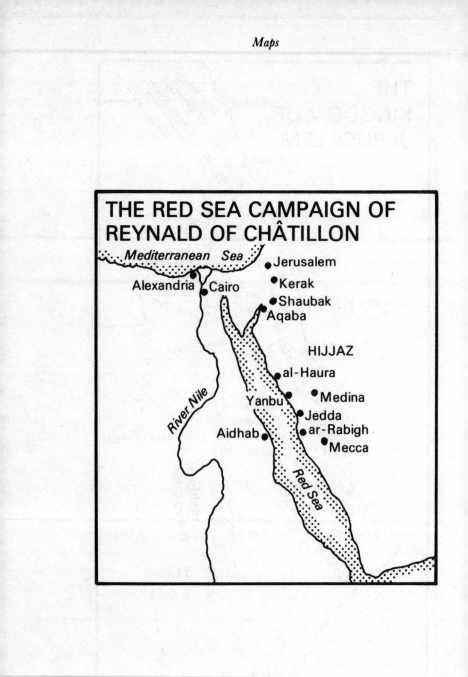

THE RED SEA CAMPAIGN OF REYNALD OF CHÂTILLON

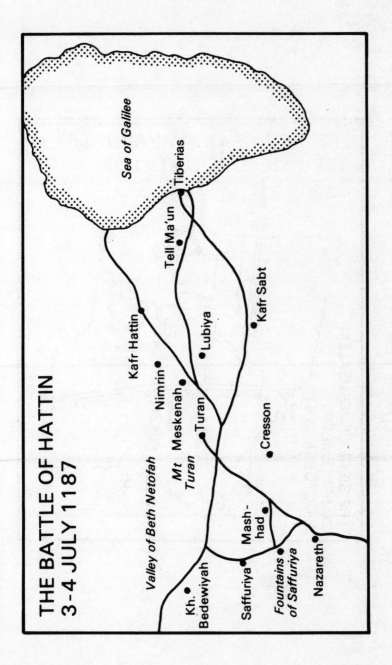

THE BATTLE OF HATTIN
3-4 JULY 1187

Sea of Galilee

Tiberias

Tell Ma'un

Kafr Sabt

Kafr Hattin

Lubiya

Nimrin

Mt Turan Meskenah

Turan

Cresson

Valley of Beth Netofah

Mash-had

Kh. Bedewiyah

Saffuriya

Fountains of Saffuriya

Nazareth

185

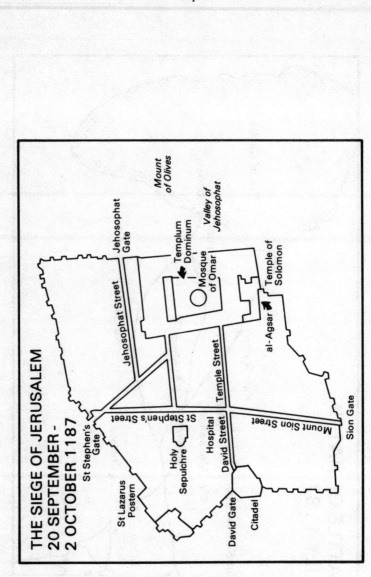

THE SIEGE OF JERUSALEM
20 SEPTEMBER -
2 OCTOBER 1187